Bifocal Vision

UNC | COLLEGE OF ARTS AND SCIENCES
Germanic and Slavic Languages and Literatures

From 1949 to 2004, UNC Press and the UNC Department of Germanic & Slavic Languages and Literatures published the UNC Studies in the Germanic Languages and Literatures series. Monographs, anthologies, and critical editions in the series covered an array of topics including medieval and modern literature, theater, linguistics, philology, onomastics, and the history of ideas. Through the generous support of the National Endowment for the Humanities and the Andrew W. Mellon Foundation, books in the series have been reissued in new paperback and open access digital editions. For a complete list of books visit www.uncpress.org.

Bifocal Vision
Novalis' Philosophy of Nature and Disease

JOHN NEUBAUER

UNC Studies in the Germanic Languages and Literatures
Number 68

Copyright © 1971

This work is licensed under a Creative Commons CC BY-NC-ND license. To view a copy of the license, visit http://creativecommons.org/licenses.

Suggested citation: Neubauer, John. *Bifocal Vision: Novalis' Philosophy of Nature and Disease.* Chapel Hill: University of North Carolina Press, 1971. DOI: https://doi.org/10.5149/9781469658070_Neubauer

Library of Congress Cataloging-in-Publication Data
Names: Neubauer, John.
Title: Bifocal vision : Novalis' philosophy of nature and disease / by John Neubauer.
Other titles: University of North Carolina Studies in the Germanic Languages and Literatures ; no. 68.
Description: Chapel Hill : University of North Carolina Press, [1971]
 Series: University of North Carolina Studies in the Germanic Languages and Literatures. | Includes bibliographical references.
Identifiers: LCCN 74028422 | ISBN 978-1-4696-5806-3 (pbk: alk. paper) | ISBN 978-1-4696-5807-0 (ebook)
Subjects: Novalis, 1772-1801.
Classification: LCC PT2291 .Z5 N4 | DCC 831/ .6

Foreword

I received generous help from many friends and colleagues in the course of my work; to list them all would efface my sole responsibility for the final shortcomings. In the last stages I particularly benefited from the suggestions of Professor Victor Lange and Professor Richard Samuel. The *Kohlhammer Verlag* kindly provided me with the printer's copy of the critical edition of Novalis' works. I received generous financial grants from Princeton University towards the research and the typing and from Case Western Reserve University towards the publication of this book. To Professor Siegfried Mews I am indebted for his kind editorial help.

J. N.

Contents

INTRODUCTION

I   Nature and Disease   1
II   Hardenberg: Life and Character   3
III   The Value of Hardenberg's Notes on Science.   9
IV   The Variety in Hardenberg's Scientific Interest   11
V   General Considerations   13

I   ASPECTS OF EIGHTEENTH-CENTURY SCIENCE

I   Locke, Bacon, and Descartes   16
II   Leibniz, Haller, and the Development of Biology   17
III   John Brown's Medical Theory   23
IV   Brown's Theory in Germany   26

II   SOURCES AND IMPULSES

I   Imagination and Hypochondria   31
II   First Studies   37
III   Schelling's Early Philosophy   39
IV   Excerpts from Kant and Eschenmayer   45
V   Hemsterhuis and Baader   52

III   THE ANTHROPOLOGY AND PHYSIOLOGY OF MAGIC

I   *Romantisirung*   57
II   The Epistemology of Magic   63
III   The Physiology of Poetry   67
IV   The Doctor as a Young Artist   70

IV   IDEAS FOR AN ENCYCLOPEDIA

I   The "Brouillon" and the other Notebooks   76

II External Unity — A. G. Werner	80
III Internal Unity — Kant, Fichte, and Lambert	83
IV The Bible Project	86
V Hemsterhuis vs. Schelling	88

V SENSIBILITY AND MEDICINE

I The Vocabulary of the Encyclopedia	95
II An Essay on Medicine	104

VI THE CASE OF *Die Lehrlinge zu Sais*

I The Importance of *Die Lehrlinge*	113
II Plans	114
III "Hyazinth und Rosenblütchen"	117
IV "Der Lehrling"	120
V "Die Natur"	121
VI The Travelers	124

VII THE LAST YEARS

I Religion and Poetry	128
II Readings and Professional Work	130
III J. W. Ritter and Galvanism	132
IV Sensibility and Disease	135
V Epilogue on "Romantic Medicine"	138

NOTES	144

APPENDICES

I Disease Chart According to Brown	171
II Brown's Disease Chart in German	173
III A Diagram of Diseases from Novalis	174
IV List of Scientific Books Read by Novalis	175

BIBLIOGRAPHY	180
INDEX	187

Introduction

I. NATURE AND DISEASE

The view that romanticism represented an irresponsible and pathological escape from the empirical world still lingers on, in spite of efforts to correct the image; in fact, the newly emerging view that romantic poets are "mythmakers" often only reinforces old stereotypes: both the commonplace and the sophisticated view give inadequate attention to the curiosity with which romantic poets approached organic and human nature. The poetic realms of Wordsworth, Keats, Shelley, Coleridge, or Novalis were created not through the exclusion but the transformation of the empirical world: if they were more intensely poetical than previous creations of the eighteenth century, they were also more directly reflecting the natural world and its newly emerging study, the sciences; if it was frequently felt that nature was a counterpart to the human mind, and science a new mode of thought threatening the primacy of poetic imagination, fear was nevertheless mingled with fascination. The romantics showed consistent efforts to master and humanize the new scientific experience because they recognized that science was to alter radically and permanently all areas of individual and social life.

Hand in hand with the interest in science went a curiosity for the physiologically or psychologically unnatural and the socially unaccepted. After the fall of the "ancien régime" and the failure of the French Revolution to realize the enlightened optimism of the eighteenth century, hopes for new syntheses seemed to lie only in radical individual efforts subjecting to scrutiny all aspects of the fragmented world—without regard to traditional tabus. These attempts are perhaps most dramatically and representatively expressed in *Faust*, although Goethe himself was clearly unwilling to carry through a radical "transvaluation of all values". Much of his wisdom—and some of his pedantry—may be ascribed to that hard-fought-for and only temporarily achieved balance between the "two souls" of Faust, in which the human mind had deep affinity with a benevolent nature, and the inherent moral qualities of organisms provided a basis for a humanism. To *this* Goethe, any human activity or thought which had no organic attachment to nature, be it Newton's physics, Kant's *Critique of Pure Reason*, or Kleist's metaphysical desperation, appeared fallacious and morbid. He described the romantics as sick because he disliked their irreverence and their unrestrained penetration into life's secrets.

Indeed, the "poète maudit" and Marquis de Sade are faces of romanticism, together with ennui, the addiction to drugs, and morbid introspection. The intent to explore the "dark recesses of the soul" informs Blake's "Sick Rose", Keats's "La Belle Dame Sans Merci", as well as Novalis' *Hymnen an die Nacht*. Morbidity is manifest, among other things, in an unusual concern for pathology itself; yet the preoccupation with disease need not always be a sign of decadence and abandon. As in the psychoanalytical theory of Freud—for which the romantics prepared the ground— in the profoundest romantic investigations of disease the clinical-therapeutic and scientific elements more than balanced the rolling "in abysses of despair and ennui".[1] The final aim was not anarchy but the conquest of hitherto uncontrolled forces and the illumination of darkness. As Thomas Mann—who was unable to decide whether to trace nazism to excessive romanticism or those opponents of romantic mentality who demanded mental hygiene—once characteristically stated: "Das Interesse für Tod und Krankheit, für das Pathologische, den Verfall ist nur eine Art von Ausdruck für das Interesse am Leben, am Menschen, wie die humanistische Fakultät der Medizin beweist; wer sich für das Organische, das Leben, interessiert, der interessiert sich namentlich für den Tod; ... Keine Metamorphose des Geistes ist uns besser vertraut als die, an deren Anfang die Sympathie mit dem Tode, an deren Ende der Entschluß zum Lebensdienste steht."[2]

The passage belongs to the speech "Von deutscher Republik" (1922) in which Thomas Mann defended the Weimar Republic by calling upon the testimony of Friedrich von Hardenberg (Novalis).[3] Mann, no less than his audience, was surprised to learn that Novalis, this "Träumer von ewiger Brautnacht", had relevant things to say both about German politics and physiology. In the nineteenth century Novalis was remembered only as an ethereal sickly poet who created the symbol of romantic yearning, the "blue flower", who mystically exalted his adolescent fiancée after her death, and died himself a premature romantic death. According to Hegel he was dominated by a noble but unhealthy yearning for the unattainable, Heine classed him with E. T. A. Hoffmann and felt that both wrote morbid poetry, in France he found followers among the purists of poetry, especially Maeterlinck.[4] Yet Novalis remarked towards the end of his life: "Ich bin überzeugt, daß man durch kalten, technischen Verstand, und ruhigen, moralischen Sinn eher zu *wahren Offenbarungen* gelangt, als durch Fantasie, die uns blos ins Gespensterreich, diesem Antipoden des wahren Himmels, zu leiten scheint."[5] Those who come to his works expecting only dark romanticism must be struck by his preoccupation with philosophy, his interest in nature and the natural sciences, and his sober acceptance of everyday life.[6] The exceedingly complex intertwining of scientific and pathological elements, which is unique for Novalis and yet in some way so characteristic of our culture ever since the romantic period, brought me originally to Novalis and prompted the first plans for this book.

II. HARDENBERG: LIFE AND CHARACTER

Friedrich von Hardenberg's life has often been mythologized, though it was relatively uneventful. He was born in 1772 at Oberwiederstedt, the small country estate of his family, near Halle. His father belonged to the prominent old Hardenberg family, but had himself only moderate means and gained his income from supervising the royal salt mines of Saxony. When he became district director in 1784, the family moved to the middle-sized town of Weissenfels, about twenty miles west of Leipzig.

Novalis entered the university of Jena in 1790 to study law. However, he seemed to bemore interested in Schiller's lectures and the trappings of student life, and finally, as result of parental pressure and perhaps a moderating intervention by Schiller himself, he moved to the University of Leipzig in the autumn of 1791. In Leipzig he made his lasting friendship with Friedrich Schlegel and continued to live a gay student life until in a moment of love-sickness he suddenly decided on a military career and left. However, parental persuasion prevailed once again and Novalis enrolled at the University in Wittenberg. This time he showed his powers and quickly obtained his degree in 1794.

The same year Novalis took a minor job in Tennstedt to gain practical experience, and encountered in the neighboring Grüningen the thirteen-year-old Sophie von Kühn. This proved to be the decisive experience of his life: they got engaged in the spring of 1795, but Sophie soon contracted consumption and she passed away in the spring of 1797. At the end of the same year Novalis went to the School of Mining Technology at Freiberg—near Dresden—and he studied there science and technology till the spring of 1799. Upon return to Weissenfels he worked in the Directorate of the salt-mines of Saxony. He was engaged for a second time when he fell sick, and he died on March 25, 1801 after prolonged sickness.

The only existing picture of him shows a small elongated head where the protruding cheekbones contrast with the long hair femininely curling over his shoulders.[7] In Friedrich Schlegel's first description one finds a similarly curious blend of traits:

> Ein noch sehr junger Mensch—von schlanker guter Bildung, sehr feinem Gesicht mit schwarzen Augen, von herrlichem Ausdruck, wenn er mit Feuer von etwas Schönem redet—unbeschreiblich viel Feuer—

> er redet dreimal mehr und dreimal schneller wie wir andre—die schnellste Fassungskraft und Empfänglichkeit.
> ...Nie sah ich so die Heiterkeit der Jugend. Seine Empfindung hat eine gewisse Keuschheit, die ihren Grund in der Seele hat, nicht in Unerfahrenheit. Denn er ist schon sehr viel in Gesellschaft gewesen (er wird gleich mit jedermann bekannt) ... (IV, 417).

The picture of robust health that emerges from the reminiscences of Tieck is even more surprising since Tieck was largely responsible for the myth of the ethereal poet:

> „Wie er auch am liebsten die Tiefen des Gemütes im Gespräch enthüllte, als begeistert von den Regionen unsichtbarer Welten sprach, so war er doch fröhlich wie ein Kind, scherzte in unbefangener Heiterkeit und gab sich selbst den Scherzen der Gesellschaft hin" (IV, 457). „Er war der gesundeste, frohsinnigste Mensch, der keckste Reiter, unermüdlicher Bergsteiger und Wanderer, schlief fast nicht, indem er praktisch und schreibend immer tätig war—aber freilich starb er, und unerwartet, an der Schwindsucht" (IV, 459).

And finally, Friedericke von Mandelsloh's remark which is in sharp contrast with Tieck's protrayal:

> [Novalis] „war zu aller Zeit körperlich krankhaft und leidend und sein früher Tod vorher zu sehen" (IV, 438).

How are we to correlate these seemingly incompatible observations? Even after allowing for inaccuracies in the recollections—Mandelsloh's were made forty years after the poet's death—and variations in individual judgement, the answer is difficult. For the disagreement on Novalis' features, his social behavior, and his health extends to all aspects of his personality and life; the volatile poet with an impulse towards the metaphysical was also a careful scholar and a conscientious high official in the Directorate of the salt-mines of Saxony. His sensibility, his exalted love, his physical suffering and early death contrast so much the toughness and discipline with which he applied himself to everyday matters or problems of philosophy that one would be inclined to believe he was among the first of those modern St. Sebastians of whom Thomas Mann has said that their art, born of suffering, represents a triumph over biological frailty and hostile environment. Indeed, if one reads the diary Novalis kept after the death of his fiancée, one is moved by his heroic and touching efforts to transcend everyday life and enter a mystic union with the beloved. And yet, a confrontation between "spirit" and "matter" or "art" and "life", as Schopenhauer later dramatized, is not typical of Novalis, and his letters seldom reveal such an agonizing self-division as is so familiar to us from the writings of Baudelaire, Flaubert, Kafka, Mann, and many others. Novalis is difficult to comprehend because he himself sensed no inconsistency in the diversity of his personality, and his poetry often appears as deceptively simple. The paradoxes of his mind and life are ultimately explainable only in terms of a supple and accommodating spiritual disposition which resolved these conflicts in Novalis himself, but which appears at times as admirable, and at others as inconsistent or naive to the skeptical modern reader.

A critical assessment of Novalis has to start with this paradoxical unity in multiplicity, for whatever aspect of Hardenberg's life or thought one takes under the magnifying glass, one quickly recognizes the outlines of his personality. The stuff of his life—his love, the course of his studies, and his final disease—seems to be incidentally encountered raw bits of experience upon which this personality printed a shape and colour of its own. Carlyle is therefore surely right when he remarks about the Sophie experience: "We cannot but think that some result precisely similar in moral effect might have been attained by many different means; nay, that by one means or another, it would not have failed to be attained."[8] On similar grounds Theodor Haering can assert that in the final analysis Novalis absorbed only those influences for which there was an a priori basis in his mind.[9] As Novalis had formulated it even more radically: "Jeder geliebte Gegenstand ist der Mittelpunkt eines Paradieses" (II, 433), which means that through the transforming power of love almost any object, event, or person may achieve ultimate significance, or saving grace.[10]

It seems then that the facts of Novalis' life, the nature of his disease, or the list of his readings would be of little value to those who wish to understand the products of his mind: the poetry and the ideas in his writing.[11] Yet, it has become clear in recent years that in the case of Novalis a precise knowledge of biographical circumstances and background material, above all an acquaintance with his readings, is indispensable for unraveling his complex, sometimes cryptic notebooks. As Novalis himself wrote about encounters with other minds. "Man studirt fremde Systeme um sein *eignes System* zu finden" (III, 278); "Ein junger Gelehrter muß mit specieller Kritik anfangen. Am fremden Faden und Gewebe lernt er eigene Ideen entwickeln und zu Fäden und einem vollst[ändigen], regelmäßigen Gewebe auszuspinnen" (III, 380).

Due to Hardenberg's early death, his contacts with other minds seldom crystallized in finished works of his own: apart from an early poem, published in the *Teutscher Merkur* in 1791, only two slim fragment collections, *Blüthenstaub* and *Glauben und Liebe*, and the cycle *Hymnen an die Nacht* were published during his lifetime. The remaining poetry and fiction—including the *Geistliche Lieder*, other poems, and the two novel-fragments: *Die Lehrlinge zu Sais* and *Heinrich von Ofterdingen*—were posthumously published by Hardenberg's friends, Ludwig Tieck and Friedrich Schlegel. This collected edition also contained fragments from the essay "Die Christenheit oder Europa" and miscellaneous notebook-material selected and arranged by Tieck under such headings as "Philosophie und Physik" or "Ästhetik und Literatur". Tieck entitled the whole last section "Fragmente"—in analogy to the collections published by Novalis himself.

The first steps towards a representative and reliable edition of Hardenberg's works were taken at the beginning of this century by Jacob Minor and Eduard Havenstein, but only in the first critical edition of 1929 were Paul Kluckhohn and Richard Samuel able to accomplish the task in a satisfactory way by returning to the manuscripts. However, this edition was still selective.

The manuscripts were auctioned by the Hardenberg family in 1930. Some of them went into unknown hands, others disappeared during the war, most of them, however, were bought by Salman Schocken and resold to the *Freies Deutsches Hochstift* in 1960. Through this last sale new possibilities opened up to the editors of the second critical edition: in the second and third volume of this edition all of Hardenberg's known notebooks were printed for the first time, with original orthography and in vastly improved chronological order. The resultant text necessitated an important revision concerning the notion and use of "fragments" in Hardenberg's writing.

The term "fragment" was defined by Friedrich Schlegel in the course of "Symphilosophieren"—a joint venture of the friends to establish a set of guidelines for the romantic artistic credo: "Ein Fragment muß gleich einem kleinen Kunstwerke von der umgebenden Welt ganz abgesondert und in sich selbst vollendet sein wie ein Igel."[12] However, Schlegel's definition is not very applicable to Hardenberg's *Blüthenstaub* or *Glauben und Liebe*: the individual pieces in these collections are seldom self-contained, their structure is dialectical and discontinuous, while their ending is open and suggestive.[13]

More important, the term "fragment" cannot be applied at all to the rest of the material in Hardenberg's notebooks—with the exception of a half-finished collection usually referred to as "Teplitzer Fragmente" (II, 596-622). These notebooks, especially the ones on science, are filled with excerpts from books or notes on them, interspersed with sketches, brief memos, or even plans for reading and daily activity. The return to the original manuscripts has made it evident that many of Hardenberg's cryptic "fragments" were artificially manufactured by Tieck, who tore passages from their context, thereby masking their origin and giving them a semblance of self-contained finality. That many of these notes become illuminated by the underlying foreign text was conclusively demonstrated by Professor Mähl, who discovered important sources for Novalis' notes and was thereby able to characterize the way in which Hardenberg's mind seized upon seemingly unimportant matters and extracted from them what it needed.[14]

With the exceptions mentioned then, Hardenberg's notebooks contain no "fragments", and one should rather refer to the material as notes being at various stages between raw material and finished product. In particular, the meaning of individual notes on science and their interrelation can only be explored by giving attention to the works and the ideas that stimulated the poet's mind: Hardenberg's natural philosophy has to be pieced together from the comments he makes on the scientific theories and practices of his day.

III. THE VALUE OF HARDENBERG'S NOTES ON SCIENCE

What may one expect from studying the scientific notes of a romantic poet? I assumed that Novalis' natural philosophy will be of interest to historians of science as well as students of literature, that his thoughts on science have an intrinsic value beyond the aid they might provide to understand his poetry. This is by no means obvious and could hardly have been defended on the basis of earlier unsatisfactory editions. Wilhelm Dilthey, an admirable critic of Novalis who was first to claim that his "fragments" were not merely confused aggregates of contradictory remarks, treasured the notebooks for those metaphysical and humanistic ideas that he found still alive and important from the point of view of his own philosophy. But he saw no intrinsic value in Novalis' scientific writings. Even in retrospect, when Dilthey included the essay in his volume *Das Erlebnis und die Dichtung*, he defended this position: "Und auch dabei muß ich bleiben, daß ich mit meiner Abschätzung des wissenschaftlichen Wertes der Fragmente damals das Richtige getroffen habe.... In den metaphysischen und geisteswissenschaftlichen Fragmenten sah ich die Bedeutung des Nachlasses. Meine Absicht war, zu zeigen, welchen Wert die letzteren auch noch für die heutigen Geisteswissenschaften haben."[15] In fact,

Dilthey felt vindicated by the first study of Hardenberg's notes on science, a dissertation by W. Olshausen which appeared in 1905.[16] Although Olshausen differed from Dilthey on specific points of interpretation, he agreed with him that Hardenberg's scientific studies were erratic and chaotic, and therefore worthless from a scientific point of view.[17]

Both Dilthey and Olshausen had to rely on very incomplete editions of Novalis' works which were particularly misleading in the presentation of the scientific material. Olshausen's contentions have been challenged on that account in several studies,[18] but only now, with the publication of all the scientific notes, a better chronological ordering, and a clearer delineation of context, can the validity of Olshausen's findings be judged. I believe that Novalis' studies were on the whole thorough and consistent and one should not judge them on the ground of occasional excentric speculations. He had a comprehensive knowledge of contemporary views and achievements in medicine and science, and his selective attention in the notebooks was not a sign of insufficient information, but a critique he applied. In emphasizing the breadth of his readings and the contemporary scientific context I kept, as far as was possible, the discussion of Novalis' conception of disease in terms of contemporary thought on pathology, physiology, and philosophy, and not, as for instance in the works of R. Unger and W. Rehm,[19] in terms of the theology and metaphysics of romanticism.

The scientific and philosophical value of Novalis' natural philosophy has been a particularly vexing question to German historians of medicine who felt torn between their scientific credo and their attachment to the cultural tradition of romanticism.[20] In the compromise which seems to be generally accepted now, Novalis' stature is vindicated by the claim that "Romantic Medicine"—a peculiar chapter in the history of German medicine covering the first decades of the nineteenth century—was decisively shaped by Hardenberg's thoughts on the nature of disease and the art of healing. Yet, this argument can hardly be construed as a compliment since to many historians of medicine the romantic period was merely an aberration from the forward march of science. As P. Diepgen put it: "Mit dem diffusen Reizbegriff ließ sich schön spekulieren. Das haben denn auch Schelling, der ihm nahestehende... Andreas Roeschlaub... und der Dichter (!) [sic] Novalis... gründlich getan, nicht ohne zahlreiche Anhänger zu gewinnen, aber ohne die wissenschaftliche Medizin auch nur im leisesten zu fördern."[21] There is no concrete evidence that Novalis had authority among doctors of medicine and we have to assume that whatever Novalis shared with the doctor-philosophers of the succeeding generation was derived from common sources and the general intellectual atmosphere of the age.

At any rate, even from a historical and scientific point of view what is at issue is not Novalis' contribution to cumulative knowledge but the consistency and reasonableness of his ideas in terms of eighteenth-century science. Historians of science recognize the inadequacy of the assumption that science develops through the gradual and uninterrupted accumulation of facts, or that it is historically possible to separate neatly discoveries from "errors" or "myths". Wrong theories might contain partial truths, valuable discoveries might result from incorrect hypotheses, and even complete errors may serve as stimuli for constructive efforts. As Professor T. S. Kuhn remarks, one ought to examine scientific attitudes in the context of their age and ask about their inner coherence and integrity: "Out-of-date theories are not in principle unscientific because they have been discarded."[22]

IV. THE VARIETY IN HARDENBERG'S SCIENTIFIC INTEREST

It has often been asserted that romanticism represents pure organicism, anthropomorphically directed among the sciences towards biology and anthropology since these define man and his position in nature. It has even been suggested by Professor Gillispie that romanticism may be defined by its preference for biology over physics and mathematics: "... we may be in a position to venture that consistent account of romanticism which eludes us in the history of politics, philosophy, and the arts. Romanticism began as a moral revolt against physics, expressed in moving, sad, and sometimes angry attempts to defend a qualitative science, in which nature can be congruent with man, against a measuring, numbering science which alienates the creator of science from his own creation by total objectification of nature. For physics romanticism would substitute biology at the heart of science."[23]

Professor Gillispie's remark may be applied to Blake and Goethe, both of whom had a long-standing quarrel with Newtonian science, and to a lesser extent to Wordsworth and Schelling who were organicists uninterested in mathematical thinking. But Novalis' conception of mathematics was more complex. He did, of course, look for an organic and personal relationship with nature. But if he wrote a little poem which anticipates a future where poetry and fables will take the place of numbers and figures (I, 344 and 360), he also remarked that letters ought to become numbers and languages mathematics (III, 50). In fact, to Novalis mathematics did not consist merely of numbers. As Käte Hamburger has shown, his idea of mathematics was related to Kant's interpretation of it, and his concepts anticipated such modern terms as function and continuity. From Kant he accepted that mathematical operations were *a priori* synthetic judgments and that consequently all the sciences should become mathematics (III, 50 and 593). In the search of unity, coherence, and certainty in knowledge, mathematics showed to him how, from a few basic principles, a universally applicable system may be constructed.

From Kant Novalis differed, however, in the interpretation he gave to synthetic judgments. If such judgments always were beyond empirical proofs, mathematical knowledge required an affirmation of faith: "In allem Wissen ist Glauben". He felt the need for reinforcing mathematics with "Glauben und Liebe" and followed the Pythagorean tradition of raising it to a mystic and divine science.

While the sciences were in need of an *a priori* mathematical structure which the pattern of the mind would supply, the study of the mind, and the body in general, necessitated the development of biology, physiology, anatomy, psychology, and the other life sciences. Medicine, as the most humane and inclusive

of the sciences, was therefore of central importance to many of
the romantics. As Schelling stated in the Introduction to the
Jahrbücher der Medicin als Wissenschaft, medicine was the crown of
all the sciences, because it studied man who was himself the
center and image of the universe. Discussing Novalis' "Naturphilosophie", one has to devote therefore greatest attention to
his notes on medicine, physiology, and psychology. These were
indeed the sciences that concerned him most: physics and
chemistry were important to him for their practical value in
the technology of salt mining and for what they revealed of the
method of science in general, but in the formation of his
philosophy they had relatively little significance. The phenomena of galvanism and magnetism form an exception, because it
was believed that these constituted a link between physical and
psychic forces.

V. GENERAL CONSIDERATIONS

It might be asked whether the picture of Novalis emerging from
this study of his notebooks will be representative, since I shall
neither discuss his best-known poetic works nor even all
aspects of his theoretical writings. Although the ideas of
Hardenberg's natural philosophy do enter into his poetry and
fiction, one has to admit that these works do not center on
science and medicine, and an exclusively scientific analysis would
damage their poetic fabric. Nevertheless, the notes on science do
play an important role in Hardenberg's intellectual development.
In spite of some older views, Novalis achieved no genuine and
lasting synthesis during his life, and very likely he had no
illusions about realizing one in general—except in an eschato-
logical future. Not only did he believe that there can be no
unique and universal mode in which men perfect themselves,
but he also saw man's crucial relation to nature from several
different angles. His earliest philosphical studies in 1794-96
centered on the works of Fichte, where nature was reduced to a
mere not-I. Emerging from, but never fully rejecting Fichte's
exaltation of the self, Novalis turned to the sciences and for a
while he inclined to agree with Schelling that nature and mind,

subject and object were corresponding to each other. The stay in Freiberg vastly enlarged his understanding of the empirical sciences, but, paradoxically, it also brought his differences from Schelling in sharper relief: philosophically he moved away from empiricism and theories of correspondence. The attempt at an encyclopedia, "Das allgemeine Brouillon", and, briefly afterwards, *Die Lehrlinge* were Novalis' attempts to construct a synthesis, to give a poetic, moral, and religious meaning to the empirical world and to its systematic explanation—science. The incompleteness of both, as well as the shift from the encyclopedic form in the "Brouillon" to the poetic form in *Die Lehrlinge*, indicates that Novalis was dissatisfied with his attempts and moved towards a more consistently poetic view of the world. In the discussion of *Die Lehrlinge* I attempt to show that the ironies and ambiguities in this work issue from a clash between contradictory states of mind. After this unsuccessful attempt the polar forces clearly separated and remained active only in a realm of their own: the empirical and scientific talents of Novalis, no longer employed in the construction of scientific philosophies, found an outlet in his technical-professional work, while his poetic and visionary self became actively engaged in the writing of poetry. The late poetic works, above all *Heinrich von Ofterdingen*, do not encompass the empirical world as the "Brouillon" or *Die Lehrlinge* set out to do: they are primarily a synthesis within a delicately woven poetic structure, incorporating, perhaps by necessity, only linguistic reminiscences of science.

It is possible to look upon this development from a different angle, and describe it not in terms of change but as a single undulating interaction of radical philosophical and historical positions. In connection with Hardenberg's reading of Schelling I attempt to show that already during his early study of Fichte there appears a pantheistic strain in his thought. According to this there is an organic unity between man and the universe, and the human mind is not radically separated from the realm of nature. Hardenberg's later preoccupation with the interaction of polarities, with the nature of organisms, and with the relationship between parts and the whole indicate that he was in search of a theory of correspondences and a holistic view of the universe. Yet, Fichte's (and Schiller's) notion that nature will have to be overcome through the assertion of human freedom never disappears from Hardenberg's thought: it dominates the "Brouillon" and his crowning poetic works. There is no unanimity in these works as to what human forces ought to propell this transformation. At times it appears as a purely ethical task, as the assertion of practical reason only, at others as a work of the imagination, of man's creative powers. Neither of these positions is consistently upheld in Hardenberg's works: he repeatedly questions the guiding power of the imagination, and towards the end of his life he becomes convinced that moral development can only result from an exposure to sin.

A complete treatment of what has been sketched here is beyond the scope of my book, even though I have tried to stress throughout Hardenberg's "bifocality". Too often in the past critics tended to overemphasize the unity of his thought, by giving exclusive attention to only one aspect of it. I hope to illuminate the variety in him, those tensions and hesitations between mind and nature or ethics and aesthetics that make him a poet of our problems too.

I

Aspects of Eighteenth-Century Science

1. LOCKE, BACON, AND DESCARTES

He that in physic shall lay down fundamental maxims, and, from thence ... shall reduce it into the regular form of science, has indeed done something to enlarge the art of talking and perhaps laid a foundation for endless disputes; but, if he hopes to bring men by such a system to the knowledge of the infirmities [of men's] bodies, the constitution, nature, signs, changes and history of diseases, with the safe and discreet way of their cure, takes much what a like course with him that should walk up and down in a thick wood... and draw a map of the country....
True knowledge grew first in the world by experience and rational operations....[1]

In more than one way, this passage from the hand of the young Locke defines a point of reference and a perfect antithesis to the romantic conception of medicine and science. It not only asserts that medicine is an empirical science based on careful bedside observations and that the "fundamental maxims" of physics and chemistry can contribute little to the art of curing, but shows also a general skepticism of the potentials of science and of the value of erecting abstract structures of the mind—a somewhat surprising view considering Locke's enthusiastic reception of Newton's discovery. The scientific method that Locke endorses here, as well as in *An Essay Concerning Human Understanding*,[2] is based on empirical observation and induction, according to the principles that Bacon had formulated eloquently some seventy years earlier in his fight against scholastic logic: "... the logic which is received, ... is not nearly subtle enough to deal with nature; and in attempting what it cannot master, has done more to establish and perpetuate error than to open the way to truth."[3] "There is none who has dwelt upon experience and the facts of nature as long as is necessary."[4]

Locke's modest claims for science were founded on Bacon's empiricism and on Descartes' theory of sensation. For in Descartes' dualistic system the physical realm (res extensio) became sharply separated from consciousness (res cogitans) and a serious problem arose when the motions of the external world were to be correlated with the perceptions of the self. Like Descartes, Locke assumed that many little corpuscles moved about in the external world, creating sensations when impinging upon the senses. But since such mechanical movements and collisions were very incongruent with our ideas of such secondary qualities as colour, sound, or temperature, the exact correspondence between the world and the self remained undefined, and science rested on shaky grounds.

II. LEIBNIZ, HALLER, AND THE DEVELOPMENT OF BIOLOGY

Neither the Baconian conception of empiricism and induction, nor the Descartian mechanical conception of the world in space became widely held in eighteenth-century Germany. At the dim beginnings of German science one perceives the towering figure of Leibniz who gave a different direction to scientific research, by opposing equally the method of induction, Locke's theory of no innate ideas, and Descartes' mechanical interpretation of the physical world. To this eminently mathematical mind the constructs of mathematics proved without doubt that certain truths do not originate from sensory experience: "... It would seem that necessary truths, such as are found in pure mathematics and especially in arithmetic and in geometry, must have principles the proof of which does not depend on examples, nor, consequently, on the testimony of the senses, although without the senses we would never take it into our heads to think of them."[5]

Leibniz believed that he delivered himself of the deceptive demon of the senses that haunted both Descartes and Locke and he set the course for a scientific method which became prevalent in Germany: with a few notable exceptions, such as Albrecht Haller, German scientists of the eighteenth century and the romantic period were more inclined to argue deductively from general principles than empirically and inductively. The success of Newtonian science only strengthened this tendency, for, by ignoring its empirical and analytical method, scientists and philosophers frequently understood only the simplicity and beauty of the final Newtonian equations, which captured such vastly different motions as the falling of an apple and the orbital revolution of planets. Newton's way of synthesizing and systematizing knowledge in a highly abstract and mathematical form fascinated those who were preoccupied with the unity of nature and the foundations of knowledge. Among them was Kant, who found *a priori* synthetic judgments exemplified in mathematics.

Equally important for eighteenth-century German science was Leibniz's rejection of mechanisms and mechanical interactions. True, he went even further than Descartes in separating mind and body by rightly contesting the Cartesian claim that the direction of a body's motion may be altered through the action of the mind. According to Leibniz, bodies obeyed only natural (efficient) causes, and coordination between mind and body was possible only because of a divinely pre-established harmony. Yet nothing would have been more alien to him than a mechanistic machine-like view of bodies. The "simple substances" of his philosophy, the self-contained and "windowless" monads, were independent of external forces and subjected only to their internal nature: "... the natural changes of the monads proceed from an internal principle, since an external cause could not influence their inner being."[6] This internal principle or force, which made the monad the source of its own internal activity and moved it teleologically from one state into another, was to Leibniz the Aristotelean entelechy. Since every such monad was a microcosm of the universe, and since each particle of matter was made up of an infinite number of simple substances, the universe was an organic structure where the tiniest part reflected the whole.

This organic view of nature became dominant in eighteenth-century German science, even though Leibniz's radical separation of body and mind was not always accepted. In the powerful "animistic" or "vitalistic" school, founded by Georg Ernst Stahl (1660-1734), it was assumed that the mind can directly intervene in the natural processes, and the entelechy was made directly responsible for all changes in organic matter,[7] including pathological ones. Stahl's colleague at Halle, Friedrich Hoffman (1660-1742), rejected the theory that a spiritual principle might guide the body, nevertheless he believed that health was regulated by a central agent. He assumed that the organic body was made up of fibres contracting and expanding upon the action of a "nervous ether" concentrated in the brain. He was thereby among the first to ascribe a central function to nerves in the body.

The emerging school of neuro-pathology was opposed by the somewhat older school that stressed the physiological function of fluids. According to the outdated Galenic conceptions, four fluids (blood, phlegm, yellow bile, and black bile) existed in the body, and the particular mixture of these determined whether the temperament of the person was sanguinic, phlegmatic, choleric, or melancholic. With the slow development of chemistry and physiology this conception was abandoned but the basic principle, that the interaction of fluids determined the constitution, was retained. The founding of iatrochemistry is usually associated with the name of Van Helmont (1577-1644), a student of Paracelsus who caught Novalis' interest (see Ch. VI). The corresponding theory of pathology, resting on the analysis of bodily humours (fluids) was termed humoral pathology.

The greatest physician of the early eighteenth century, the Dutch Hermann Boerhave (1668-1738), was neither an adherent of the humoral pathologist school nor an advocate of animism, but an empiricist without a theory, collecting "true knowledge" through "experience and rational operations" by working in hospitals and laboratories. This too was the method of his most gifted student, Albrecht Haller (1708-1777), who is chiefly remembered today in literary history for his poem "The Alps". But Haller was above all a scientist and a scholar, the dominating figure in the early history of the university at Göttingen, where he lead the scientific society and contributed prodigiously (around ten-thousand reviews!) to the *Göttingische Gelehrte Anzeigen*. He was also the founder of modern physiology, principally through his famous experiments which separated irritability, the muscles' capacity to answer stimulation, from sensibility, a reaction to stimuli involving not only the muscles but the whole nervous system and even the soul. As Haller reported to the scientific society at Göttingen on April 22, 1752:

> I call that part of the human body irritable, which becomes shorter upon being touched; very irritable if it contracts upon a slight touch ... I call that a sensible part of the human body, which upon being touched transmits the impression of it to the soul; and in the brutes, in whom the existence of a soul is not so clear, I call those parts sensible, the Irritation of which occasions evident signs of pain and disquiet in the animal.[8]

Everybody agreed that these were important experiments, but there was little consensus concerning their meaning and historians of medicine still disagree widely on the issues in the debate ensuing from Haller's paper. Some believed that by establishing sensibility as the transmission of physiological impulses to the soul Haller's theory supported Stahlian animism; on the other end, Lamettrie, the author of *L'homme machine* (1747), claimed that Haller's concept of irritability actually disproved the soul and affirmed the exclusive existence of mind—a conclusion which greatly chagrined the pious Haller. In England, Robert Whytt defended a form of animism and violently fought Haller's separation of irritability and sensibility by claiming that the soul was diffused throughout the nervous system and always responsible for muscular movements. Whytt was supported by a professor from Prague, Georg Prochaska (1749-1820), whose book on physiology was in Novalis' possession.[9]

The reaction to Haller's experiments was generally favorable in Germany for they seemed to confirm the widely held belief that physical and psychological phenomena were inseparable from each other. Sensibility appeared as the "missing link", the palpable evidence for the unity of life: at last, the Descartian dualism seemed defeated by the irrefutable evidence emerging from the laboratory of the physiologist. It was still in the wake of Haller's experiments that in 1774 F. C. Medicus coined the term "Lebenskraft", a mysterious, immaterial agent guiding the life and the development of organisms.[10] The stage was now set for the biology of the "Goethezeit", according to which everything was interrelated and alive, striving to unfold the potentials dormant in the womb of nature.

In fact, a friend of Goethe and one of the first evolutionists formulated this principle most clearly and coherently. J. F. Blumenbach (1752-1840) saw nature as an unceasingly changing being that regenerated, reproduced, and organically developed, so that the related organs, the species of nature, continually showed their kinship. The vision of organic unity in nature led him to initiate the study of comparative anatomy, a science which recognized everywhere a basic vital force that drove life from the seed towards its teleological end: "[ich bin überzeugt], daß in allen belebten Geschöpfen ... ein besondrer, eingebohrner, lebenslang thätiger würksamer Trieb liegt, ihre bestimmte Gestalt anfangs anzunehmen, dann zu erhalten, und wenn sie ja zerstört worden, wo möglich wieder herzustellen."[11] Blumenbach named this force "Bildungstrieb" (*nisus formativus*), which indicates that he regarded it not merely as a symbol of unity in nature but as an assertion of individuality in the sense in which Goethe's "Bildung" meant a harmonious and ultimately self-centered development of individual potentials; as in Goethe's understanding of life, in Blumenbach's biology the dynamic indestructibility of "Gestalt" was claimed.

But scientific concepts should in some way be observable or measurable, and attempts to find a physically measurable correlative for the "Bildungstrieb" in galvanism or magnetism remained unsuccesful. It was not a scientific "discovery", but an index to the intellectual climate of the age: in the decades following it emerged as a useful expression of organic drive which was felt to be operating in individual lives as well as in the movement of history.

For instance, "Bildungstrieb" provided the biological pattern to Herder's historical scheme in *Ideen zur Philosophie der Geschichte der Menschheit*, where it was claimed that a unique force pervaded the universe and moved the tiniest part of it. Following Blumenbach,[12] Herder imagined that this universal power was constitutive in a number of component forces, each with a peculiar function and value within a hierarchical order. Production and reproduction as muscular activities were on the lowest level; higher forms were supposed to exhibit a more delicate structure, and a division of labor guided by the nerves and the brain. The latter was the center and director of receptivity and activity.[13] This way Herder combined Haller's ideas on sensibility and irritability with Blumenbach's conception of a unitary force, and projected a vast dynamic movement along an evolutionary scale.

Herder's impact upon the German intellectual life of the last two decades in the eighteenth century is well-known and need not be discussed here; Novalis entered his university studies with a copy of the *Ideen*—the only book in his library at that time which had some relevance to scientific problems.[14] Later he also acquired a copy of a speech by the biologist C. F. Kielmeyer (1765-1844) which seems to be a codified version of Herder's sketchy ideas on the hierarchy of organic forces.[15] Kielmeyer recognized five different properties unequal in value but all of them indispensable for the maintenance of life. On the lowest level were the mechanical forces of secretion and propulsion providing for the proper distribution, absorption, and secretion of fluids. Above these vegetative forces rose the tripartite hierarchy of "higher" properties, an arrangement that owes much to the experiments of Haller for Kielmeyer defined these properties as *sensibility*, the passive property of internalizing external impulses, *irritability*, the contractility of muscles, and finally the *reproductive capacity* of the organism.[16] Although Kielmeyer's speech was hailed by Schelling as epochmaking (Sch, I, 633), it was never seriously adopted in scientific investigations, perhaps because the list seemed arbitrary. Like Blumenbach's theory, Kielmeyer's scheme became important, however, in the emerging "Naturphilosophie", where it met with medical and biological speculations also related to Haller's experiments but originating from England.

III. JOHN BROWN'S MEDICAL THEORY

Although the conclusions of Haller's experiments were not universally accepted in England, they were received with interest and subjected to scrutiny; as a consequence, the functioning of the nervous system received increased attention in medical research and thinking. The word "neurosis" was coined in the *Synopsis Nosologiae Methodicae* (London, 1769) of the Scot William Cullen (1710-1790),[17] professor of chemistry and medicine at Edinburgh and founder of the medical school at Glasgow. Cullen was among the originators of the neuropathologist school of medicine by claiming that the nervous system regulated the organism, and nervous atony and spasm were responsible for diseases.

It remained, however, for a student and later opponent of Cullen, John Brown (1735-1788), to simplify and popularize these ideas. This odd genius founded an illustrious family which includes Ford Madox Brown the painter and Ford Madox Ford,[18] opened an odd chapter in the history of medicine, and exerted a remarkable influence on the intellectual life of Goethe's age.

Brown's *chef d'oeuvre*, the *Elementa Medicinae*,[19] appeared a year after its author graduated from medical school, to answer the momentuous question posed by the author himself: "whether the medical art, until then conjectural, incoherent, and, in the great body of it, false, was not, at last, reduced to a demonstrated science, which might be called the science of life."[20]

This rhetorical question, prompted in Brown by the shining success of Newton, he answered himself in a modest footnote: "That question has been answered in the affirmative by every one who had been at due pains to understand the doctrine."[21]

This "science of life" rested on the central idea that in "all states of life, man and other animals differ from themselves in their dead state, or from any other inanimate matter in this property alone: that they can be affected by external agents, as well as by certain functions peculiar to themselves."[22] Thus internal and external stimulations enter the organism much the same way as ideas enter consciousness in Locke's theory of ideas. But whereas the Lockean stimuli impinge on a *tabula rasa*, in Brown's definition the organism was not quite passive with regard to external stimulation (a central feature of his philosophy for Schelling and Novalis), for at the outset of life it was supposed to have received a fixed quantity of *excitability*: "We know not what excitability is, or in what manner it is affected by the exciting powers. But whatever it be, either a certain quantity, or a certain energy of it is assigned to every being upon the commencement of its living state."[23] External agents, such as heat, food, and air, and internal stimuli, due to thinking and the emotions, constantly feed upon this excitability, which recovers a part, but never the totality of its loss during rest or sleep. According to Brown, internal and external stimuli constitute together the exciting powers, and if excitability or either of the two exciting powers is withdrawn, life ceases, for "nothing else is necessary to life."[24] Paradoxically, the exciting powers support life but simultaneously exhaust it—which gives a touch of melancholy to Brown's theory: "It is not therefore true, that some powers are contrived by nature for the preservation of life and health, others to bring on diseases and death. The tendency of them all is indeed to support life, but in a forced way, and then to bring on death, but by a spontaneous operation."[25]

Brown believed that the health of an organism depended solely on the proper amount of stimulation, sicknesses could therefore arise only from a lack or an overdose of it and had to be one of two types: overstimulation brought the body into a state of excitement called sthenic, while organisms with a debility in stimulation and excitement were said to be asthenic. The two states also differed insofar as the extreme of the sthenic state converted into exhaustion, called Indirect Debility (or indirectly asthenic state), while the extreme of the asthenic diseases directly led to death.

Since all diseases merely depended on the quantity of stimulation, the aim of healing was to reestablish the proper amount of it: stimulation and excitement were to be reduced in sthenic diseases and increased in asthenic ones.[25] Brown considered most diseases asthenic, and therefore his cure usually consisted in the application of stimulating and strengthening medicaments and foods—a positive contribution to the medical practice of the time, still steeped in debilitating methods such as bloodletting.[26]

Yet Brown's fortifying cure was a mixed blessing. He believed that "spirituous or vinous drink ... stimulates more quickly, and more readily, than seasoned food, and its stimulus is in proportion to the quantity of alkahol which it contains." More important: "... there are stimuli, which possess an operation as much quicker, and more powerful, than these just now mentioned ... the highest of all, as far as experiments have yet reflected light upon the subject, is opium."[27] Perhaps these stimulating yet life-consuming powers inspired Brown's resigned and poetic meditation on human fate: "... life is a forced state; ... the tendency of animals, every moment, is to dissolution; ... they are kept from it by foreign powers, and even by these with difficulty, and only for a little; and then, from the necessity of their fate, give way to death."[28]

The "foreign powers" caught up with Brown—in 1788 still poor and neglected—and the years to come did not bring him more recognition in England. Yet his works were embarking upon a curious new life all over the world: in the United States his fellow-student from Edinburgh, Benjamin Rush, published an edition of the *Elements* which was followed by five more; there were several Spanish translation both in Spain and in Mexico; in Italy the reception was so serious that versions of his theory dominated Italian medical thinking into the third decade of the nineteenth century; in France it was published and according to Walter Scott even Napoleon was a confirmed believer in the theory. One medical authority claims, however, that Brown's treatment had more casualties than all the Napoleonic Wars.

IV. BROWN'S THEORY IN GERMANY

Brown's theory had its most serious intellectual impact in Germany. Although Blumenbach, Goethe, Kielmeyer, Herder, and many others may be regarded as forerunners, romantic science and medicine did not come to full life until Brown's ideas invaded Germany. The precise date of this is, however, somewhat obscure. During his tour in 1798-99 Coleridge noted with curiosity that in Germany, where foreign ideas were as a rule taken up quickly, Brown's theory had found only a late reception.[29] We know now that this remark, copied almost verbatim from the *Allgemeine Literatur Zeitung*, was not quite correct. As early as 1790 an article in Rosier's *Journal de Physique* described a medical theory ominously resembling the *Elementa*, deviating from it only insofar as it ascribed the degree of irritability (excitability) in the body to the quantity of oxygen in it.[30] The article was written by a German, Christoph Girtanner, and received much critical attention in Germany; but a few years later the plagiarism was discovered and Girtanner had to defend himself by claiming that he had written a parody of Brown which the sullen Germans had missed.[31] Later he became serious enough to write a two volume critique of Brown's work and to close the affair with the feeling of victory: "Nunmehr aber, nachdem ich meinen mächtigen Gegner durch die Waffen der Vernunft bekämpft, und ihn so zu Boden geworfen habe, daß er nicht wieder aufstehen kann, trete ich, mit dem angenehmen Gefühle des Siegers, von dem Kampf-Plaze ab, und hänge, gleich den Gladiatoren des alten Roms, meine Waffen-Rüstung auf."[32]

Another entry in Coleridge's notebook throws light both on himself and on the philosophical conditions prevailing in Germany when Brown's ideas penetrated there. Answering Girtanner's accusations that Brown attributed universal validity to ideas which were built on induction and analogy,[33] Coleridge wrote that "Brown was no Kantian & probably held nothing but high degrees of Probability possible."[34] Once more, Coleridge's remark holds only partially: although Brown was indeed no Kantian, he was, for all practical purposes, turned into one by German philosophers and physicians. To the same objection by Girtanner, an avid supporter of Brown remarked in the spirit of Kant: Excitability was no object of spatial perception but an a priori concept of the mind and that both induction and analogy were indispensable modes of understanding in all the natural sciences.[35]

In 1798, when Girtanner believed he had eliminated Brown from the ring, the *Elements of Medicine* actually enjoyed rising reputation in Germany. Its most loyal defender was M. A. Weikard (1742-1803), a former court physician to Empress Catherine of Russia. He had published a German translation of the *Elements* in 1795 together with his own *Entwurf einer einfachern Arzeneykunst*[36] which also dealt with the teachings of Brown. In the following two years Weikard added to these a handbook and a magazine,[37] all of which were to disseminate the "dogmas" in a fittingly dogmatic manner; he was a passionate but untalented and intolerant disciple of the new gospel, advocated the discarding of nosology and diagnostics, and held all former medical knowledge in contempt. His ruthless, personal attacks against members of the establishment and critics of the new system polarized opinions, and while they alienated many of the older doctors they won him a significant section of the young students. The spirit of revolution was smuggled with Brown into Germany.

Of Weikard's medical practice we possess a charming little souvenir in Justinus Kerner's *Das Bilderbuch aus meiner Knabenzeit*. The young Kerner, who suffered of a nervous stomach, was once brought to the "Wunderdoktor" of Heilbronn and was subjected to a lengthy examination, at the end of which he fainted. Weikard, the "Wunderdoktor", until then evidently undecided whether to call the disease sthenic or asthenic, now unhesitatingly declared that the disease was asthenic and prescribed for it "Hoppelpoppel" and "Pfefferkorn". Since "Hoppelpoppel", a Russian concoction of tea, egg yolk, and cherry brandy, did not appeal to the young Kerner, he promtly decided to throw up whenever it was administered to him. The "Wunderdoktor", in turn, remarked with firmness and decorum upon departure: "Furchtbare Asthenie durch zu schnelle Entwickelung ist es, sonst nichts ... und da müssen nur stärkende Mittel gereicht werden"[38] — which might have been the correct diagnosis after all.

For all his zeal, Weikard probably did more harm than good, and the fad would have quickly passed, had more imaginative minds not seized, developed, and reinterpreted the dogma. A. F. Marcus and A. Röschlaub were engaged in such a revaluation at the clinic of Bamberg, which became the center for the study of Brown's theory. Marcus, the chief physician, published the *Prüfung des Brownischen Systems der Heilkunde* between 1797 and 1799, a book consisting of bedside observations and case histories interpreted in terms of Brown's theory.[39] Röschlaub, in turn, published the *Magazin zur Vervollkommnung der theoretischen und practischen Heilkunde* which became the mouthpiece of Brown's followers after the quick foundering of Weikard's magazine.

Even more important was the appearance of Röschlaub's *Untersuchungen über Pathogenie*, a book which started from Brown's premises but subtly and perhaps unknowingly readjusted them according to German philosophical ideas. The young Schelling was deeply impressed by it even though he disagreed with its mechanistic premises, and when he decided that his medical knowledge needed reinforcement he went to observe Marcus and Röschlaub at work. He spent the ill-fated summer of 1800 in Bamberg while Karoline Schlegel and her daughter, K. Böhmer, stayed in the nearby Bocklet; it was rumored that Schelling applied Brownian cure to the girl who suddenly died at the end of the summer — at least this is what the *Allgemeine Literatur Zeitung* asserted years later in its war against the romantics.[40] Schelling remained, however, a friend of the physicians at Bamberg and became with Marcus co-editor of the *Jahrbücher der Medicin als Wissenschaft* (1806-08). By that time both Marcus and Röschlaub became followers of his "Naturphilosophie".

Goethe too had his experience with Brown's treatment, though this was considerably milder. As recorded in the *Tag- und Jahreshefte*, Goethe once accepted from a young friend a Brownian medication with opium against pains in his chest. The pains deceptively ceased for a brief period but soon returned with increased vigor.[41] As a result, both Brown and Röschlaub found their way into the pantheon of Goethe's enemies:

> Wenn ich nun im holden Haine
> Unter meinen Freunden wandle,
> Mögens meine Feinde haben,
> Die als Kegel ich behandle.
> Kommt nur her, geliebte Freunde!
> Laßt uns schleudern, laßt uns schieben;
> Seht nur, es ist jedem Kegel
> Auch sein Name angeschrieben....
> Brown steht hinten in dem Grunde,
> Röschlaub aber trutzt mir vorne,
> Und besonders diesen letzten
> Hab ich immer auf dem Korne.[42]

Goethe's criticism was shared by others, and most medical authorities expressed some reservations about the new ideas. The opposition grouped around the dignified C. W. Hufeland (1762-1836), a court physician at Weimar who published the influental *Journal der practischen Arzneykunde und Wundarzneykunst* and *Bibliothek der practischen Heilkunde*, and ran a series of critical articles on the Brownians and their theory. As a student of Blumenbach Hufeland was not unfavorably disposed towards theories of excitability (which did seem to be a form of "Lebenskraft"), but the Brownian movement in Germany appeared to him as a misguided revolution. He claimed that in science development was evolutionary and not revolutionary,[43] and he shared with Locke the view that medicine ought to be put together piecemeal, by the slow accumulation of bedside observations. *A priori* constructs of pure reason had no place in medicine, for its theories were always contingent upon experience.⁴⁴ Even worse, the adherents of Brown, like the Jacobins in France, were not heralds of a new freedom, but would-be dictators of a new dogma and oppressors of the mind's freedom to inquire.⁴⁵

Hufeland was of course right in regarding the Brownians as a group of zealots in defence of a "dogma" which promised all too easy solutions for life, death, and disease. But he was too deeply steeped in seventeenth-century rationalism to recognize that only on the elementary level did science develop through the evolutionary process of collecting facts. The history of eighteenth-century science was dotted with important discoveries which were made in the name of an imaginative scheme or a theory which later proved to be wrong. It remained for the romantics to recognize the role that imagination, conviction, and even partisan fanaticism have in the apparently objective and neutral sciences. As Wordsworth put it, the poet "considers man and nature as essentially adapted to each other, and the mind of man as naturally the mirror of the fairest and most interesting properties of nature"—thus theory need not wait till all empirical evidence is collected. Novalis was acquainted with Hufeland's magazines,⁴⁶ but the editor's approach seemed pedestrian and pedantic to him: Hufeland's "Makrobiotik", a popular work on how to prolong life through moderation, upheld a "principle of mediocrity" (II, 464) against which Novalis developed his own vision of qualitatively raising and projecting humanity into the infinite.

II

Sources and Impulses

1. IMAGINATION AND HYPOCHONDRIA

In the only source about Novalis' early youth, a biography which was drawn up by his brother Karl, one finds an interesting note on his nature and development:

> Er war der erste Sohn und das 2te Kind frommer Eltern; in seinen ersten Kinderjahren war er schwächlich doch ohne schwere Krankheit bis in das 9te Jahr, auch schien er bis dahin keinen außerordentlichen Geist zu versprechen, und nur die vorzügliche Liebe und zärtliche Anhänglichkeit zu seiner Mutter zeichnete ihn vor seinen andern Geschwister aus; ... In seinem 9ten Jahre bekam er die Ruhr, und als Folge dieser Krankheit eine Atonie des Magens die nur durch die schmerzhaftesten Reizmittel und eine langwierige Cur konnte gehoben werden;—Jezt schien sein Geist auf einmal zu erwachen; ...[1]

The medical terminology in Karl's report clearly indicates the penetration of Brownian medicine into the parlance of everyday. Since the theory was yet unknown at the time when Novalis had actually fallen sick (but was widely used when Karl wrote his reminiscences), the trustworthiness of the report—at least from a medical point of view—is open to question. It seems therefore unwarranted to conclude, as K. J. Obenauer did, that the description of this disease and its remarkable similarity to a passage in Book VI of Goethe's *Wilhelm Meisters Lehrjahre* signified a latent mystic potential in the poet.[2] From a variety of reports we get the picture of a rather healthy and normal child that showed no extraordinary signs of introspection and withdrawal. His main interest did, however, foreshadow his ultimate field of excellence: a list of books he took to Jena at the beginning of his university studies contains almost exclusively works from men of letters and perhaps only some papers of Herder foreshadow Hardenberg's later interest in science. A somewhat later note, probably from Leipzig, lists plans to study theater, philosophy, law, history, and languages, but mentions none of the sciences. It is therefore more than likely that he had neither training nor any great knowledge in these fields by the time he received his law degree in Wittenberg.[3]

While medicine was a discipline which needed special concentration, sickness was a universal experience into which Novalis was initiated early in his life. His concern with hypochondria demonstrates well that personal experiences in his early life interacted later with philosophical and scientific attitudes.

In the *Nachlese* there is a report on a premature childbirth in 1783 which seriously upset the psychological balance of Novalis' mother:

> Zwar schwand die Lebensgefahr nach einigen Wochen, aber es blieb eine Art Hypochondrie zurück, die zeitweise in Schwermuth auszuarten drohte und, verbunden mit körperlicher Hinfälligkeit, die sonst so kräftige, lebensfrische Frau für mehrere Jahre unfähig machte, sich um ihren Haushalt zu bekümmern. Es traten Monate ein, wo sie entweder in völliger Theilnahmlosigkeit verharrte oder durch alles aufs Aeußerste erregt und geängstigt wurde (p. 17).

As the context indicates, hypochondria denoted in the eighteenth century states of mental depression which affected the physiological functioning of the body, diseases which would today be called psychosomatic. Although there is no way to know how the mother's hypochondria affected Novalis, her illness was surely one reason why the mysteries of hypochondria were foremost in his mind and became indicative of the problematic nature of the imagination itself. A second biographical factor was the prolonged sickness of Erasmus, who suffered from various diseases and passed away on April 14, 1797, a month after the death of Sophie.

Novalis referred to hypochondria for the first time when he reported to his father that Erasmus, who was studying with him in Leipzig, had an attack [sic] of this disease during Christmas of 1792 (IV, 36). Soon after, when Novalis left Leipzig to embark on a military career, he wrote a letter to Erasmus. It may be thought that the paternal tone of this letter reflects admonitions that Novalis himself received at this time from his father. But it is more true to say that the rules of conduct given to Erasmus are meant for Novalis: he was critical of those traits in Erasmus which he found questionable in himself. Hence the discussion of Erasmus' hypochondria reflects Novalis' own uncertainty concerning the use and the value of the imagination:

> [der Natur] getreulich folgen, nie ungeduldig zu sein, immer das Gute anzuerkennen, was wir haben, und nicht von der kranken Empfindung und Phantasie Parallelen ziehn zu lassen, die höchst unnütz, schädlich und unwahr sind, nicht zu raffinieren auf Empfindung oder Situation, nichts unterdrücken, was gesundes, wahres Gefühl ist, ... das ist das, was uns zu tun übrig bleibt.... *Reine Willenskraft*, ohne alles Gewühl von raffinierten Gefühlen, ist das, wodurch wir einzig leben und handeln können.... Sie ists, wodurch wir gesund sind und werden. ... Wo kranke Phantasie, da ist auch kranke Empfindung und kranker Verstand. Eins wird durch das andre gesund. So wirkt auch Gesundheit des Kör-

> pers und der Seele ineinander, obgleich nie oder
> höchst selten Krankheit des Körpers wesentlich
> nachteiligen Einfluß auf das Gemüt haben kann,
> wenn reine, feste, ewige Willenskraft da ist....[4]

Even if one discounts some of the excesses, which are due to the didactic form and purpose of the letter, this is a remarkable document in romantic literature that sharply contrasts with the self-assured and at times jubilant affirmation of the imagination one is accustomed to in the writings of Wordsworth, Keats, Shelley and others. Within Novalis' *oeuvre*, however, the letter represents not merely a juvenile stage which he overcame later, but a recurring theme which may be followed through the notebooks and letters. It has been insufficiently realized that although Novalis later assigned a positive and important function to the creative imagination—which he denoted with Fichte's "produktive Einbildungskraft"[5]—he nevertheless retained to the very end of his life an ironic distrust of the imagination, of his own poetic talents, and of the value of poetry. He remarked that the seat of his own harmful qualities was the imagination (IV, 110), and he described it as an amoral if not immoral force which, like dreams, prefers the night and times of loneliness when the moral and intellectual powers relax their hold on consciousness. Hence he felt the constant need to curb it.

Since the letter to Erasmus repeatedly mentions "kranke Phantasie" and "kranke Empfindung", one might at first sight be inclined to agree with Professor Haering that one ought to distinguish between a healthy and a decadent form of "Empfindung" and that Novalis judges only the diseased version as harmful. But Novalis indicates only the symptoms and the results; is there a way of knowing when he means the healthy and when the diseased form? Let us return to the letter to Erasmus for clarification:

> Kannst Du so viel über Deine Einbildungskraft
> gewinnen, wie mir es sehr möglich scheint, daß sie
> Dir nicht immer andere Zustände vorspiegelt, die

> eine gewisse, bloß idealische Behaglichkeit haben, und hingegen der Vernunft und Empfindung so untergeordnet ist, daß sie Dir bloß zur Verschönerung und inneren Unabhängigkeit von der Außenwelt dient: so wirst Du mutig und fest die Bahn gehen, die Dir der Genius Deines Schicksals jetzt hier vorzeichnet (IV, 45); Nur nicht zuviel überhaupt und zuviel untereinander gelesen. ... Schiller gar nicht. ... Philosophie und Verse sind jetzt für Dich nichts nütze und die letztern werden es nie sein. ... Rousseau gar nicht (IV, 48).

Knowing that Hardenberg had a deep respect for Schiller and devoted his own life to poetry and philosophy, it could hardly be maintained that he talks here about the "decadent" form of imagination.[6] It seems much more reasonable to assume that there was only one kind of imagination for Novalis, which appeared in different lights according to the circumstances and his disposition; the judgements of the letter have to be taken as partial truths, as inversions of equally valid positive views. In fact, the clash between the negative „bloß" and the positive expressions "idealische Behaglichkeit" and "innere Unabhängigkeit von der Außenwelt" suggests that even within the letter there is ambiguity. All we can say is that Novalis condemns here the harmful *effects* of the imagination: the sickly fantasy, and the refined aesthetic enjoyment of sophisticated feelings which undermines the willpower and results in hypochondria.

Probably in the fall of 1797, the theme of hypochondria emerged again amidst thoughts about Sophie and the philosophies of Kant and Fichte: "Hypochondrie ist eine sehr merckwürdige Kranckheit. Es giebt eine kleine und eine erhabene Hypochondrie. Von hier aus muß man in die Seele einzudringen suchen. /Übrige Gemüthskranckheiten./" (II, 395). Although Novalis did not spell out the distinction between minor and sublime hypochondria—the blur manifests the ambiguity of his thought—the split evidently served to separate the petty disease from that useful cognitive function which by now Novalis attributed to hypochondria. He not only believed, as Freud did later, that the study of this peculiar form of self-deception leads us to a knowledge of character, he also recognized in hypochondria the workings of a creative force that can objectify emotions. The idea was repeated in a note from the first half of 1798: "Über Hypochondrie und Eifersucht—2 sehr merckwürdigen Phaenomenen zur Kenntniß der Seele etc." (II, 555).

Amidst notes written a few months later, Novalis went a step further and specified the forces that may be harnessed through hypochondria: "Die *Hypochondrie* bahnt den Weg zur *körperlichen* Selbstkenntniß—Selbstbeherrschung—*Selbstlebung*" (II, 607). The typically disjunct mode of Novalis' prose proceeds here from "Selbstkenntniß" through "Selbstbeherrschung" to "Selbstlebung". While "Selbstkenntniß" merely reiterates the idea that hypochondria may provide us with knowledge, the antithetical terms "Selbstbeherrschung" and "Selbstlebung" suggest that Novalis took now a wider perspective of this disease. He did so probably in response to an open letter by Kant to Hufeland entitled "Von der Macht des Gemüths durch den bloßen Vorsatz seiner krankhaften Gefühle Meister zu seyn", in which Kant regarded hypochondria as a mere sign of excessive sensibility that should be overcome through reason and determination.[7] Novalis held a very different view. Not only did he believe that hypochondria may be utilized for useful purposes, but he saw in it a proof that factual knowledge was inseparable from morality and faith: hypochondria was both "Selbstkenntniß" (knowledge) and "Selbstlebung" (moral action). The need to bring these two together was first expressed by him amidst excerpts from Hemsterhuis—"Wir *wissen nur*, insoweit *wir machen*"[8]—and this theme became subsequently important in the notebooks. Characteristically, in the passage on hypochondria the link between knowledge and action is "Selbstbeherrschung", the "reine Willenskraft" of the earlier letter to Erasmus. In opposition to Kant Novalis held then that the potentially dangerous imagination may be rendered productive and creative by fusing it with the disciplined will; this implication is spelled out and developed in an other note: "Absolute Hypochondrie—Hypochondrie muß eine *Kunst* werden—oder Erziehung werden" (II, 614). Hypochondria is defined here both as a form of future artistry—because its cultivation would necessitate the shaping power of the artist—and a moral excercise. As a result this psychological aberration could be transformed into an educated form of the imagination.[9]

In summary, hypochondria was to Novalis the sign of genius, but also of excessive imagination and of mental derangement. Indeed, one may define Novalis' often discussed concept of "magic" as a mental activity so intense and so imaginatively deranged that it becomes the order of the world. It is Rimbaud's "immense et raisonné dérèglement de tous les sens" applied not only to the task of the poet but all of human consciousness: "In der Periode der Magie dient der Körper der Seele, oder der Geisterwelt. /Wahnsinn—Schwärmerey./ Gemeinschaftlicher Wahnsinn hört auf Wahnsinn zu seyn und wird Magie. Wahnsinn nach Regeln und mit vollem Bewußtseyn" (II, 547).

II. FIRST STUDIES

Hardenberg's study of the technical sciences, such as geology, mineralogy, and mining technology, may be traced to the circumstances of his life, while his concern with mathematics was essentially philosophical. What initiated his study of medicine? It has often been suggested that biographical circumstances forced upon him this interest, even though medicine had no relation to his professional work. These assumptions were apparently supported by A. C. Just, Novalis' superior and friend from Tennstedt, who was the first to link Sophie's disease and Hardenberg's interest in medicine: "Ihre Krankheit hatte ihn indes veranlaßt, sich mit der Arzneiwissenschaft näher bekannt zu machen" (IV, 429). Yet Just was sensible enough to realize that the medical studies, which extended over a considerable period of time, were at best only initiated by this tragic experience and that the deeper reasons were probably internal and philosophical: "Zwei Studien waren es, deren eine er nun vorzüglich zu treiben wünschte: Arzneiwissenschaft oder Bergwerkskunde. Zu jener zog ihn die Neigung, zu dieser bestimmte ihn die Pflicht. Schon mit den herrschenden Systemen und neusten Entdeckungen der Heilkunde bekannt, wünschte und strebte er, sie auf ein einfaches Prinzip begründen und ihr dadurch Gewißheit geben zu können" (IV, 431).

Reading the letters and notes of Novalis from the first half of 1797, one indeed feels that Novalis did not turn to science and medicine because these promised to give him immediate aid in combating disease and suffering, but because he attempted, as Just said, to base them upon a simple principle. In February he wrote to Erasmus:

> Dein Entschluß, Algebra zu studieren, ist gewiß sehr heilsam. Die Wissenschaften haben wunderbare Heilkräfte—wenigstens stillen sie, wie Opiate, die Schmerzen und erheben uns in Sphären, die ein ewiger Sonnenschein umgibt. Sie sind die schönste Freistätte, die uns gegönnt ward. Ohne diesen Trost wollt ich und könnt ich nicht leben. Wie hätt ich ohne sie seit anderthalb Jahren so gelassen S[ophiens] Krankheit zusehn und außerdem so manchen Verdrießlichkeiten ausgesetzt sein können? Es mag mir begegnen was will; die Wissenschaften bleiben mir—mit ihnen hoff ich alles Ungemach des Lebens zu bestehn.[10]

Two weeks later the imminent death of Sophie made him write that the realm of science was as dead and barren as the world itself (IV, 179), but at the end of March, i.e. after Sophie's death, he reported to Just that he studied the sciences this time from "a higher point of view".[11] The course of these studies was not even interrupted by Sophie's sickness and death, for sporadic diary entries between January and April 1797 record readings in mathematics and philosophy, and specifically refer to the names of Schelling and Pascal.[12] The study of Schelling's works must have continued after Sophie's death, for in a letter to Schlegel (June 14) we find the remark: "Mit Schelling such ich je eher, je lieber bekannt zu werden. In *einem* Stücke entspricht er mir mehr als Fichte. Ich will bald wissen, was ich an ihm haben kann" (IV, 208). In addition, there are several entries about Schelling in the diary that Novalis kept after the death of Sophie, between April 18 and July 6: "Gestern früh schrieb ich philosophische Gedanken von Wert auf, las in Schellings Briefen über Dogmat[ismus] und Kriti[zismus]... [June 28]; Nachmittags blättert ich in Schellings 'Ich' ... [June 30]; Ich las früh in Schelling ... [July 1]; Sonntag früh Schelling ... Abends Bösen getroffen—Schellings 'Ideen' erhalten... [July 2]."[13]

All these scattered remarks indicate that by the middle of 1797 Novalis was familiar with Schelling's early works, including the *Ideen*, the first work which showed that after his arrival at Leipzig in 1796 Schelling turned to the natural sciences and attempted to form a coherent "Naturphilosophie". The turn to "Naturphilosophie" accelerated Schelling's alienation from Fichte, hence Novalis' interest in Schelling was a sign of his own separation from Fichte. After the thorough studies of Fichte's works in 1795-96 Novalis also entered upon a new phase of his intellectual development, freeing himself from the coldness and abstractions of the *Wissenschaftslehre*.[14] In Schelling's works he found not only a philosophical approach to nature but also an inclination towards Spinoza's ecstatic and mystic love of the universe, elements which were altogether absent from Fichte's philosophy of the self. The paths of Schelling and Novalis diverged soon after the initial encounter, but Novalis remained the only major figure in the romantic movement who shared with Schelling an interest for science and medicine and an understanding of them.[15]

III. SCHELLING'S EARLY PHILOSOPHY

The title of Schelling's first important work, *Vom Ich als Princip der Philosophie*, shows that he started as a disciple of Fichte. Yet in even this work the author's respect for Spinoza throws a curious light on his espousal of Fichte's idealism. The *Philosophische Briefe über Dogmatismus und Kriticismus* of the same year puts this duality in Schelling's mind in a sharper relief: although the work purported to defend criticism (i.e., Fichte's idealism), Schelling confessed later that these letters were written not so much against dogmatism as against some followers of Kant who fashioned from their preceptor's philosophy a moral proof for the existence of God. To Schelling, their argument was logically circular and morally timid compared to consistent dogmatism which quietly surrendered the self to the cosmos: "Der consequente Dogmatismus geht nicht auf Kampf, sondern auf Unterwerfung, nicht auf gewaltsamen, sondern auf freiwilligen Untergang, auf stille Hingabe meiner selbst ans absolute Objekt..." (Sch, I, 208).

Although Schelling finally rejected this dogmatic submission so supremely exemplified in Spinoza's philosophy, he could do so only practically, i.e., for personal and not for theoretical reasons. Moreover, the rejection was mellowed by the profound admiration that Schelling expressed for the aestheticism and heroism which he discovered in Spinoza's submission to the forces of the universe: "Die stille Hingabe ans Unermeßliche, die Ruhe im Arme der Welt, ist es, was die Kunst auf dem andern Extreme jenem Kampfe entgegenstellt: stoische Geistesruhe, eine Ruhe, die den Kampf erwartet, oder ihn schon geendigt hat, steht in der Mitte" (Sch, I, 208).

A major portion of Schelling's essay is taken up with the attempt to understand Spinoza's "quiet surrender to the unfathomable". To the student of Fichte for whom the highest philosophical principle was the "courage to be", it was quintessential to unravel Spinoza's heroic "courage to suffer and to disintegrate". Schelling's search revealingly yielded two major points, each of which became important in his own philosophy: in Spinoza Schelling had found material for his organic views and his concept of "intellektuale Anschauung".

Both of these elements in Spinoza's philosophy became important to Novalis: against Fichte's disdain for the not-I he worked out an organic view of nature, and his frequent use of "intellektuale Anschauung" is traceable to Schelling's—and not Fichte's—use of it.[16] Spinoza's sensibility became of growing importance to Schelling and Novalis once they turned to the philosophy of nature and the study of science.[17]

Novalis was also in agreement with Schelling's judgement that Spinoza's passive subservience ran counter to the "highest demand" of critical philosophy: "Be!". This is probably the meaning of a somewhat cryptic remark by Novalis, in which he entertained the idea of synthesizing Spinozism with hylozoism (the teaching that all matter is self-animated) (II, 529). While Fichte asserted that the original act of the absolute self was self-generated, and that even the empirical self was a morally free agent, in Spinoza's philosophy thought and action were predetermined. Novalis, however, believed that all philosophy was a self-ignition of the mind so that the resultant chain of thought was determined by the shape of the acting intelligence (II, 530).

Even after departing from Schelling, Novalis returned to Spinoza: there are notes in the "Brouillon" on Spinoza and Plotinus which were occasioned by Novalis' reading of D. Tiedemann's *Geist der spekulativen Philosophie* in the fall of 1798. Although Tiedemann traced Spinozism to the cabbala and neo-Platonic thought, both of which were alien to his cast of mind, he mentioned it in his discussion of Plotinus and gave it a rather fair and detailed description in the sixth volume of his work. He pointed out that since, according to Spinoza, everything was attribute and modification within God, there could be no emanation or "chain of being" in his philosophy. Perhaps this ubiquitousness of God and this tight universal organization in Spinoza's philosophy appealed to Novalis as "wollüstiges Wissen", sensuous and immediate knowledge. For this insight he valued the Dutch philosopher more than such contemporaries as Ritter, Baader, and Schelling (IV, 263).

Schelling's *Ideen zu einer Philosophie der Natur*, which Novalis read during the summer of 1797, directs our attention to more specifically scientific matters, for with this work Schelling quietly departed from Fichte and turned to "Naturphilosophie". The question to which he addressed his essay (and all later works on the philosophy of nature) was still within the context of Fichte's philosophy, but his method and his answer were certainly incompatible with Fichte's solution. In the *Wissenschaftslehre* the question of how the mind knows about things outside was unfolded through a chain of dialectical arguments which started with the first and unconditional statement about the primeval act of positing.[18] Schelling's epistemology started, however, with a critique on one hand and the body of empirical knowledge on the other, working its way back to a hypothesized primeval unity of dialectical opposites, such as spirit and matter, object and subject (Sch, I, 706). In this search for original unity Schelling ignored the unity of consciousness in Fichte's absolute self and turned first to such dogmatist solutions as Spinoza's unity of an infinite substance and Leibniz's "pre-established harmony". Eventually he found these too unsatisfactory and turned his attention to organisms. He thought that each organism contained its own reason of existence, that it was its own cause and effect (Sch. I, 690). In a surprising deviation from idealistic thought Schelling assumed in this work that the idea of an organism resided in the phenomenon itself: "Daß ihr aber jede Pflanze als ein Individuum denkt, in welchem alles zu Einem Zweck zusammenstimmt, davon müßt ihr den Grund in dem Ding außer Euch suchen; ... ihr müßt also einräumen, daß die Einheit, mit der ihr es denkt, nicht bloß logisch (in euern Gedanken), sondern real (außer euch wirklich) ist" (Sch, I, 693). Nature appeared then as a huge supra-organism where every part contained a degree of life and the parts were subordinated to each other through an organizing and animating principle, the world-soul.[19] Since, according to Schelling, human consciousness was part of this purposeful organization which united spirit and matter, nature expressed the laws of the mind not incidentally or through the mediation of a third entity—e.g., the God of Descartes' philosophy—but through the postulated primeval unity which necessitated that nature be the inverse side of human consciousness. Hence Schelling hoped to resolve the ancient problem of mind and matter, and the possibility of knowing about things outside of us: "Die Natur soll der sichtbare Geist, der Geist die unsichtbare Natur seyn. Hier also, in der absoluten Identität des Geistes in uns und der Natur außer uns, muß sich das Problem, wie eine Natur außer uns möglich sey, auflösen" (Sch, I, 706).

With this well-known statement in the Introduction, the *Ideen* reached a crescendo and outlined the aim and content of the coming papers on the philosophy of nature. The main body of the essay plunged into the chaotic profusion of contemporary science, in an attempt to fashion from it a coherent system that would conform to the ideas of the Introduction. Unfortunately, in spite of the expressed desire to build on the body of existing knowledge, Schelling fell prey to the dangers of philosophical speculation about science, distorted, overrated, and ignored ideas, and exposed himself to criticism. The essay treated of the inorganic realm only, and the planned second part about organisms was never written, although the *Weltseele* may be regarded as a substitute.

What could have interested Novalis in this uneven, at times disjointed, at times fuzzy, and yet even today immensely stimulating work of Schelling? Above all, the *Ideen* was an example to him of how the body of empirical sciences may be treated within a single vision and comprehension. In addition, Schelling's book was probably the first among Novalis' readings in which the latest achievements and speculations in the empirical sciences were discussed, and thus the work probably served him as a guide in entering this foreign territory. For instance, Schelling gave great praise to a work by the still unknown C. A. Eschenmayer, stating that he had applied the Kantian principles of dynamics to the empirical sciences in a true philosophical temper (Sch, Suppl. I, 320). A few months after reading the *Ideen* Novalis made excerpts from the German version of Eschenmayer's Latin dissertation, probably upon Schelling's praise. Similarly, Novalis' reading of Kant's *Metaphysische Anfangsgründe der Naturwissenschaft* might be traced to Schelling's *Ideen*, where frequent reference was made to this work.

Beyond these cases of mediation, the *Ideen* provided a new and detailed presentation of two concepts which preoccupied Novalis later: 1. the concept of the organism; 2. the duality of primeval forces (attractive and repulsive) which, according to Schelling, structure the universe and all components of it. To be sure none of these were unique to Schelling: romantics in general uphold organic theories in poetry and philosophic thought. Yet, Schelling was the first among the professional philosophers to gather up a wealth of empirical evidence into a single encompassing idea to which he was able to give eloquent expression in his papers on the philosophy of nature. Schelling was also a former follower of Fichte and a student of Kant; his "Naturphilosophie was therefore a response to the *Kritik der reinen Vernunft* and the *Wissenschaftslehre,* two works which had formed the intellectual background from which Novalis had to emancipate himself. Indeed, when Novalis reported to Schlegel on June 14, 1797 that he struggled his way through Fichte's "furchtbares Gewinde von Abstraktion", he also indicated that this was related to the reading of Schelling's works (IV, 208).

This early enthusiasm for Schelling did not last; by the end of the year the remarks on Schelling's conception of nature became increasingly critical. While the exact nature of the differences will have to be discussed later, it might be said in anticipation that Novalis agreed with Schelling on the local and temporal significance of such concepts as the dualism of forces and the organism, but he did not accept them as the universal and final forms of reality. Thus, for instance, as an immediate reaction to his reading of passages from Schelling and Spinoza he could remark in the "Brouillon": "Unser Geist soll sinnlich wahrnehmbare Maschine werden—nicht in uns, aber außer uns. /Umgekehrte Aufgabe mit der Äußern Welt./" (III, 252)—for this was in accordance with the principles of his own philosophy. Similarly, he could agree with Schelling that organisms cannot be explained without accounting for the spirit's secret tie with the body: "Leben ist vielleicht nichts anders, als das Resultat dieser Vereinigung—die *Action dieser Berührung*" (II, 643). But when Novalis interpreted the universe as a purposeful organism, he was likely to posit its animating soul not in the organism itself, as Schelling did, but outside it. In other words, he conceived of a rational God as coordinator of a "preestablished harmony", and not of an entelechy moving the universe from "inside". The difference is made clear in the first sentence of the last quoted note which was probably made in reference to Schelling: "Den Organismus wird man nicht ohne Voraussetzung einer *Weltseele,* wie den Weltplan nicht ohne Voraussetzung eines Weltvernunftwesens, erklären können" (II, 643).

The case is similar with Schelling's idea that the interaction of two basic universal forces constitutes the dynamism of everything living. This idea, apparent already in the *Ideen* but worked out only in the *Weltseele*, was, of course, transferred from Newtonian celestial mechanics into the sphere of organic living. Consequently, Schelling considered these forces to be chemical and internal rather than mechanical and external (Sch, Suppl. I, 193). In many of Novalis' remarks on polarity such a background of mechanics or electricity is evident: "Zentripetalkraft —ist das synthetische Bestreben—Centrifugalkraft—das analytische Bestreben des Geistes..." (II, 589); "Alle Dinge haben eine Centrifugaltendenz—Centripetal werden sie durch den Geist..." (II, 581). But additional factors provided for disagreement. Schelling's dual forces not only represented a dialectic more concrete than Fichte's abstract confrontation of plus and minus or reality and negation, they also seemed to be modern correspondences to ancient mystic, Zoroastric, and Gnostic notions about the dualistic reality underlying the universe. It is with respect to these last associations that Novalis disagreed with Schelling. While he accepted the universality of dual forces on the spatial and temporal level, he could not posit these as ultimate realities. Since his conception of evil lacked concreteness he had no affinity with dualistic ethical theories, and since he was profoundly monistic he was instinctively drawn to the emanation theory of Plotinus. The quoted fragment about centripetal and centrifugal forces continues: "... Streben nach Einheit—Streben nach Mannichfaltigkeit— durch wechselseitige Bestimmung beyder durch Einander— wird jene höhere Synthesis der Einheit und Mannichfaltigkeit selbst hervorgebracht—durch die Eins in Allem und Alles in Einem ist" (II, 589).

IV. EXCERPTS FROM KANT AND ESCHENMAYER

The study of Schelling's *Ideen* was only one of many signs suggesting that Hardenberg had a serious interest in the natural sciences even before he departed in December 1797 to study at the mining academy of Freiberg. The change in outlook and interest may already be observed in his notebooks from the fall of this year, where among studies and excerpts from Fichte and Hemsterhuis we also find excerpts from Kant's *Metaphysische Anfangsgründe der Naturwissenschaft*, from a book by the anatomist S. Sömmering, and from C. A. Eschenmayer's *Säze aus der Natur-Metaphysik auf chemische und medicinische Gegenstände angewandt*.[20] In topic and tenor, particularly through the fusion of scientific and philosophical thoughts, these works have much in common, and so it seems only appropriate that in Novalis' notes the excerpts from the *Metaphysische Anfangsgründe* should form the beginning and the end of the MS (cf. II, 342).

Kant erected his philosophical scaffold of the natural sciences in the Introduction of the *Metaphysische Anfangsgründe*, where he distinguished between "historische Naturlehre", containing only systematically ordered facts, and "Naturwissenschaft". The latter he subdivided once more: "Die Naturwissenschaft würde nun wiederum entweder *eigentlich*, oder *uneigentlich* so genannte Naturwissenschaft sein, wovon die erstere ihren Gegenstand gänzlich nach Principien a priori, die zweite nach Erfahrungsgesetzen behandelt."[21] Accordingly, Kant asserted that a true science (eigentliche Naturwissenschaft) rests on mathematics, for mathematical knowledge is neither wholly empirical nor metaphysical (constructed of pure concepts), but *a priori* and synthetic, i.e. metaphysical concepts are complemented by an *a priori* intuition. Hence the famous statement which reaffirms the tradition of Leibniz in German philosophy of science: "Ich behaupte aber, daß in jeder besonderen Naturlehre nur so viel *eigentliche* Wissenschaft angetroffen werden könne, als darin *Mathematik* anzutreffen ist."[22] Accordingly, since contemporary chemistry and medicine contained only a collection of empirical data and no mathematics, Kant excluded them from the pure sciences.

Kant's definitions, especially his charges against chemistry, became the subject of many scientific treatises; the treatment of chemistry in Schelling's *Ideen*, for instance, shows a strong influence by Kant—even though Schelling's view of nature was essentially amathematical—and in Schelling's later *Weltseele* and *Erster Entwurf* one finds an attempt to give a priori if not mathematical foundations to medicine. Hardenberg's reaction to Kant's work was somewhat more complex. He had a better knowledge and understanding of mathematics than Schelling and he certainly recognized its great value in constructing scientific theories. About chemistry he knew something from his studies with the well-known scientist Wiegleb in January 1796. Yet he maintained a fundamental reservation with respect to Kant's position; this may be seen in two of his notes concerning chemistry: "Das chymische Princip—die Idee der Chymie—die Materialien der Chymie sind Zerstreute Glieder der ursprünglichen Idee der Chymie—das beseelende Princip—wodurch die Chymie zur Kunst a priori wird—muß ich hinzubringen" (II, 584 f.); "Kann die Chymie Kunst werden? Hauptfrage. Sie solls durch Moralitaet werden" (III, 253).

To Novalis, Kant's question of how to turn chemistry into an a priori science is not identical with the question of applying mathematics to it, for he is in search of the "idea of chemistry", a "beseelendes Princip" that would turn the science into an art. Like Shelley, Novalis assumes that poetry "is at once the centre and circumference of knowledge; it is that which comprehends all science, and that to which all science must be referred". The transformation should be achieved by imprinting upon the material the structure of the self (this is the Fichtean element in Hardenberg's thought) and the end product would be created artistically: "Kunst". But this does not amount to a rejection of mathematics, since Novalis admits the synthetic nature of mathematical knowledge. The argument is implicitly directed against Kant's separation of mathematics from the synthetic postulate of practical reason which Novalis had already questioned upon reading the *Metaphysische Anfangsgründe*. If pure mathematics and the pure natural sciences use the forms of external intuition, could there be an analogous science relying on internal intuition? Is there extra-sensuous cognition? Could there be other ways open to reach out from the self to other beings or to be affected by them (II, 390)? The title "Glauben und Liebe" implies already Novalis' affirmative answer (cf. II, 421), and in a sense the "Brouillon" represents a more elaborate reply.

The purpose of Eschenmayer's little booklet was to prepare the philosophical foundations for the backward empirical sciences, especially chemistry and medicine, by working out the principles of "Naturmetaphysik", a link through which the applied sciences were to be secured to the philosophical ground. Following Kant, Eschenmayer declared that every science ought to be based on rational principles that follow from the metaphysical foundations. But chemistry and medicine had only empirical principles deduced from experience, and such principles were hypotheses, permitting only limited generalizations and necessitating further secure proofs even if they happened to be correct.[23] Eschenmayer attacked a problem that Kant posed, but he employed Fichtean ideas insofar as he accused the chemists and doctors of positing at the pinnacle of their disciplines such unprovable concepts as affinity and excitability. Following Fichte, Eschenmayer stated that only the philosopher may posit the ultimately unprovable first principle from which all further knowledge be deducible, and he set out to form a "Naturmetaphysik" to fit the concepts of chemistry and medicine within the logical chain of Fichte's argument.

Eschenmayer's classification and analysis of the various sciences, as well as the terminology, followed Kant, albeit with some surprising results. Since Kant associated the category of quality with dynamics and Eschenmayer believed that chemistry was the science of qualitative material relations, he came for the wrong reason to a half-truth and analyzed chemistry in terms of the attractive and repulsive forces of Newtonian dynamics. (He could not know that modern chemistry would explain chemical properties with the forces that electric charges exert upon each other.) According to Eschenmayer, all matter was a particular configuration of two ever-present forces, and the qualitative differences between substances were ultimately reducible to quantitative force-relations.[24] To this structuring of nature he gave the name "dynamische Naturphilosophie", a term which, to my knowledge, he uses for the first time, since Schelling's works on "Naturphilosophie" appeared only later. Eschenmayer, however, was looking back to Fichte and associated the duality of forces in dynamics with the transcendental acts of positing and counterpositing, thereby giving to the principles of chemistry an ontological foundation in the very structure of consciousness.[25] Hence Eschenmayer's broadly conceived dualistic view of nature complemented Novalis' readings in philosophy and science and this might explain why he returned to Eschenmayer's theory in his later notebooks.[26]

No less important to Novalis was the second part of Eschenmayer's book, which dealt in a similar way with questions of medicine: as the first part attempted to give foundations to chemistry, so the second part, entitled "Etwas für die Pathologie", set out to give philosophical grounding to the art of healing which, as Novalis ironically remarked later, collected experience by filling cemeteries. Eschenmayer's procedure exactly followed the pattern of his analysis of chemistry. Here, as there, he accepted as the basis of his "Naturphilosophie" the Fichtean categories of Reality and Negation and went out in search of medical concepts that could be subsumed under them. Given the climate of medical thought in Germany, it was inevitable that he should adopt the Brownian concepts of stimulation and excitability, and the division of diseases into sthenic and asthenic: Brown's theory of medicine lent itself well to dialectic interpretations. If matter was built upon the polar forces of attraction and repulsion, analogously, life was an interaction of the principles of excitability and stimulation — medicine was thereby grounded in *a priori* philosophy (II, 333).

Unlike Weikard, Eschenmayer did not merely transmit Brown's ideas; he unintentionally distorted the original doctrines by giving to excitability as much power in the sustenance of life as to stimulation. Besides, as a would-be philosopher Eschenmayer had only contempt for Brown's "mere empiricism". Eschenmayer, as well as Röschlaub and Schelling, acknowledged that Brown's principles were the starting point for a true science of medicine, but he accused Brown of insufficient philosophic acumen,[27] and felt that his inadequate theoretical grounding was detrimental both to medical philosophy and praxis. Specifically, Eschenmayer thought that Brown committed an error when he refused to speculate on the nature and meaning of excitability, and he was looking for a third and synthetical principle to complement Brown's dialectic.

Novalis' excerpts from Eschenmayer's book do not cover the section on medicine, but since his notes on the first part contain two important remarks on Brown, we must assume that at the time of their writing Novalis already had some knowledge of his theory.[28] The first of these notes refers to Eschenmayer's chapter on the principles of mechanics, where it was asserted that all changes must have an external reason, thereby paraphrasing Newton's Second Law of Dynamics, the law of inertia, which was articulated in a slightly different form in Kant's *Metaphysische Anfangsgründe*.[29] In his excerpts Novalis added a question mark to the sentence and noted on the margin: "Vid. Browns System—contra Fichte" (II, 383)—which means, first of all, that he associated a mechanical principle with Brown's theory. Although this did not run counter to the spirit of Eschenmayer's book, there the law of dynamics was not streched to cover medicine.

Hardenberg's note and question mark becomes meaningful if we associate the law of inertia with the basic tenet of Brown's theory, namely that "life is a forced state", that "the tendency of animals, every moment, is to dissolution" and that "they are kept from it by foreign powers" which both support and exhaust life. In Fichte's philosophy, however, the Absolute Ego posits itself in a sovereign act and the Empirical Ego is morally free, so that only the coward and philosophically inferior dogmatists submit to external determinism:

> Der Streit zwischen dem Idealisten und Dogmatiker ist eigentlich der, ob der Selbständigkeit des Ich die Selbständigkeit des Dinges, oder umgekehrt, der Selbständigkeit des Dinges die des Ich aufgeopfert werden solle.[30] Wer in der Tat nur ein Produkt der Dinge ist, wird sich auch nie anders erblicken; und er wird recht haben, solange er lediglich von sich und seinesgleichen redet. ... Wer aber [als Idealist] seiner Selbständigkeit und Unabhängigkeit von allem, was außer ihm ist, sich bewußt wird, ... der

bedarf der Dinge nicht zur Stütze seines Selbst, und
kann sie nicht brauchen, weil sie jene Selbständig-
keit aufheben, und in leeren Schein verwandeln.[31]

Thus this innocuous little marginal note leads us not only to the central problem of Novalis' thoughts on medicine, but to the root of romantic thinking in general. The question mark was directed not so much against Newton's law of mechanics as against its extension into the organic and human realm. It indicates that Novalis was skeptical about Eschenmayer's and Brown's procedure to explain higher forms of life in terms of the lower and unconscious events in nature. In Novalis' view organisms could not be explained by mechanics, unless inanimate matter was conceived as an organism (III, 740) and hence he consciously and anthropomorphically reversed Brown's procedure and planned to introduce medical theories into mechanics (III, 179). Since, as we saw, Novalis projected an organic structure into Fichte's lifeless not-I, the marginal note implies also a criticism of Fichte. Yet whatever the differences were at this point or later between Hardenberg and Fichte, in the "debate between the Idealists and Dogmatists" Novalis always inclined towards the former, and consequently the confrontation of Brown and Fichte has to be read as principally directed against the philosophy underlying Brown's medical theory. The profound hostility against mechanistic theories which Novalis shared with the other romantics is evident throughout the notebooks. A few months after reading Eschenmayer's book he wrote: "Aller Anfang des Lebens muß antimechanisch—gewaltsamer Durchbruch—Opposition gegen den Mechanism seyn" (II, 575); and later in the "Brouillon" he remarked specifically about Brown: "Das Individuelle, *propter Genesin*, und *falsche* des Br[ownschen] Systems ist seine Neigung zur Mechanik" (III, 407).

We may conclude that Novalis consistently opposed Brown's theory on the ground that its mechanical foundations were incompatible with life, and held up against it the sovereignty of the organism. Yet to Novalis, as to Eschenmayer and many others, the *Elements* represented the first attempt to treat medicine philosophically, and as such it merited a philosophical critique. In addition, the theory was attractive because it contained a rudimentary form of romantic dialectic, by confronting externality with internality, subject with object, and stimulation with excitability.

The second marginal note to the Eschenmayer excerpts indicates that Novalis felt the need to modify Brown's dialectic by raising the active power of excitability (the subjective internal force) above stimulation (the objective external component). While Eschenmayer, directly relying on Kant, defined matter as mobility[32] ("Beweglichkeit"), Novalis remarked in the margin, once more switching from the inorganic to the organic: "Vid. Brown—Erregbarkeit" (II, 385). This association between mobility and excitability, which recurs in Novalis' later notes (III, 559), says in effect: as inorganic matter is defined by its intrinsic mobility, so organisms are determined by their excitability and not by the external stimulants.

We find therefore in these first little notes a sophisticated and differentiated view of medicine, which does not permit any summary statements about Novalis' initial acceptance or rejection of Brown's theory. One has to hold this, for instance, against the theory of Th. Haering, which attempts to force the dynamics of Novalis' philosophy into an all too simple developmental scheme, and maintains that an initial acceptance of Brown's ideas was followed by a later critical rejection.[33] But since already these early remarks on Brown and medicine constitute a system of acceptances and rejections, this view is untenable; in fact, as Novalis' knowledge and understanding of medicine deepened, he adhered to the specific tenets of this differentiated view with considerable consistency.

V. HEMSTERHUIS AND BAADER

Approximately at the time when Novalis prepared the excerpts from Kant and Eschenmayer, he also made extensive excerpts from the works of the Dutch philosopher Franz Hemsterhuis and attempted to correlate these with his other readings. Although Hemsterhuis did not write on science, his psychology and his conception of history left a deep imprint on all aspects of Novalis' philosophy.[34]

While Hemsterhuis is little known today, Novalis' admiration for his sensitively written neo-Platonic dialogues and letters was shared in various degrees by a great many contemporaries, among them Herder, Goethe, and even Diderot.[35] As F. Schlegel reports, Novalis was inspired by Hemsterhuis' notion of the "golden age" as early as 1791. This concept was discussed in *Alexis ou de l'âge d'or*, an essay that attempted to prove that the golden age was both a fact of historical past and a possibility for the future. Could man ever become as pure as he was in the cradle of history? Hemsterhuis' answer was contained in the psychology expounded in *Simon ou des facultés de l'âme*. He recognized four faculties: 1. "la velleité"; the basic material that has to be formed and educated somewhat analogously to Dante's "simple little soul"; 2. the imagination, which Hemsterhuis considered to be the receptacle of all impressions coming from outside—not a creative imagination; 3. the intellect, originally a vague intuition which became reason by excercising comparison, composition, and dissection; and finally 4. the "organe moral", which consisted of a passive part exposed to the passions, above all love and hate, and of an active part whose task was to judge and modify impressions, and shape the course of action.[36] In the earlier *Sur les désirs* Hemsterhuis stated that the passions of the passive moral sense arose from the soul's constant desire to unite with external objects, and from the frustration that the senses as intermediaries inevitable cause. As Novalis noted in his excerpts, if the senses could be by-passed a perfect union would become possible: "Ohne Organe würde die Seele *im Moment* von dem unendlichen Object durchdrungen —beyde würden Eins—und der Wechselgenuß vollkommen seyn" (II, 361).

More important than the question of physical sensation was Hemsterhuis' theory of the active moral sense and the need for its training. He was convinced that the intellect has become the despotic overseer of all faculties; the way to raise mankind was therefore through activating morality and harmoniously developing all faculties. Novalis' early theory of magic does not yet contain a fully developed conception of how morality ought to interact with the physical world, yet there is clearly a connection between his Hemsterhuis excerpts and the later "Brouillon"; for it is stated in both that the relation between physiological and psychological phenomena may be utilized for asserting the spiritual forces and morally transforming nature.

Franz Xaver von Baader (1765-1841) is remembered today primarily as a theologian, but he was also a scientist in his early days and he even discovered a method of making glass. Novalis knew only his early works on "Naturphilosophie": he owned his *Beiträge zur Elementar-phisiologie* (Hamburg, 1797), and *Ueber das pythagoräische Quadrat in der Natur oder die vier Weltgegenden* (Tübingen, 1798), and he also read the very early *Vom Wärmestoff*.[37] Starting with scientific questions, Baader reached for "higher philosophy" and tried to amalgamate his classical, religious, and humanistic learning with the latest ideas in the sciences. For instance, his work on the Pythagorean square, inspired by Schelling's *Weltseele*, set out to show that the ubiquitous polar forces of Schelling's philosophy were identifiable with fire and water; adding to these a coordinating principle, namely earth, and a fourth one permeating the three, namely air, Baader believed he had shown that the universe was made up of fire, water, earth, and air. Novalis' remark about the essay seems to be just: "... nichts wie derbe, gediegene Poesie, aber freilich in grobe Bergarten eingesprengt und schwer zu säubern und auszuhauen."[38]

The *Beiträge zur Elementar-phisiologie*, a work which Novalis read during the fall of 1797, is almost equally perplexing and annoying because of its inflated dependent clauses and copious footnotes which all but obliterate the central thoughts, its highly personal vocabulary, and its conjectures, many of which must have made little sense even in view of the limited knowledge then available. Yet, if one takes the trouble to "clear and to carve out", one meets the marks of a highly original mind. Baader concerned himself with the nature of interacting forces and attempted to oppose mechanistic explanations with a dynamic philosophy. Mechanistic explanations seemed to him excusable only in those cases where the interacting bodies were completely lacking autonomy, i.e., internal spontaneous capacity to act. But within Baader's anthropomorphic view of nature the number of such bodies was low indeed—even the interaction of sea and wind to form waves he read as the creation and annihilation of selves.

Baader's own argument ran the following way: the concept of force is always a synthesis between the form of external intuition (space) and internal intuition (time). While forces are additive in the perception of space, in the inner form of perception they are multiplicative and exponential, because forces are dynamically interrelated through a principle called "Gliederung" which arranges for a division of labor. In Baader's understanding this "Gliederung" vouchsafed for the anthropomorphic construction of nature: "Da nun Gliederung nur aus einem Princip (systematisch) möglich ist, da ferner das hiezu erforderliche Durchgehen eines Vielerlei nicht im äussern Sinne... sondern nur im innern ... stattfinden oder geschehen kann, so bürgt uns ersteres für die Vernünftigkeit der Natur als Bildnerin ... sowie letzteres für ein unserem inneren Sinnenstoff analoges Innere in jedem Körpergebilde."[39]

Baader opposed both pure mechanism and the radical separation of object and subject, for he believed that even among the lower orders of nature an inner principle of change existed. External stimulation was therefore only the releasing spark for self-generated action: "Ueberall leuchtet nun hiebei der Urtheilskraft der Satz vor, dass die äussere (räumlich-berührende) Ursache bloss als Reiz, Funke oder Same zu betrachten sei, welcher der inneren Naturkraft (Einbildungskraft im weitesten Sinne) nur das Schema zu einer bestimmten Synthesis darbietet ... welches jene (das bildende, weibliche, und hernach gebärende Vermögen) fasst, eigentlich empfängt, in sich entzündet und fortbildet."[40]

Baader's theory of "Gliederung" and his belief in self-generated activity became important for Novalis when he attempted to formulate his answer to mechanistic philosophies.[41] Like Baader, he came to believe that bodies obeyed a central principle similar to the entelechy of the Leibnizian monad: "Jeder Körper wird durch eine *Monade* zusammengehalten und bestimmt."[12]

The most important case of agreement between Hardenberg and Baader reveals a remarkable affinity: in fighting pure rationalism and Kant's separation of action and knowledge both Baader and Novalis believed that "Glauben und Liebe" have to form the basis of all knowledge. Pure knowledge as such does not exist, human wisdom is ultimately a participation in divine knowledge and its acquisition requires faith. The laws of nature are, in turn, the manifestation of divine love: "Liebe ist das allgemeine Band, das alle Wesen im Universum an und ineinander bindet und verwebt. Man nenne es nun allgemeine Schwere, Attraction, Cohäsion, Affinität...."[43] Hence Novalis could remark with approval about Baader: "Seine Zauber binden wieder,/ Was des Blödsinns Schwert geteilt" (IV, 241).

III

The Anthropology and Physiology of Magic

1. *Romantisirung*

Die Welt muß romantisirt werden. So findet man den urspr[ünglichen] Sinn wieder. Romantisiren ist nichts, als eine qualit[ative] Potenzirung. Das niedre Selbst wird mit einem bessern Selbst in dieser Operation identificirt. So wie wir selbst eine solche qualit[ative] Potenzenreihe sind. Diese Operation ist noch ganz unbekannt. Indem ich dem Gemeinen einen hohen Sinn, dem Gewöhnlichen ein geheimnißvolles Ansehn, dem Bekannten die Würde des Unbekannten, dem Endlichen einen unendlichen Schein gebe so romantisire ich es—Umgekehrt ist die Operation für das Höhere, Unbekannte, Mystische, Unendliche—dies wird durch diese Verknüpfung logarythmisirt— Es bekommt einen geläufigen Ausdruck. romantische Philosophie. *Lingua romana.* Wechselerhöhung und Erniedrigung (II, 545).

The demand "Die Welt muß romantisirt werden" is one of the best known statements of Hardenberg's poetic and philosophical intent, but its meaning is seldom deciphered in terms of the notes with which it is woven into a pattern, the MSS from the first half of 1798, especially those which follow this quotation. These notes deal with the "Romantisirung" from all possible angles, particularly from the point of view of physiology, psychology, anthropology, and poetry. My purpose is to demonstrate that, although fragmentary, these notes are unified through the ideas of "Romantisirung" and "Magie", both of which are developed in connection with Hardenberg's scientific and medical studies.[1]

"Romantisirung" aims at "Wechselerhöhung und Erniedrigung": at raising the everyday into the realm of the mysterious and at a palpable representation of the supernatural. Shelley must have meant something similar to "Erhöhung" when he wrote that poetry "lifts the veil from the hidden beauty of the world, and makes familiar objects be as if they were not familiar", while the "Erniedrigung" roughly corresponds to the Goethean conception of the symbol in literature.

Although the "Romantisirung" will have to be more than merely an artistic act, it is prefigured in the artist's creativity, which is therefore exemplary for all human activity: "Dichtkunst ist wohl nur—willkührlicher, thätiger, produktiver Gebrauch unsrer Organe..." (III, 563). The conviction that the future will necessarily realize the projected "Romantisirung" is rooted in Hardenberg's vision of history according to which the coming age will self-consciously reconstruct the Golden Age. "Romantisirung" is an attempt to reinvest in poetry that religious and magic power which provided the men of the Golden Age with a mythology and gave to their everyday life a transcendental incantation. If the future is to resemble the past in harmony and beauty, it will have to reconstruct the primeval unity of theology, ethics, and aesthetics: the act of poetry will have to regain its universal and metaphysical power, while purposeful everyday activity will have to acquire an artistic quality. Hardenberg's poetics is the unfolding of the first program, while his physiology, anthropology, psychology, and medicine describes the second of the complementary parts of "Romantisirung". In the course of this chapter I shall first outline the theory and its epistemological implications, then further illuminate it under the complementary aspects of poetics and medicine.

Novalis' approach to the sciences is historical and programmatic, inasmuch as he starts from the given conditions but is mainly concerned with the dormant future possibilities. How can human lives be heightened and refined? Accepting the traditional dualism of body and soul Novalis conceives of the natural world and the spiritual realm ("Geisterwelt") as two domains to which the human components are subordinated. The two realms are interrelated through a network of associations which, at present, unfortunately enable the body to dominate the soul. However, within Novalis' vision of history this state of affairs is only temporary and many signs indicate that the spirit will assert itself to form a free association with the body: "Dennoch sind häufige Spuren eines umgekehrten Verhältnisses anzutreffen, und man bemerckt bald, daß beyde Systeme eigentlich in einem Vollkommnen Wechselverhältnisse stehn sollten, in welches jedes von seiner Welt afficirt, einen Einklang, keinen Einton bildeten. Kurz beyde Welten, so wie beyde Systeme sollen eine freye Harmonie, keine Disharmonie oder Monotonie bilden" (II, 546).

The balance of components in this harmony is described by Novalis in various ways which do not always agree. In the group of notes under discussion the association between body and soul is usually governed by the latter. From the medical point of view this is only tantamount to that inversion of Brown's ideas which was already observable in the marginal notes to the Eschenmayer excerpts: if Brown proclaimed that external stimulation was far more important than the stimulation resulting from the activity of consciousness, in the state envisaged by Novalis the senses would primarily, but not exclusively, react to the changes of inwardness: "In der Periode der Magie dient der Körper der Seele, oder der Geisterwelt" (II, 547).

In asserting that the senses might be directed inward, Novalis belongs to the neo-Platonic tradition, and to the romantic generation that was in search both of extra-sensory experience and of modes in which the imagination might objectify itself in the external world.[2] Novalis is unique among the romantics because of his thorough scientific learning and the corresponding concreteness and practicality of his proposals. The moving diary he kept after Sophie's death and the notebooks on science are both in search of a method to penetrate the extra-sensuous realm. One finds in both empirical material collected from acute self-observation, a mixture of medieval asceticism and modern impassioned research, which precipitated in notes and maxims as the following: "Es giebt mancherley Arten von der vereinigten Sinnenwelt unabhängig zu werden. 1. durch Abstumpfung der Sinne. ... 2. durch zweckdienliche Anwendung, Mäßigung, und Abwechselung der Sinnenreitze. /Heilkunst./ 3. durch Maximen a. der Verachtung [Novalis originally wrote "Gleichgültigkeit"] und b. der Feindlichkeit gegen alle Empfindungen. ... 4. theilweise durch Aushebung gewisser Sinne oder gewisser Reitze, die durch Übung, und Maxime einen beständigen, überwiegenden Einfluß erhalten" (II, 549).

Such a neutralization of the "external senses"—the development of "neutral regions" in the body as Novalis described the process elsewhere—would permit concentration upon the "interior senses". The latter are of course not merely sensors of time, as in Kant's philosophy, but include in general all faculties which have as yet no "objective correlatives". As a result of such a concentration one might not only refine sensitivity, but could also creatively employ the refined senses to form new parts for the body: "Wir würden nur Veränderungen hervorbringen können—die Gedanken ähnlich wären, und wir würden ein Bestreben fühlen, uns jene Sinne zu verschaffen, die wir jezt äußre Sinne nennen. Wer weis ob wir nicht nachgerade, durch mannichfache Bestrebungen Augen, Ohren etc. hervorbringen könnten, weil dann unser Körper so in unsrer Gewalt stände, so einen Theil unsrer innern Welt ausmachte, als jezt unsre Seele."[3]

Although passages of this kind are often regarded as poor science fiction, recent experiments and theories seem to confirm them in several respects. Thus, for instance, we know now that if for some reason the senses are deprived of stimuli, consciousness will eventually attempt to replace them through hallucinations and visions. Even more surprising, these symptoms of sensory deprivation bear resemblance to the apparitions of certain kinds of mental derangement such as schizophrenia; in both, the command of the senses is switched from the external world to internal forces.

This switch may be brought about in an artificial way, through the application of certain drugs, such as mescaline or LSD.[4] Novalis, who was familiar with the stimulating power of opium from Brown's theory, might have had his own experience with narcotics, as the praise of the "brown juice of poppy" in the second hymn to the night suggests.[5]

The skepticism and ambiguity concerning the excessive or exclusive use of the imagination, so outspokenly described in the early letter to Erasmus, is evident also in this context. The spiritualization of human sensibility remained for Novalis a delicate and somewhat questionable operation, and it is therefore a misrepresentation of his ideas to say that he merely envisaged a turning inward by "switching off" the external senses. Such popularizations usually arrive at the banal conclusions that Novalis was a late mystic or an early escapist, but they cannot account for the complexity of his life and work. What Novalis envisaged was, in Fichtean terminology, the simultaneous existence of an absolute, practical, and empirical self (II, 547), which means that the moral activity of the empirical self was to be potentialized so that it become identical with the original act of positing—without, however, giving up the specifically human and empirical aspect of life.

Of the different versions of this abstract Fichtean formula only those will be mentioned here that use the language of science and medicine. Already among the excerpts from Hemsterhuis' *Simon* we find a passage in which the dangers of excessive sensibility are noted: "Der moralische Sinn /die sensible Seite des Herzens/ ist die schönste, aber auch gefährlichste Seite unsers Wesens. Seine zu große Lebhaftigkeit veranlaßt leicht Täuschungen" (II, 376). In one of the important *Blüthenstaub* fragments this idea is developed further in terms of Novalis' own theory of the organs. Once more the dangers of an absolute spiritual domination are emphasized: "Eine allzugroße Dienstfertigkeit der Organe würde dem irdischen Daseyn gefährlich seyn. Der Geist in seinem jetzigen Zustande würde eine zerstörende Anwendung davon machen. Eine gewisse Schwere des Organs hindert ihn an allzuwillkührlicher Thätigkeit, und reizt ihn zu einer regelmäßigen Mitwirkung, wie sie sich für die irdische Welt schickt. Es ist unvollkommener Zustand desselben, daß ihn diese Mitwirkung so ausschließlich an diese Welt bindet. Daher ist sie ihrem Prinzip nach terminirt" (II, 451). Although the phrase "in seinem jetzigen Zustande" seems to leave the question of the future open, Novalis' repeated references to earthly existence suggest that he deemed it necessary to retain a balance between spirit and matter even under future circumstances, for it is this bond that defines the nature of human existence.

One may say, therefore, that the projected "higher" existence in Novalis' philosophy does not fall beyond human boundaries; within the "great chain of being" it would still be accommodated between Kleist's marionette and Rilke's angel, between mechanical existence and pure consciousness: "Die höhere *Phil*[osophie] behandelt die *Ehe von Natur und Geist*" (III, 247). The point is crucial and needs further emphasis, for even such a meticulous and intelligent scholar as Professor Strohschneider-Kohrs fell victim of traditional views, in asserting that Magic Idealism is tantamount to the transcendence of the empirical world: "Anderseits ist in Novalis' Vorstellung vom magischen Idealismus das Denkmotiv der absoluten Annihilation des Empirischen schon eingeschlossen: zu der Erzeugung von Welt gehört auch die totale Rückführung des Empirischen in die Identität des Geistes."[6] In support of this thesis Professor Strohschneider-Kohrs adopted the phrase "indifferente Einheit von Welt und Ich" from Hugo Kuhn and asserted that Hardenberg's philosophy rests on such a point of indifference: "[Novalis] faßt den Indifferenzpunkt ... in mystisch bestimmter Abwandlung als den Urgrund und das Zeugungswunder von Sein, Welt und Ich ineins."[7]

If there were such a point of indifference, then Professor Strohschneider-Kohrs could claim with justification that Hardenberg's philosophy is void of irony, for irony always depends on the interplay between distinct categories. Although it is somewhat difficult to grasp what exactly is meant by the "Zeugungswunder von Sein, Welt und Ich", one feels sure that the "Indifferenzpunkt" does not correspond to Novalis' conception of the "neutral zones" discussed above. Since the latter are to be developed with the expressed intention of refining the contact between the self and the world, there can be no "absolute annihilation of the empirical world" in Hardenberg's philosophy. His irony issues precisely from the dynamic and dialectic interplay between body and soul, self and world, present mechanism and future magic. Isolated extremes are always simplifications of complex situations: "Aus Trägheit verlangt d[er] Mensch *bloßen* Mechanism oder *bloße* Magie. Er will nicht thätig seyn—seine *prod*[*uctive*] *Einb*[*ildungs*]*Kr*[*aft*] brauchen,, (III, 408).

II. THE EPISTEMOLOGY OF MAGIC

Nowhere do the dialectical elements of Novalis' thought appear more clearly than in his theory of knowledge. To the question of how we know about matters outside of our consciousness, Novalis replies that it is through intuition and analogy—two forms of cognition which implicitly assume that mind and self are distinct from the matter of the world. Neither claiming an identity between self and world, nor separating them as radically as Fichte in his *Wissenschaftslehre*, Novalis conceives of an alienation and adoption process issuing in knowledge: "Ich kann etwas nur erfahren, in so fern ich es in mir aufnehme; es ist also eine Alienation meiner selbst und eine Zueignung oder Verwandlung einer andern Substanz in die meinige zugleich: das neue Product ist von den beiden Factoren verschieden, es ist aus beiden gemischt."[8]

This alienation and adoption process corresponds to the "Wechselerhöhung und Erniedrigung" of the "Romantisirung", for alienation, the objectification of the self, means the spirit's descent into matter, while adoption means transformation (had Novalis known Hegel he might have said "Aufhebung") of sensuous matter through the "magic" power of the self. Since the processes dialectically complement each other as activity and passivity, diastole and systole, or "Tun" and "Leiden", neither their source nor their sum can be an "Indifferenzpunkt".

What are the physiological factors and what function do the senses have in this learning process which is based on intuition and analogy? In a note entitled "Von der *unsinnlichen*, oder *unmittelbaren* Erkenntniß" (II, 550), Novalis gives his answer: the senses are media which transmit, but also distort the primary data they receive. In the terminology of physics, they are impure conductors.[9] As already indicated by some earlier notes, Novalis considered the possibility of making the senses into "insulators", by turning them inward so that they might produce a world, perhaps identical with the existing one, without sensory impressions. In such a system the senses would not be conductors, but insulators and mirrors, or, as Novalis put it, they would become "absolute senses": "Ein absoluter Sinn wäre Mittel und Zweck zugleich" (II, 550). Such would perhaps be the structure and nature of an Absolute Ego. Novalis, however, suggests the retention of the conducting function of the senses (in other words, he would still insist on certain functions of the Empirical Ego); as a result the nature and function of the senses would become twofold:

> Ich bekäme eine zugleich mittelbare und unmittelbare—repraesentative und nicht repraesentative, vollkomne und unvollkomne—eigne und nicht eigne, kurz antithetisch synthetische Erkenntniß und Erfahrung von dem Dinge. Das Glied, oder der Sinn würde zugleich Glied und NichtGlied seyn, weil ich es durch meine Belebung auf gewisse Weise vom Ganzen abgesondert hätte.
> Nenn ich das ganze Ding Welt, so würde ich ein integrantes Glied der Welt in mir, und das Übrige außer mir haben. Ich würde mir in theoretischer Hinsicht, in Rücksicht dieses Sinns, als abhängig und unter dem Einfluße der Welt erscheinen (II, 551).

This theory, which recurs in Novalis' polemic against Schelling's *Weltseele* (III, 109), gives also the epistemological foundation to Magic Idealism: if the body is largely under the powers of the soul but nevertheless remains a part, a variation, of the empirical world, a knowledge of the macrocosm may be derived through analogies from the direct and intuitive knowledge of the microcosm, which is one's own body.[10] Examining this relationship from a different angle, another thesis in Hardenberg's philosophy becomes evident: since the body serves both as a source of information about the world at large and as a tool with which the self can modify this world, in the body action and cognition represent merely two aspects of the same operation: "Ich selbst weis mich, wie ich mich will und will mich, wie ich mich weis—weil ich meinen *Willen will*—weil ich abs[olut] will. In mir ist also Wissen und Willen vollkommen vereinigt" (II, 552). As formulated elsewhere: "Wir wissen etwas nur— insofern wir es *ausdrücken*—i.e. *machen* können."[11]

Thus the complementarity of doing and knowing follows from the dialectic between the "Wechselerniedrigung und Erhöhung", and the alienation and adoption. Together they represent a conscious opposition to the philosophies of Kant and Fichte, where object and subject are radically separated: "Sich nach den Dingen, oder die Dinge nach sich *richten*—ist Eins" (II, 589).

The theory raises, however, an important problem: theoretically at least, one can conceive of a spiritual domination of the body, and one may even imagine that one day the senses will serve the soul and accept its commands—although technological advances have not brought this moment closer. But precisely because of the modifications that the body might have to endure in the course of this transformation, we have no safeguards that nature would retain that consistency which permits the macrocosm to be seen in terms of the microcosm. In other words: the spiritual modification of the body might lift it completely from the realm of nature, so that future observations on it would not necessarily tell anything about the structure of the universe. As a passage from *Die Lehrlinge* indicates, Novalis was aware of the problem, although he had no definite answer for it: "Es frägt sich, ob wir die Natur der Naturen durch diese spezielle Natur wahrhaft begreifen lernen können, und in wiefern unsre Gedanken und die Intensität unsrer Aufmerksamkeit durch dieselbe bestimmt werden, oder sie bestimmen, und dadurch von der Natur losreißen und vielleicht ihre zarte Nachgiebigkeit verderben" (I, 97).

Magic Idealism does not represent, therefore, a logically binding theory of knowledge of the kind that Fichte's *Wissenschaftslehre* offers; it is a hybrid, a bridge between consistent but radical answers. It envisages a state where the mind might know its material substratum as intimately as it knows itself; thereby it displaces, without overcoming, the crucial boundary between consciousness and externality. Ultimately, Novalis deviates from the young Schelling and sides with Descartes and Leibniz because he resorts to a supreme being and a preordained harmony which secure the tie between mind and matter, and provide a foundation for knowledge. In describing this coordination Novalis mixes elements of the traditional Christian conception of God with Fichte's transcendental self, and the notion of the "Weltseele".[12]

Hardenberg makes no attempt to resolve the contradictions between freedom and constraint, or individuality and universality. He describes a precarious and paradoxical balance which is intimately tied up with a vision of history, and he assumes that the development of the individual correlates with this movement on the universal scale, or, more exactly, that the self can "animate" the changes of the world on the basis of an a priori unity between self and world: "Die Welt hat eine ursprüngliche Fähigkeit durch mich belebt zu werden—Sie ist überhaupt a priori von mir belebt—Eins mit mir. Ich habe eine ursp[rüngliche] Tendenz und Fähigkeit die Welt zu beleben— Nun kann ich aber mit nichts im Verhältniß treten—was sich nicht nach meinem Willen richtet, oder ihm gemäß ist—Mithin muß die Welt die ursp[rüngliche] Anlage haben sich nach mir zu richten —meinem Willen gemäß zu seyn" (II, 554).

This a priori unity between self and world vaguely resembles Professor Strohschreider-Kohrs' "point of indifference". But in Novalis' conception it is a transcendental unity infinitely removed from history and the empirical world, and the only claim he makes as to its empirical reality is that, on the basis of a correspondence, consciousness may act upon the world without disturbing the inner structure of it: "Meine *geistige* Wircksamkeit—meine Realisation von Ideen—wird also keine *Decomposition*, und Umschaffung der Welt—wenigstens nicht, insofern ich *Mitglied* dieser bestimmten Welt bin—seyn können, sondern es wird nur eine *Variations Operation* seyn können—Ich werde unbeschadet der Welt und ihrer Gesetze—mittelst derselben—sie für mich ordnen, einrichten und bilden können" (II, 554).

III. THE PHYSIOLOGY OF POETRY

Curiously, among the main works of Kant Novalis ignored the *Critique of Judgment*, that work which could have been most relevant to his poetic calling. Yet the omission is not accidental. Novalis had hardly more than a passing interest for such Kantian aesthetic questions as the nature of the beautiful and the beautiful in nature—like Hegel, but unlike Kant, he was only concerned with man-made beauty. To him, the essence of art lay in the mode of its creation—an aspect to which Kant's analytic method did not do full justice. As Croce remarks with somewhat undue severity, Kant "knows a reproductive imagination and an associative, but he knows nothing of a genuinely productive imagination, imagination in the proper sense."[13]

In turn, it might be said of Novalis that he knows only of "a genuinely productive imagination"; in fact, "produktive Einbildungskraft" is a key word in his vocabulary. Wackenroder's description of the artistic process, as given in "Raffaels Erscheinung" of *Herzensergießungen eines kunstliebenden Klosterbruders*, was closer to Novalis' views than Kant's treatment of the imagination. Quoting from a letter of Raphael, Wackenroder asserts that a painting is not the reproduction of what the artist had seen in the realm of appearances, but an attempt to shape matter according to an inner vision. Hence the source of art is not nature but the spiritual realm, which finds outlet through the individuality of the artist: "Da man so wenig schöne weibliche Bildungen sieht, so halte ich mich an ein gewisses Bild im Geiste, welches in meine Seele kommt."[14] In this interpretation, Raphael's Madonna is a copy of an ideal or a Platonic form, and the artist is reduced to a medium through which inspiration operates. While Wackenroder raises art from the degrading "imitation of an imitation" to an "imitation of the real", he leaves the artist as a passive tool in the hands of higher powers: the image "comes" into the soul of Raphael, it is properly speaking not his own making. The position parallels the famous complaint of Keats that the artist, qua artist, may have no personality of his own.

Novalis shares with Wackenroder and Keats the view that art is a product of the imagination and not an imitation of nature—"ja keine Nachahmung" was his advice to his brother Karl (IV, 336). But as to the artist's role in the creative process, he holds a significantly different view. According to him, art, as to a lesser extent all human activity, is a personal and individual expression of the creative genius inherent in man. The artistic product carries therefore the imprint of the mind's pattern, the shape of the imagination. Although it may, and in the highest cases should, achieve universality, it does so indirectly and almost incidentally, through the postulated preordained harmony between the self and the world.

The issue is a crucial one, and the position that Novalis takes has at least two important consequences: 1. since art is primarily a product of the self—and not the objectification of an impersonal inspiration—Novalis, unlike some other romantics, perceives no qualitative difference between the poetic act and other human activity; 2. he regards the involvement of the self as total, and devotes careful attention to physiological, as well as psychological, aspects which might play a role in creativity; the artist, to him, is "Werckzeug und Genie" (II, 525).

These views might be illuminated through a few additional comparisons. In the Preface to the "Lyrical Ballads" Wordsworth asserted that "the human mind is capable of being excited without the application of gross and violent stimulants" and that the "Poet is chiefly distinguished from other men by a greater promptness to think and feel without immediate external excitement, and a greater power in expressing such thoughts and feelings ..."[15] This comes close to Novalis' conception of writing, although there are still important differences. The "thoughts and feelings" of poetry are, according to Novalis, not only not "immediately" excited from outside, they are not even recollections in tranquillity—they are in the literal sense brought forth from a source within the self: "... der Künstler hat den Keim des selbstbildenden Lebens in seinen Organen belebt—die Reitzbarkeit derselben *für den Geist* erhöht und ist mithin im Stande Ideen nach Belieben— ohne äußre Sollicitation—durch sie heraus zu strömen—Sie, als Werckzeuge, zu *beliebigen* Modificationen der wircklichen Welt zu gebrauchen..." (II, 574). The difference lies not merely in the "Keim des selbstbildenden Lebens" which is to Novalis the hallmark of the artist, but even more in the general transforming power that he attributes to the artistic imagination: the organs of the artist—his hand, his eyes, his voice—are conceived as tools which may modify the external world in a sovereign way.[16]

Yet, the difference between Wordsworth and Novalis is not as great as the comparison indicated. For Novalis is usually careful to place his analysis in a historical context and he describes the imagination not so much as a power existing but as a power to be. At present the genius of the artist does not modify the world at large, only the piece of stone to be sculptured, the language to be moulded into poetry, and, perhaps, in the sense of Rilke's "Du mußt dein Leben ändern", the life of those who come in contact with the finished work. The artist is further advanced in the art of objectifying his spiritual impulses than others, but his activity does not separate him from the rest of mankind, for "Romantisirung" is the development of artistic and creative faculties in all men. As Novalis says in the fragment quoted above: "Fast jeder Mensch ist in geringen Grad schon Künstler..." (II, 574).

Briefly considering Novalis' thoughts on the differences between the various arts may further illuminate his position. It has been noted that Novalis' poetry and prose show a subtle melody and rhythm, although they lack the visual clarity and plasticity of Goethe's style. This stylistic inclination towards musicality was probably reinforced by Novalis' opposition to imitation: the sounds of music show little resemblance to naturally occurring noises, while the plastic arts were traditionally (before the advent of abstract art) some form of imitation. One might therefore expect a preference for music in Hardenberg's aesthetics. Yet, to him, the creative process in art was not an internalization, but an objectification of inwardness: "Der Musiker hört eigentlich auch active—Er hört heraus. Freylich ist dieser umgekehrte Gebrauch der Sinne den Meisten ein Geheimniß, aber jeder Künstler wird es sich mehr oder minder deutlich bewußt seyn" (II, 574). If every art attempts to impose the pattern of consciousness upon raw material, the forms of art are only distinguished by their tools, signs, and media ("Werckzeug", "Chiffer", and "Stoff"). Since the signs of musical notation are arbitrary and independent of material conditions, the composer is not faced with the resilience of matter, this task is left to the performer. But brush, brushstroke, and canvas are all materials of nature, and their use requires a technique as well as an inner vision of shape. The painter's task is therefore not only more difficult than that of the composer, but also much more representative of the universal problem that the magic idealist will have to face in his imaginative transformation of the world. Novalis concludes: "So viel, dünkt mich, werde daraus gewiß, daß die Mahlerey bey weiten *schwieriger*, als die Musik, sey."[17]

IV. THE DOCTOR AS A YOUNG ARTIST

Novalis holds that artistic creativity is exemplary for all human activity in the envisaged future, and consequently he attempts to establish a relation between art and the creative element in various professions, among them medicine. He calls poetry the laboratory where the future remedy of mankind is tested: "Poësie ist die große Kunst der Construction der transscendentalen Gesundheit. Der Poët ist also der transscendentale Arzt" (II, 535). Inverting this statement, Novalis demanded from physicians that they become artists in their profession, and from men in general that they become a virtuoso of their bodies. In medicine, as in all other realms, he saw universal principles at work, and in the fight of various schools of thought he recognized fundamental issues at stake. The humoral pathologists he linked with the materialists ("Stoffseher") who saw life in terms of interacting fluids. The neuro-pathologists, in turn, were "die atomistischen mechanischen Formseher" who interpreted organic life in terms of the motion and collison of solids. In the "Actionisten" who, like Fichte, rose above the restricting conditions of the natural world, he saw a possible synthesis (II, 646). He occasionally counted John Brown to these actionists or "schaffende Betrachter, Seheschöpfer" because Brown held a "dogmatic" philosophy with the personal courage and the conviction of an Idealist: "Das Beste am Brownischen System ist die erstaunende Zuversicht, mit der Brown sein System, als allgemeingeltend, hinstellt" (II, 545).

Hence, in spite of his philosophical reservations, Novalis accepted Brown's vocabulary; in the remaining part of this chapter I shall give a few examples of how he redefined this vocabulary to fit his own philosophy. For example, Novalis changed the original categories of internal and external stimulants into direct and indirect: "Der Reitz von Außen ist indirecter, der Reitz von Innen directer Reitz" (II, 561). This harmless substitution did indeed fit better his own theory of sensation, since he held that the body performed a mediating role between consciousness and the external world, so that all external stimuli impinged upon the mind indirectly.[18] Moreover, he believed that external stimuli played only a secondary role in defining consciousness, since the decisive impulses came from the operation of the mind itself: as if the self were to contain in an undefined and raw form all its future, and stimulation would only act as a trigger for the particular act. As Baader stated, stimulation was merely an "ignis mas", a "Samen", while the self had been defined in a primeval hylozoistic act. Novalis agreed with Baader that mechanical causation was mere appearance effacing the original transcendental act of begetting. In tracing this original act of creation both were in search of an "Urmaterial", an unformed medium of dormant potentials, which they came to identify with a primitive fluid.[19] The self-begetting of this fecund medium became for them an emblem for all reproduction and consequently both of them raised the female principle above the purely triggering function of the male. To my knowledge it has not been noted so far that in Baader's *Elementar-phisiologie*, as later in Hardenberg's *Die*

Lehrlinge, this primitive fluid was associated with the veil of Isis.[20]

These physiological considerations had important consequences in pathology. If external stimulation was only of secondary importance in defining the state of a body, the causes of a disease were not so much in the environment as in the constitution, while deficiencies in a constitution were ultimately related to the irregularities in a man's psychological make up — as Novalis' speculation about hypochondria and madness already indicated. These are the considerations that later led Novalis to see a link between disease (a physiological aberration) and sin (a moral and psychological failure).

Perhaps the most important improvement that Novalis proposed to make over the medical works he studied was the introduction of a theory of constitutions. The outline was as follows:

1. Constitution mit mangelnder Reitzbarkeit. (indirect asth[enisch])
2. Constit[ution] mit überflüssiger Reitzbarkeit. (direct asth[enisch])
   a. C[onstitution] mit überflüssiger Incitation (direct sthenisch)
   b. C[onstitution] mit mangelnder Incitation (indirect sthenisch.) (II, 573).

The note belongs to those which Novalis found yet unsatisfactory and crossed out, but he must have regarded the classification as important because the scheme is sketched out in a recently published little drawing (also crossed out), and the concept introduced by him, the term "indirectly sthenic", recurs in a "Brouillon" note relating to Röschlaub's *Untersuchungen*.[21]

A superficial comparison between Hardenberg's sketch and the chart that usually accompanied the *Elements* (Appendices I-III) would suggest that Novalis merely wanted to round off Brown's somewhat asymmetrical pattern by introducing a fourth type of disease. But by doing so he also redefined some basic principles: in the new classification diseases were either due to irregular amounts of excitability or unhealthy environments; the former became the internally caused asthenic diseases, the latter the externally conditioned forms of "Sthenie". Although the new category was a form of "Sthenie", Novalis' real concern were the asthenic diseases, which, in his scheme, were caused by internal physiological or psychological disorders. Brown's "dogma" that most diseases were asthenic[22] achieved thereby a new meaning and Brown himself became the physician of the age because he recognized the "Zeitgeist" and identified the dominant asthenic disposition corresponding to it: "Die herrschende Konstitution ist die Zärtliche—die Asthenische. Das Heilsystem ist das natürliche Produkt der herrschenden Constitution..." (II, 604).

Novalis' remarks about the dominant constitution of the age are merely medically dressed expressions of that almost universal self-conscious modernism of the "Goethezeit" which found more eloquent expression in Hölderlin's poetry, Schiller's *Über naive und sentimentalische Dichtung* or later in Hegel's philosophy. While the Greek temperament expressed itself in "noble simplicity and quiet grandeur", the modern constitution, as Novalis noted, was typified by easy excitability, delicacy, sensitivity, and slight femininity (II, 579, 602, and 604). To this observation he even brought a personal testimony: "Zuviel Abstraction erzeugt Asthenie—zu viel Reflexion Sthenie. Ich muß viel reflectiren und nicht viel abstrahiren. Ich bin schon reitzbar genug" (III, 289). Carrying this medical analysis even further, in the "Brouillon" he asked whether this asthenic disposition of the age was a constitutional deficiency (direct weakness) or due to the exhausting external conditions (indirect weakness): "Wichtige Frage, ob die Menschheit im Zustande der directen oder indirecten Schwäche sey" (III, 419)?

The usefulness of this terminology, as well as the restlessness of Hardenberg's mind, is shown by the undue haste with which these idioms became landmarks and general signposts on the philosophical map he was charting. Epic poetry became indirectly asthenic, lyric poetry directly asthenic, while drama was both directly and indirectly sthenic: "Die Dramatische [Poesie ist] die vollständig Gesunde, ächt Gemischte."[23] Somewhat earlier, however, a "Trauerspiel", as well as life, was described by a transition from sthenic to asthenic or vice versa.[24] In another sketch Novalis quickly moved from contemplating a "medical view of the French Revolution" to the asthenic nature of the Chinese, and finally to a plan to write a history of mankind in terms of medicine.[25]

More interesting and important is a fragment that immediately followed the classification of constitutions and did not explicitly use any medical term: "Plato macht die *Liebe* schon zum Kinde des *Mangels, des Bedürfnisses*— und des *Überflusses*" (II, 573). The occasion for this remark was not the passage from Plato's *Symposium* (203 A-204 A), as suggested in the critical edition (II, 775), since Novalis' references to Plato were probably made on the basis of reading secondary works.[26] In this case Novalis' source was Schlegel's 69th "Lyceum" fragment which appeared in 1797: "Es gibt auch negativen Sinn, der viel besser ist als Null, aber viel seltner. Man kann etwas innig lieben, eben weil mans nicht hat: das gibt wenigstens ein Vorgefühl ohne Nachsatz. Selbst entschiedne Unfähigkeit, die man klar weiß, oder gar mit starker Antipathie ist bei reinem Mangel ganz unmöglich, und setzt wenigstens partiale Fähigkeit und Sympathie voraus. Gleich dem Platonischen Eros ist also wohl dieser negative Sinn der Sohn des Überflusses und der Armut."[27] Since Novalis' note captures most of Schlegel's last sentence, there can be no doubt about the background and we only have to ask what interested him in the statement, since he was not concerned with Schlegel's "negative sense". The words "Mangel" and "Überfluss" suggest that the note may be related to thoughts on medicine, and this assumption is confirmed by another note in the same MS where sthenic and asthenic loves are compared. What could have Novalis meant by these odd terms?

In Hardenberg's theory, constitutions are described by a "deficiency" or "excess" in excitability or stimulation. Love in a constitution of low excitability will express itself through dispassionate tenderness and yearning, while a highly excitable constitution will burst into flames of passion. The distinction allows for an interesting reading of the *Hymnen an die Nacht* and some "Teplitzer" fragments which describe a "deficiency" or "excess" of light—the metaphor of love.[28] The night of the hymns represents a realm beyond sensuous experience where extrasensory perception is aided by the juice of poppy (opium) and the "golden flood of grapes" (I, 133). This realm is only "indirectly" dim, because the beloved, the "dear sun of the night" (I, 133) spreads an overabundance of light over the firmament. In a fragment written in Teplitz Novalis did indeed distinguish between directly and indirectly asthenic nights. The first was simply lacking in illumination, whereas the latter was characterized by an excess of light and likened to an organism with an "excess of self-stimulation".

Precisely such an excess in internal stimulation will lead to that imaginative derangement of the senses in which the visions of the hymns are experienced: "Die Nacht ist zweyfach—Indirecte und directe Asthenie—Jene entsteht durch Blendung—Übermäßiges Licht—diese aus Mangel an hinlänglichen Licht. So giebt es auch eine Unbesonnenheit aus Mangel an Selbstreitz—und eine Unbesonnenheit aus Übermaaß an Selbstreitz—dort ein zu grobes—hier ein zu zartes Organ. ... Die Nacht und Unbesonnenheit aus Mangel ist die Häufigste. Die Unbesonnenheit aus Übermaaß nennt man Wahnsinn" (II, 620).

IV

Ideas for an Encyclopedia

> „Was ist die Natur? — ein encyclopaedischer systematischer Index oder Plan unsers Geistes. Warum wollen wir uns mit dem bloßen Verzeichniß unsrer Schätze begnügen — laßt sie uns selbst besehn — und sie mannichfaltig bearbeiten und benutzen" (II, 583).

1. THE "BROUILLON" AND THE OTHER NOTEBOOKS

The last sketches of the "Vorarbeiten zu verschiedenen Fragmentsammlungen" date from September 1798, when Novalis had already started to jot down miscellaneous notes under the title "Das allgemeine Brouillon": "Was mir nebenher einfällt, wird in das *allg[emeine] Brouillon* mit hineingeschrieben" (III, 280). He continued to write into this notebook till March 1799, shortly before his return from Freiberg to Weissenfels. The "Brouillon" was, of course, not the only notebook Novalis kept during his stay at Freiberg: the so-called "Freiberger naturwissenschaftliche Studien", printed for the first time in their entirety in vol. III of the new critical edition, contain a large number of detailed notes on specific scientific works of the time.[1] Since the "Brouillon" often reuses themes and ideas from these and older notes, one might be tempted to merge it with other notebooks, and perhaps even follow E. Wasmuth who collected all of Hardenberg's "fragmentary writing" and subdivided it according to subject matters.

But such an arrangement would be misleading, not merely because it is often difficult to determine to what subject a many faceted Novalis-note belongs. The "Brouillon" neither contains direct excerpts and notes as other notebooks from Freiberg do, nor is it made up of polished fragments as *Blüthenstaub* or *Glauben und Liebe*. Both its form and its content will best be dealt with if we attempt to reconstruct the outline and the aim of this collection, which occupies a distinct place in Hardenberg's development.

As already the title (= general outline, scheme) indicates, the "Brouillon" meant to bring together a wide spectrum of knowledge to show the interrelations and the underlying higher unity. In the "Kant-Studien" of 1797 Novalis already defined philosophizing as a scientific and poetic treatment of the sciences (II, 390), and half a year later the notion reappeared in that letter to A. W. Schlegel which accompanied the first version of the *Blüthenstaub* fragments. In this letter Novalis expressed the hope of escaping from the "Strudel der Empirie" through his old inclination towards the absolute, and asserted that in the future he would only engage in poetry: "... die Wissenschaften müssen alle poetisiert werden—von dieser realen, wissenschaftlichen Poesie hoffe ich recht viel mit Ihnen zu reden. Ein Hauptgedanke dazu ist die Idee der Religion in meinen Fragmenten" (IV, 229). Both a fragment written in Teplitz (II, 601) and a letter to F. Schlegel (IV, 233) contemplated a "symbolic treatment" of the natural sciences. In the "Brouillon" itself Novalis noted programmatically: "Romant[ische] poët[ische] Ansicht d[er] W[issenschaften]" (III, 377).

Although these remarks do not necessarily refer directly to the "Brouillon", there can be no doubt that this was conceived as a symbolic, poetic, and religious treatment of the sciences. What exactly was the meaning that Novalis attached to his project? His first notions lead us back to the notes he wrote preceding the conception of the encyclopedia, notably to the "romanticizing of the world" and to some of the early notes on medicine, where an imaginative reconstruction of the world was advocated: "Das Beste am Brownischen System ist die erstaunende Zuversicht, mit der Brown sein System, als allgemeingeltend, hinstellt—Es muß und soll so seyn— die Erfahrung und Natur mag sagen, was sie will. Darinn liegt denn doch das Wesentliche jedes Systems, seine wircklich geltende Kraft" (II, 545). In the notebooks written in conjunction with the "Brouillon" this idea was repeated in much more general terms: "Der Begriff Materie, Phlogiston, Oxigène, Gas, Kraft, etc. gehören in eine *logische Physik*—die nichts von concreten Stoffen weis—sondern mit kühner Hand eigensinnig in das Weltchaos hineingreift—und eigne *Ordnungen* macht. *Plotins Physik*" (III, 179). This symbolic conception of science, which Novalis attributes to Plotinus, points to prevalent twentieth-century theories because it recognizes that, contrary to the popular conception, the terminology of science is not a representation of materials and material objects, but rather a mental and imaginative aid that helps us in ordering the "Weltchaos". Today Novalis could refer to the notions of wave, electron, or orbit to show that physical concepts do not correspond to a uniquely defined material reality beyond consciousness. He saw the task of science in developing a system of concepts or regulative norms that could be applied to nature: "Wir werden erst Physiker werden, wenn wir *imaginative*—Stoffe und Kr[äfte] zum regulat[iven] Maaßstab der Naturstoffe und Kr[äfte] machen" (III, 448). Novalis called the process of generating a system of "imaginative materials and energies" "active empiricism" (thätiger Empiricismus), and meant by it an essentially creative endeavor; physics, as well as poetry, experimented with "images and concepts in the imagination (III, 443) until these lost their arbitrariness and became pure representations of a divine idea. Hence the process may also be called "experimenting in God" (III, 443)—Novalis found this expression while reading Tiedemann—and the resultant body of science may be described as "theological physics".

Considering the "Brouillon" as an attempt at a symbolic, poetic, and religious treatment of physics, with the philosophy of Plotinus and the medical theosophies of the sixteenth century (Paracelsus and his followers) as precursors, it comes as a surprise that Novalis regarded Goethe as the greatest physicist of his age: "Göthe soll der Liturg dieser Physik werden—er versteht vollkommen den Dienst im Tempel" (III, 469). This remark from the "Brouillon" has antecedents in an earlier letter and in the essay-fragment on Goethe, probably written in the first days of September 1798. Conceived in the mixed spirit of respect and criticism which characterizes most of Hardenberg's writing on Goethe, the essay praised Goethe's scientific talents:"Auch dürfte man im gewissen Sinn mit Recht behaupten, daß Göthe der erste Physiker seiner Zeit sey..." (II, 640). Professor Samuel is probably correct in observing that here, as in the more explicit letter, Novalis praises Goethe's science with a contrast to Schelling in mind (II, 519). But the praise is shrewdly qualified ("dürfte", "im gewissen Sinn", "mit Recht") and seems to be based on methodology rather than basic issues. For Novalis emphasizes Goethe's ability to deal penetratingly with an insignificant subject until the presentation became highly polished and "comfortable"—praise in which the undertone of irony cannot be ignored.[2] It was, nevertheless, this penetration and care which compared favorably with the "immaturity" of Schelling's *Weltseele* (IV, 238).

Novalis seems to have attributed to Goethe a "Naturanschauung" which was his own rather than Goethe's. He believed that the great physicist looks at nature as the artist does at antiquity: he constructs a model of nature as the modern artist forms an ideal image of Greece: "... man irrt sehr, wenn man glaubt, daß es Antiken giebt. Erst jezt fängt die Antike an zu entstehen. Sie wird unter den Augen und der Seele des Künstlers. Die Reste des Alterthums sind nur die specifischen Reitze zur Bildung der Antike. Nicht mit Händen wird die Antike gemacht. Der Geist bringt sie durch das Auge hervor—und der gehaune Stein ist nur der Körper, der erst durch sie Bedeutung erhält, und zur Erscheinung derselben wird" (II, 640). Accordingly, Novalis praised in Goethe the ability to abstract with unusual accuracy, "without ever failing to *construct* simultaneously the object" (II, 641). This is indeed Novalis' physics, (the essay actually applies the term "activer Empirismus" to the method), and not Goethe's view of nature, for in Goethe's scientific studies, as well as in his poetry, one finds a reverence for the natural construction of objects which often led him to contempt for abstractions and for higher religious significations. Instead of an ideal reconstruction of nature, Goethe aimed at empathy, a blending into the organic unity of the universe.

II. EXTERNAL UNITY — A. G. WERNER

The work that went into the making of the "Brouillon" concerned form and method as much as it did subject matter. When Novalis had come to suspect that the "symbolic treatment of the sciences" was too ambitious a plan for complete and satisfactory execution he decided to focus his work on methodology, giving only examples from the particular fields of knowledge (III, 356). He did indeed devote increasing attention to the very nature of his undertaking, and as a result the "Brouillon" has become to a large extent a critique of its own nature and intentions (III, 357); a number of notes bear the title "Enzyklopaedistik" and others refer back specifically to the project itself. As part of this self-examination Novalis consulted, or planned to study, a wide range of encyclopedic works, among them the great French encyclopedia of Diderot and d'Alembert, from which he made excerpts, G. G. Fülleborn's new *Encyclopedia philologica*, Rousseau's *Dictionnaire de musique*, J. K. G. Jacobson's *Technologisches Wörterbuch*, and W. T. Krug's encyclopedia of the sciences.[3] His preoccupation with the form of the project is evident also in a note of the "Brouillon": "Meine Hauptbeschäftigungen sollen jezt 1. Die Encyclopaedistik. 2. ein Roman. 3. der Brief an Schlegel seyn. Im leztern werde ich ein Bruchstück aus 1. so romantisch, als möglich, vortragen. (Soll es eine Recherche (oder Essai), eine Sammlung Fragmente, ein Lichtenbergischer Commentar, ein Bericht, ein Gutachten, eine Geschichte, eine Abhandlung, eine Recension, eine Rede, ein *Monolog* oder *Bruchstück eines Dialogs* etc. werden?)" (III, 277 f.). Since we do find in the "Brouillon" fragment-like notes, essays, commentaries, and review notes, we may surmise that this lengthy list of possible formats was not merely a sign of Hardenberg's indecision, but a planned feature of his encyclopedia[4] bearing resemblance to Schlegel's "progressive Universalpoesie". The latter aimed at the reunification of literary genres and the fusion of philosophy with literature by envisaging the saturation of the arts with "all kinds of learned material".[5]

Novalis was well aware that the variety in form was seriously endangering the internal and external unity of his project and he was in search of unifying schemes. Most useful was what he learned from A. G. Werner (1749-1817), his friend and teacher at Freiberg. Werner, although still regarded as the greatest figure in the history of the academy, is remembered among laymen chiefly because of his erroneous Neptunian theory, which asserted, like Thales in *Faust II*, that the continents of the earth emerged from the sea in an evolutionary process. But Werner's solid and enduring achievement was the founding of oryctognosy (mineralogy) which he chiefly accomplished with his book *Von den äußerlichen Kennzeichen der Foßilien*.[6] As may be expected, such a systematic book was of particular value to Novalis, who needed a system of classification for the construction of his "Brouillon". The idea of the project itself might have come to him in the lectures of Werner who taught a course on "Enzyklopädie der Bergwerkskunde" during Novalis' stay in Freiberg (cf. III, 738).

Indeed, the "Brouillon" abounds in little memos which meant to remind Novalis of the need to study Werner's system of classification.[7] Surprisingly, however, most of these notes are highly polemic, advocating the revision of the oryctognostic classification (III, 358), the criticism of Werner's Introduction to the work (III, 358), or even the joint revision of Werner's system and the "Brouillon" itself (III, 359). To understand the meaning of these remarks, one has to turn to Novalis' extensive notes on Werner's book, which were recently published for the first time (III, 135-161).

As the title of Werner's book indicates, he was concerned with the external characteristics of minerals. It was, however, Werner's conviction that no matter how carefully and systematically one would construct and order these external features, they could not serve as a basis of a true classification of minerals, for such a classification had to rest on their internal, chemical composition. Werner himself was very skeptical of the possibility of establishing a necessary relationship between external features and internal composition, because he felt that the observable characteristics were only arbitrarily and haphazardly expressing something about internal makeup (III, 856 f.). He nevertheless wrote this book on external characteristics because he preferred to have his minerals well described and ill classified than vice versa.

Novalis objected to several specific points in Werner's system. Quite correctly, for instance, he was unwilling to accept Werner's rigid separation of the animal and plant kingdoms from that of minerals, or the somewhat rigid distinctions concerning the study of minerals. But he was most interested in the relation between external signs and internal structure (or symptoms and chemistry) for he sensed that it was here that a critique of a higher science must start. Werner was dogmatic, inasmuch as he believed that any meaningful association between internal and external features may only be established *a posteriori*, i.e., when complete information about both realms was already available (III, 139). An idealist (Novalis calls him a person of magic knowledge, a prophet), on the other hand, would apply a synthetic method whereby changes in form would give him the key to internal transformations. Novalis remarked quite correctly that it is anthropomorphic to believe that internal changes do not show up in scientifically observable external changes; such a belief attributes a free will to minerals and denies the possibility of science.

The basic weakness of Werner's system of classification was its empirical method, which Novalis considered subjective and arbitrary. His opinion is only seemingly paradoxical; for he thought that Werner's scheme was similar to the botanical system of Linné, where the empirically found facts were arranged into an orderly array of empirically established categories. Such a nominalistic system could not show why and how the classification was an internal and logical necessity. Lacking the "principle of necessity" and the "principle of completeness", Werner's system remained a "useful" but "prosaic oryctognosy".[8]

Instead of merely wanting to replace Werner's "dogmatism" by an "idealistic" method, Novalis was looking for a dialectic that would synthesize the two. As in his interpretation of Goethe's physics, the observed object was to be simultaneously an a priori idea in the mind of the observer (III, 357 f.), and the "compelling concept of a fossil" (III, 388) was to be constructed through a both theoretical and practical method of investigation (III, 144 f.). A method of empiricism and abstraction could uncover that binding relationship between chemical composition and external appearance which Werner denied (III, 141), for individuality and universality were always dialectically present in appearance and internal structure (III, 140).

III. INTERNAL UNITY—KANT, FICHTE, AND LAMBERT

A unifying form for the "Brouillon" was, of course, never found, and the shifts in Hardenberg's plans—first from the encyclopedic project to the inhomogeneous *Die Lehrlinge zu Sais*, and then from *Die Lehrlinge* to *Heinrich von Ofterdingen*—suggest that he became gradually convinced that only poetry could provide that external form for which he was looking. In any case, the unifying element of the "Brouillon" is not the external but the internal arrangement of its subject matter, for the project is grounded in the conviction that knowledge, however immense, is both unique and universal, and that neither nature nor the human mind is split by irreducible contradictions. According to Novalis, there is an inner core of truth somewhat analogous to general mathematical statements,[9] which reduces the bewildering variety found in the empirical world:

> Doppelte Universalität jeder wahrhaften W[issenschaft]—Eine entsteht, wenn ich alle andern W[issenschaften] zur Ausbildung der Besondern benutze. —Die Andre, wenn ich sie zur Universalwissenschaft mache und *sie selbst unter sich* ordne—alle andre Wissenschaften, als ihre Modificationen betrachte. Den Ersten Versuch der leztern Art hat Fichte mit der Phil[osophie] unternommen. Er soll in allen W[issenschaften] unternommen werden (III, 269).

The passage suggests that Novalis took from Fichte that transcendental foundation in which he found Werner's system deficient, and attempted to apply Fichte's mathematical and logical but abstract rigor to the empirical sciences.

To these two processes, namely the deduction of a specific science from the general framework of all sciences, and the universalizing of a single field, Novalis often applied the mathematical terms of "logarithmisiren" and "potenziren", and he even defined romanticizing as a "qualitative Potenzirung" (II, 545). Such terms as "Logologie" (Logik × Logik = Logik^2). "Philosophie der Philosophie", "Kritik der Kritik", or "Poesie der Poesie" show that Novalis had actually attempted to establish Fichtean "potentialized" categories which would symbolically incorporate in their name the self-conscious and reflective way in which the world was reconstructed by Fichte's empirical self. For it was the method of Fichte's *Wissenschaftslehre* to start from the arbitrarily selected statement $a = a$, and to arrive through the use of logic and "intellectual intuition" to the ideally posited first principle of philosophy which states that "the ego simply posits in an original way its own being". The trouble with Fichte's procedure was that the individual consciousness "potentialized" itself to the truth of the absolute self without touching the specific truth of the sciences that cover the empirical world: "Der W[issenschafts]- *Lehrer* behandelt blos W[issenschaft] im Ganzen—Hat blos mit W[issenschaften], als solchen zu thun. / Die W[issenschafts]Lehre ist eine wahrhafte, unabhängige, selbstständige Encyklopädik.—W[issenschaft] d[er] W[issenschaften]. / W[issenschafts]L[ehre] ist *System des wissenschaftlichen Geistes*—die *Psychologie*, wenn ich so sagen darf—der Wissenschaften im Ganzen" (III, 249). The issue mentioned here was already discussed by Eschenmayer, and this note in the "Brouillon" does indeed pick up themes from the Eschenmayer-notes.

Like Fichte's *Wissenschaftslehre*, the "Brouillon" meant to reflect a transcendental unity, but instead of analyzing the structure of consciousness it turned to the empirical world and attempted to show that the homogeneous pattern of knowledge turns the consideration of any subject, be it medicine, physics, geology, psychology, or music, into a paradigm of universal truth: "*Alle W[issenschaft]* ist *Eine*" (III, 356). If Fichte had sketched the "Psychologie der Wissenschaften", the universal application of his method was still wanting; the "Fichtisiren", as Novalis called his own procedure earlier (II, 524), aimed precisely at that: it wished to treat the various concepts in the sciences as Fichte treated the concept of the self: "Behandl[ung] jedes Begr[iffs]—nach der Fichtischen Ichformel" (III, 405). In a similar way, Novalis performed experiments with Kant's question whether *a priori* synthetic judgments are possible. When he gave ten different physical and metaphysical interpretations to Kant's fundamental question (III, 388), he wished to demonstrate that all forms of knowledge are related to a unified philosophical chain into which they enter organically through a method of "potentialization" (III, 346), and he tried to prove against Kant himself that there are no divisions between the sensuous, the moral, and the metaphysical realms. Seen from this angle, the "Brouillon" may be read as a series of thought-experiments in which Kant's and Fichte's ideas are tested upon the empirical world: "Es ließe sich eine äußerst instructive Reihe von specifischen Darstellungen des Fichtischen und Kantischen Systems denken z.B. eine poëtische, eine chemische, eine mathematische, eine Musikalische etc. ... Ich habe eine Menge Bruchstücke dazu" (III, 336).

The third volume of the second critical edition contains a new section entitled "Studien zu Tiedemanns 'Geist der spekulativen Philosophie' und Lamberts 'Neuem Organon'" (III, 129-134). As mentioned before, the rather cryptic notes on Tiedemann's work in this section led Professor Mähl to significant discoveries about the background material of the "Brouillon". The excerpts from Lambert's *Neues Organon*[10] contain less explosive information and only a few, rather insignificant, personal notes from Novalis; nevertheless they raise some interesting questions.

Lambert was a follower of Wolff and Locke and had an almost boundless confidence in the power of reason: in the *Neues Organon* he set out to discuss the ways in which truth may be separated from error, and he proposed that ultimately all human knowledge may acquire the certainty of logic and mathematics. As Novalis quoted him in the excerpts: "Man sollte daher allerdings *jede* Aufgabe in den *Wissenschaften* auf *blos logische Aufgaben* reduziren können" (III, 131). The unfolding of this principle resulted in a book which one critic called the "most comprehensive theoretical formulation of a 'mathesis universalis' in the history of philosophy."[11] Such claims are no doubt excessive, yet they make Hardenberg's interest in the work clear; indeed, in spite of scarce direct references to Lambert's work, Hardenberg's encyclopedic project was surely stimulated and influenced by Lambert's ideas. In the larger sense the *Neues Organon* shows once more that the main current of eighteenth-century German philosophy of science and epistemology—from Leibniz through the generation of Lambert and culminating in Kant—had anticipated and prepared an important aspect of romantic thought: rationalism and romanticism shared the belief that all knowledge was of the same pattern and shaped by the same principles.

IV. THE BIBLE PROJECT

When Friedrich Schlegel wrote to Novalis on October 20, 1798 that the goal of his literary projects was to write a new bible and to follow the footsteps of Mohamed and Luther (IV, 239), Novalis responded with enthusiasm. Schlegel's plan seemed like a decisive sign of success for their "Sym-organization" because Novalis too had "potentialized" himself from the study of science and its vessel, the book, to the bible—the prototype of all books (IV, 240). Yet, as Schlegel recognized, their plans were quite different;[12] Schlegel's friendship with Schleiermacher led to a project that was literally, and not merely symbolically, religious: "Nun habe ich aber eine Bibel im Sinne, die nicht in gewissem Sinne, nicht gleichsam, sondern ganz buchstäblich und in jedem Geist und Sinne Bibel wäre, das erste Kunstwerk dieser Art, da die bisherigen nur Produkte der Natur sind. ... Mein biblisches Projekt aber ist kein literarisches, sondern— ein biblisches, ein durchaus religiöses." (IV, 247).

This is not the place to analyze Schlegel's hazy notion about the religion he was to proclaim and the prophet he was going to become through his bible-project. In relation to Novalis' ideas on the bible it is important to note only that although Schlegel's book was to be strictly religious, the project was not unrelated to his essay, *Über das Studium der griechischen Poesie*: Schlegel was planning a self-conscious, artistically constructed book which could become for modern man what the "spontaneously" written bible was for ages past, thus rendering a concrete answer to his own call for a new mythology. The call was not unknown to Novalis, and he himself had felt the need for renewing the foundations of faith. As he indicated in a letter to Just (IV, 256), he was emancipated from the traditional "theology of historical-critical reason" and could not take the bible as a "pledge of God and immortality" (IV, 257). Instead of documents, his faith rested on the proofs that his imagination constantly supplied, and he regarded the bible as an "Urbuch", a symbol and prototype of all books. Consequently, his bible could not be religious in the narrow sense, but had to unite religion with morality, poetry, and the knowledge of the empirical world, as the bible mirrored the primeval unity between the poet and the priest. In Novalis' conception, the age needed not a modern bible, but a theory that would universalize the spirit of the "Urbuch": "Die Theorie der Bibel, entwickelt, gibt die Theorie der Schriftstellerei oder der Wortbildnerei überhaupt—die zugleich die symbolische, indirekte Konstruktionslehre des schaffenden Geistes abgibt" (IV, 240).

In what way was the "Brouillon" project affected by Hardenberg's ideas on the bible? In contrast to the arbitrary external unity offered by Werner's classification, and the internal but abstract unity of Fichte's method, the bible rendered both an internal and external unity through the poetic treatment of its subject. It imposed unity not through a mathematical scheme or an abstract philosophical argument but through the concrete representation of lives and events. Although the "Brouillon" remained an inadequate realization of a vague idea, Novalis' later turn to poetic representations shows how he eventually conceived of this "theory of the bible", from which he hoped to generate "grandiose truths and ideas", to prepare the way towards a "true process of reunion" (IV, 240 f.). In the "Brouillon" itself he wanted to apply the idea of the bible to the sciences, so that his work could be called a "scientific bible" and a "real and ideal model", in short: a "Keim aller Bücher" (III, 363). In this sense Novalis could characterize his project as a "description of the bible", a "Bibel Kunst und Naturlehre", and his aim was to raise his book to the art of the bible (III, 365). Indeed, the creative construction of a Book was a task for all those who strove for perfection: "Eine Bibel schreiben zu wollen—ist ein Hang zur Tollheit, wie ihn jeder tüchtige Mensch haben muß, um vollständig zu seyn" (III, 491).

V. HEMSTERHUIS VS. SCHELLING

> Die Wissenschaften sind nur aus Mangel an Genie und Scharfsinn getrennt—die Verhältnisse zwischen ihnen sind dem Verstand und Stumpfsinn zu verwickelt und entfernt von einander.
> Die größesten Wahrheiten unsrer Tage verdanken wir solchen Combinationen der Lange getrennten Glieder der Totalwissenschaft (II, 368).

This meditative excursion amidst the Hemsterhuis-excerpts foreshadows the "Brouillon" and suggests that the philosophy of Hemsterhuis was another formative element in the making of the encyclopedia. The second sentence of this passage and other quotations from *Lettre sur l'homme*, *Simon*, and *Alexis* were indeed inserted word for word into the "Brouillon" (III, 275).

Hemsterhuis believed that the postulated unity of knowledge would only be established, if reason, the faculty of the sciences, becomes subordinated to the moral sense that resides in the heart and develops through social intercourse.[13] Novalis became acquainted with this concept of the moral sense in the fall of 1797, but neither his notebooks from the earlier part of 1798 nor his ideas on magic, as outlined in the preceding chapter, show that it impressed him; his notebooks from that time reflect rather his scientific studies in Freiberg, his interest in medicine, and a residual attachment to certain ideas of Fichte. However, by the end of summer 1798 moral, scientific, and philosophical concerns began to illuminate each other: in a letter to F. Schlegel from July 20 Novalis suggested that one might treat physics symbolically and he divulged that he had come upon the idea of a "moral astronomy" in Hemsterhuis' sense and discovered the "religion of the visible cosmos" (IV, 232). The letter states that

Christian religion and everyday life were among the "central monads" of Hardenberg's meditations at the time, and so "moral astronomy" may be associated both with religion and with the rituals of everyday circumstance. Indeed, among the fragments written during August in Teplitz there are several passages where religious and moral concepts are fused with common life—a life that Novalis calls "Priesterdienst" (II, 608): communal eating, for instance, is described as a symbolic act of union (II, 620), and the tangible world in general is conceived as an "Universaltropus", an image of the spirit (II, 600).

What exactly is meant by "moral astronomy"? In a note from late summer 1798, Novalis stated once more that the imagination was independent of mechanical laws and capable of replacing the external senses (II, 650). In this particular passage he arrived at the assertion by contemplating the association that Hemsterhuis postulated between the visible and invisible worlds: "Alles Sichtbare haftet am Unsichtbaren—Das Hörbare am Unhörbaren—Das Fühlbare am Unfühlbaren. Vielleicht das Denkbare am Undenckbaren—. Das Fernrohr ist ein *künstliches, unsichtbares Organ.* /Gefäß./" (II, 650). Now the last sentence strikes one as odd. Why should the telescope be an "artificial, invisible organ"? Our clue is given by a passage in Hemsterhuis' *Lettre sur l'homme* where the demoralizing effects of the disintegrating geocentric astronomy are described. Hemsterhuis contrasts the weakening of faith and loosening of morals consequent to the invention of the telescope (i.e., the improvement of the external senses) with the constructive intention of the Pythagorean sect to improve their internal sense of morality: "Ils tenterent une modification de la société, dont la base seroit, non la perfection de l'organe de la vue, ni de celui de l'ouïe, ni de celui du tact, mais celle de l'organe moral."[14] Although Novalis made no excerpts of this passage, he noted the Pythagorean refinement of the moral sense and asked if there were telescopes for it (II, 367). The question is in accordance with the description of the telescope as an "artificial, invisible organ", for in both the reference is not to the physical instrument which gives power to the eye, but to that "invisible organ" which may enhance the effectiveness of the moral sense: through self-observation and training such an instrument could "telescope" the action of the internal sense. Hence moral astronomy consists of the "reasons of the heart" aided by the technical power of the mind, while the "moral" telescope is an instrument to fortify the unstable heart and to achieve moral wisdom.[15]

Expressions such as "moralische Heilkunst" (III, 276) indicate that the "Brouillon" intended to establish also a reverse relationship between morality and science, by giving a moral meaning to empirical knowledge. Following Hemsterhuis, the "Universalwissenschaft" or "Wissenschaft im großen" of the "Brouillon" would have been a science saturated with the moral law: "Die magischen W[issenschaften] entspringen, *nach Hemsterhuis*, durch die Anwendung des moralischen Sinns auf die übrigen Sinne—i.e. durch die Moralisirung des Weltalls, und der übrigen Wissenschaften" (III, 275). That magic should be in the service of a moral idea is the specifically new thesis of the "Brouillon" with respect to earlier notes where magic merely designated the possibility of achieving internal control of the externally oriented sense. As if discovering a new dimension beyond the earlier concept of magic, Novalis could say now that the final purpose in the art of magic was to develop the sense of moral responsibility (III, 250).

This shift in Hardenberg's thinking carried him further away from Kant. If earlier notes already reflected his endeavor to eliminate Kant's distinction between knowing and believing or knowing and moral action, the idea of the "moral sciences" in the "Brouillon" sharpened the polemic and defined Novalis' position more clearly. The central argument against Kant was that although God and nature, or morality and nature, were indeed distinct under the existing circumstances, the inevitable movement of history was to bring about a moralization of nature, a moral subjugation of natural forces: "Gott und Natur muß man hiernach trennen—Gott hat gar nichts mit der Natur zu schaffen—Er ist das Ziel der Natur—dasjenige, mit dem sie einst harmoniren soll. Die Natur soll *moralisch* werden und so erscheint allerdings der Kantische Moralgott und die Moralitaet in einem ganz andern Lichte. Der moralische Gott ist etwas weit Höheres, als der magische Gott" (III, 250). Both in the "Brouillon" (III, 248) and in the plans for *Die Lehrlinge* (I, 111) man appears as the "Messiah of nature" because he is destined to liberate the universe from the yoke of mechanical determinism by following the poet-prophet.

The shift from a "magical God" to a "moral God" marks also Novalis' decisive departure from Schelling's early "Naturphilosophie". One ought to be discriminating, however, in evaluating their relationship. Although Novalis might have had later personal reasons for disliking Schelling, especially on account of Karoline Schlegel's relationship with Schelling, the initial differences were only philosophical and not very clearly defined. Of their first meeting on December 1, 1797 Novalis reported to the Schlegel brothers that it was a success and they agreed to begin a correspondence.[16] The impression that Schelling made on Novalis was perhaps more due to the quality of his mind than to agreement about aims and methods, because Novalis' later remarks on Schelling's works were mostly negative. But one should read these in their context: the oft-quoted critical remarks on Schelling appear almost exclusively in his correspondence with the Schlegels,[17] particularly with Friedrich, who was unfavorably disposed towards Schelling. Since Friedrich's attitude towards Schelling betrayed an excess of jealousy from the very beginning—Schelling was three years younger and significantly more successful— and since his reports about Schelling's new works were always accompanied by some disparaging remarks,[18] Novalis made some rather striking adjustments to the opinions of his addressee by avoiding a polemic and harmonizing with his tone— as he always did in his correspondence.[19] This may also reveal why Novalis wrote to Friedrich that he "boldly explained" to Schelling "our" (i.e., Novalis' and Friedrich's) displeasure at the *Ideen*.

Nevertheless there were real differences and serious issues at stake. In retrospect these were not, as Schelling and Steffens believed, due to Hardenberg's allegedly "fragmentary and restless" nature,[20] since Schelling's own escapades in the fields of medicine, chemistry, and physics are often more undisciplined than certain speculations of Novalis. It seems more important that the young Schelling consistently refused to subordinate his concept of nature to any supernatural idea or being. His *Weltseele*, which appeared in the spring of 1798, carried in its title a concept which was not beyond nature, merely the unseen coordinating principle inherent in it. In short, Schelling's "Weltseele" was a Spinozistic concept.

The early notes of Novalis do not explicitly reject this worship of nature, and the notion of magic is merely an attempt to define the power that consciousness may acquire over matter; but after the study of Hemsterhuis' enthusiastic and metaphysical treatment of nature Schelling's philosophy must have appeared to Novalis as somewhat prosaic. Like Schelling, Hemsterhuis considered the attractive and repulsive forces as fundaments of nature, but he saw a personal God and a "preordained harmony" holding and coordinating them.

The most interesting comment within Novalis' extensive study of the *Weltseele* makes it clear that Novalis was unwilling to concede to Schelling a radical dualism between mind and matter, even on the empirical level (III, 114). He agreed with Hemsterhuis in matters of ultimate priorities: "Mit dem bloßen Stoff den Anfang in der Philos[ophie] der Wissenschaften zu machen ist eben so einseitig und antinomisch und unkritisch, als mit der *bloßen Bewegung* anzufangen. Mit dem Menschen anzufangen ist schon kritischer ... mit Gott anzufangen—ein Maximum der Kritik" (III, 343); "Die Wissenschaft fängt nicht mit einem Antinom—Binom—sondern mit einem *Infinitinom* an" (III, 432). That this last remark was directed specifically against Schelling, we know from a letter by Steffens in which he complained to Schelling that Novalis posited an "Urinfinitismus" instead of an "Urduplizität" at the heart of nature, and thereby "misunderstood" the basic principle of "Naturphilosophie" (IV, 463).

Thus Hardenberg's increasing differences with Schelling may partly be traced to his renewed interest in Hemsterhuis' philosophy: when he announced his plans for a "moral astronomy" and a symbolic physics, he added that he hoped to surpass Schelling in these fields; similarly, his second thoughts about Schelling's "Weltseele" were related to the moral redefinition of nature. If nature and morality were as yet separate and the "Weltseele", according to Schelling, was the intrinsic principle of the physical world, then it had to be separated from the moral concept of God: "Will ich nun Gott oder die Weltseele in den Himmel setzen? Besser wär es wohl, wenn ich den Himmel zum moralischen Universo erklärte—und die Weltseele im Universum ließe" (III, 250). As Professor Mähl noticed, another solution offered itself, once Novalis learned about Plotinus' philosophy. Here the upper "Weltseele" was defined as the immediate emanation of the divine hypostasis and was separated from the lower "Weltseele", the spirit of the sensuous world. The use of the concept "Weltseele" in the later notes of the "Brouillon" should be associated therefore with the neo-Platonic tradition rather than with Schelling's work of that title.[21]

In passing it might be mentioned that while the "Brouillon" marked Hardenberg's alienation from Schelling, it showed his affinity with Schiller, particularly his *Über die ästhetische Erziehung des Menschen* (1795) which Novalis must have read—although his notebooks show no direct references to it. Like Novalis, Schiller accepted the dualism in man as a necessary part of the human condition and described a distant goal which had common features with the physiology and psychology of Magic Idealism: "[des Menschen] Kultur wird also darin bestehen: erstlich: dem empfangenden Vermögen die vielfältigsten Berührungen mit der Welt zu verschaffen und auf seiten des Gefühls die Passivität aufs höchste zu treiben: zweitens: dem bestimmenden Vermögen die höchste Unabhängigkeit von dem empfangenden zu erwerben und auf seiten der Vernunft die Aktivität aufs höchste zu treiben."[22] The decisive point of agreement, however, was that both Schiller and Novalis foresaw a moral development in which man would transform himself and nature,[23] and that they saw art as the mediating force in this transformation. As Schiller stated, the realm of art lies both in the natural world of change and the motionless sphere of moral freedom and it is in this joint aesthetic realm that man's primeval "Spieltrieb" may be effective: "Der sinnliche Trieb will, daß Veränderung sei, daß die Zeit einen Inhalt habe: der Formtrieb will, daß die Zeit aufgehoben, daß keine Veränderung sei. Derjenige Trieb also, in welchem beide verbunden wirken ... der Spieltrieb also würde dahin gerichtet sein, die Zeit *in der Zeit* aufzuheben."

V

Sensibility and Medicine

I. THE VOCABULARY OF THE ENCYCLOPEDIA

"Romanticism was above all a renewal of human sensibility" writes Pierre Trahard in his monumental work on eighteenth-century French sensibility, and one is inclined to accept his definition, not because it is precise, but because his notion is as complex as romanticism itself.[1] For the concept of sensibility that M. Trahard traces through the torturous ways of eighteenth-century France and opposes to the classic ideal seems as a one-dimensional projection of an idea that moved over the frontiers and the artificial compartments of human thought. One only has to consider the precise and experimentally measurable phenomenon that Albrecht Haller investigated just about mid-century, or the literary and social associations of the term in England (here it had simultaneously retained its narrowly defined physiological meaning) to be convinced of this.[2] Thus on his "sentimental journey" Laurence Sterne addressed himself to sensibility as the "source unexhausted of all that's precious in our joys, or costly in our sorrows", referring to the God-given gift of charity and good-heartedness, while Dr. Johnson could write in a very different sense: "I was on Saturday at Mrs. Montague's, who expressed great sensibility of your loss." Finally, reading Byron's description of the "motley court" of romance "Where Affectation holds her seat,/ And sickly Sensibility", one is inclined to say that romanticism was more a crisis of this notion than a renewal of it.³

With these considerations we have come surprisingly close to the ambiguous meaning that Novalis attaches to the term, because in his mind the various shades of "sensibility" were fused together to form a complex encyclopedic concept. The first strand came to his attention in the writings of Hemsterhuis, who had regarded sensibility as the passive component of the moral organ, the heart, and defined six stages between perception and action, subordinating the first two receptive ones to the heart. As Novalis summarized it, sensibility was the hearts's capacity to like and dislike: "1. / Das Herz / welches H[emsterhuis] hier für Gefühl von Lust und Unlust—für Sensibilitaet nimmt— / begehre oder verabscheue" (II, 371). In *Simon* Hemsterhuis went considerably further. He identified the active and passive components of the moral sense with the faculty of judgment and the imagination respectively, and advocated a proper balance between the two: "Ein Mensch mit sehr viel Sensibilitaet des moralischen Organs, aber ohne Activitaet desselben—ist der Tugend und des Lasters gleich fähig" (II, 375); "Der moralische Sinn / die sensible Seite des Herzens / ist die schönste, aber auch gefährlichste Seite unsers Wesens" (II, 376). Even more important, Hemsterhuis believed that an imbalance in the two components could be redressed through constant training and education.

The argument about the dangers of excessive sensibility and the teaching about the training of it must have struck a chord in Novalis, since, as his letters to Erasmus show, these were problems he confronted in his youth. Yet, curiously, once he finished making excerpts from the works of Hemsterhuis he dropped the subject for a while: the early notebooks from Freiberg (which often relied on material from the previous year) do not touch on the concept of sensibility, as they are not, in general, concerned with the moral transformation of nature. In the "Brouillon" and the accompanying notebooks the term emerges again in a changed context and with different shades of meaning: "Gehört etwa die Sensibilitaet schon der Seele an? (Reitzbarkeit und Sensibilitaet haben einen sehr bemercklichen

Einfluß auf die Organisation" (III, 249); "Reitzbarkeit und Sensibilitaet stehn in ähnlichen Verhältnissen, als Seele und Körper..." (III, 316).

The coupling of sensibility and irritability in both remarks suggests that the concepts are taken here in their physiological sense, and that we have to turn to medical literature to understand their meaning. "Irritability" and "sensibility" were as fashionable then as "id" and "ego" in the recent past, and Novalis must have read about them in at least five or six different publications,[4] but the meaning and significance that he attached to them leave little doubt that the immediate occasion was offered by the works of Schelling. Indeed, the terms appeared first in Novalis' notes on Schelling's *Weltseele*. Following Kielmeyer, Schelling defined sensibility as the highest organic force, and irritability as the lower expression of the same general power, so that irritability and sensibility were in an inverse mathematical relationship (III, 114). Although inversely proportional to each other, both sensibility and irritability were regarded by Schelling as "negative conditions of life",[5] not because they were merely receptive faculties, but because he recognized only one positive principle, the "Weltseele", which guided and coordinated the interaction of the dialectically opposed negative principles: "Die negative Bedingung des Lebensprocesses ist ein Antagonismus negativer Principien, der durch den continuirlichen Einfluß des positiven Princips (der ersten Ursache des Lebens) unterhalten wird" (Sch, I, 575).

A more detailed interpretation necessitates acquaintance with Schelling's notion of "capacity". Following Girtanner, Schelling believed that irritability, the lower of the two reciprocal factors, was physiologically measurable through the oxygen capacity of the nerves in the organ: large or numerous nerves were supposed to increase the capacity for oxygen, thereby making the organ more irritable and less uniform in its function, and vice versa.[6] On the basis of this theory it was argued, for instance, that the heart should have few nerves because the organism could not endure its irregular operation; in turn, the physiologically observable sign for great sensibility became the scarcity of nerves:

> So hat also die Natur, indem sie die Bewegung der Willkür ganz zu überantworten schien, sie durch Erhöhung der Sensibilität der Willkür wieder entzogen; denn die Bewegungen der empfindlichsten Thiere sind auch am wenigsten willkürlich, und umgekehrt, die größte Willkür der Bewegungen ist in den trägen Geschöpfen. So nimmt mit steigender Sensibilität des Nervensystems das Willkürliche (Abgemessene) der Bewegungen durch die ganze Reihe der Organisationen, und sogar in Individuen derselben Gattung (nach Verschiedenheit des Geschlechts, Klimas, Temperaments u.s.w.) regelmäßig ab (Sch, I, 631).

This odd claim, that high sensibility should be marked by few nerves, becomes more comprehensible upon considering that to Schelling sensibility was not so much a sensitivity to stimulation as a sign of mental development, and that the mental level of a race was, according to a thesis of Sömmering (Sch, I, 630), inversely proportional to the abundance of nerves. Stated in a different way, Schelling believed that with the development of sensibility the animal organism would gradually lose that arbitrariness in operation which is the inevitable consequence of abundant nerves, and thereby blend more harmoniously with the laws of reason. Novalis' characteristic reaction to this theory was: "Vereinigung der höchsten Sens[ibilitaet] und höchsten Irritabilitaet" (III, 114), which meant that he was in search of a state in which extreme subjectivity would harmonize with the laws of reason.

The following two remarks may serve as a starting point in analyzing Novalis' concept of capacity: "Zersezt besteht die Erregbarkeit aus Sensibilitaet und Reitzbarkeit—oder Beweglichkeit und Capacitaet" (III, 323); "Allzu große geistige Beweglichkeit und Sensibilitaet deutet auf Mangel an Capacitaet..." (III, 559). In both of these remarks Brown's "excitability" is resolved into "irritability" and "sensibility", and also into two other contending tendencies, namely "mobility" and "capacity"—in analogy to the concepts of mobility and inertia in mechanics ("Beweglichkeit" was the basic property of matter for Kant and Eschenmayer). The two different ways of resolving excitability yield an association between irritability and capacity or sensibility and mobility. According to the second note, excessive sensibility and mobility are characteristics of an unstable constitution; the same theory is upheld in another note: "Die Trägheit steht mit der *Sensibilitaet* in umgekehrten [sic] Verhältniß—vielleicht also in Geradem mit der *Irritabilitaet*—und ist nichts anders, als diese" (III, 179)? Yet another note shows that Novalis followed Schelling in recognizing a "scale of life" which was arranged according to the organism's oxygen capacity: "Die Capacit[aet] [der?] Mat[erie] (Oxigène. *organischer Stoff*) ist unterschieden—daher es eine Leiter des Lebens giebt...." (II, 556). These various statements yield a chart that can be contrasted graphically with Schelling's theory:

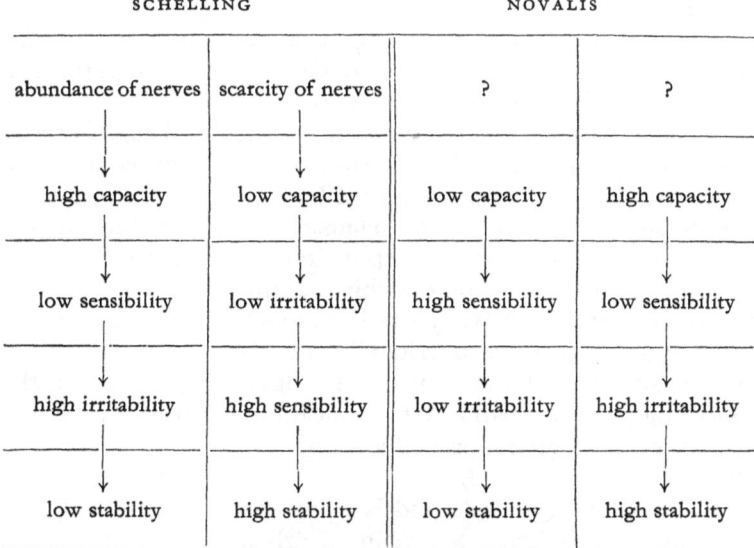

The gist of the comparison is that Novalis accepted Schelling's terms of sensibility and capacity but inverted the meaning attached to them. While Schelling associated capacity with irritability and instability, Novalis regarded it as a measure of constitutional stability,[7] emphasizing once more the inherent constitutional factors in health and disease and adding a new parameter to Brown's physiology. Like a pendulum with a short suspension, or a highly elastic body that quickly bounces back to its original shape, a constitution with high capacity would be highly sturdy and quick to return to its steady state of health. In other words, capacity was meant to measure a body's capability to suffer and to regenerate.[8]

This interpretation of "capacity" permits a few more concrete observations relating to the already mentioned differences between Schelling and Novalis. In *Weltseele* sensibility was the highest expression of organic life so that through it the organism was liberated from the yoke of local and mechanical conditions and placed under the direct guidance of the "spirit of nature".[9] But since this guiding and coordinating principle was merely the spirit of nature itself, Schelling erected a closed system where the highest development, sensibility, remained a wholly natural phenomenon. No God or other supernatural being hovered above Schelling's natural world.

Novalis, in turn, saw in sensibility a faculty feeling its way towards regions beyond the natural order. In contrast to Lamettrie who concluded from Haller's experiments that there was no soul, Novalis held with Hemsterhuis that sensibility was a high moral and spiritual expression of man, not yet fully developed and not wholly within nature.[10] In this sense he could ask if sensibility was part of the soul (III, 249), or he could make an analogy between irritability and the body on one hand, and sensibility and the soul on the other (III, 316). As the following passage illustrates, the education of sensibility was the key to the advocated moral education:

> Synthesis von Seele und Körper—und Reitzbarkeit und Sensibilitaet. Sie gehn natürlich jezt schon in einander durch Indifferenzsfären über—unendliche Erweiterung dieser Indifferenzsfären—Realisirung, Ausfüllung der *Null* ist das schwierige Problem

d[es] Künstlers der Unsterblichkeit. Die Indifferenzsfäre ist das Maas d[er] Constitution. Willkührliche Glieder sind *Sinne* im strengern Sinn. Vermehrung der Sinne und Ausbildung der Sinne gehört mit zu der Hauptaufgabe d[er] Verbesserung des Menschengeschlechts, der Graderhöhung der Menschheit.

Wir sahen vorhin, daß Bildung und Vermehrung der Seele das wichtigste und erste Unternehmen ist. Äußere Reitze haben wir schon in unsrer Hand—und mit ihnen die Reitzbarkeit—es kommt nur vorzüglich auf Vermehrung und Bildung der Sensibilitaet und zwar auf die Weise an, daß die Reitzbarkeit und der äußre Reitz nicht dabey leiden, nicht dabey vernachlässigt werden—denn sonst webt man ein sehr zerreißbares Gewebe, und ein Gewebe der Penelope ... (III, 318).

It may be claimed that the "multiplication and education of the senses" is still identical with the program of magic to develop freely usable organs, and that the described synthesis of body and soul is in accordance with the earlier aim to endow the soul with a dominating power without severing its ties with the physical world. But here the training of the senses has a moral aim: the new layer of meaning over the original theory of magic is evident even in the new vocabulary which includes "irritability" and "sensibility" but not "magic". Similarly, the "Indifferenzsfären" which the "artist of immortality" ought to develop, have now become signs of constitutional stability and denoted with "capacity". The spheres of neutrality indicate the strength of the constitution, because they enable the body to use external impulses freely. High capacity (stability) may be maintained in spite of a high level of irritability if the formation of zones of "numbness" is balanced by refining some organs to extreme sensibility; the one-sided cultivation of sensibility would lead to an unstable constitution ("ein Gewebe der Penelope"), while the exclusive expansion of neutral regions would lead to a regression to an animal state.

Hence Novalis saw sensibility as a historical and teleological force that was destined to liberate man from Schelling's natural world; through its right cultivation man could develop—but also destroy—his potentials, and raise himself from his fallen state to a second millenium. It is typical of Hardenberg's bifocal vision that he attached to this utopia very immediate and practical tasks in terms of a rather prosaic notion. His prescription was not, as one might expect, a cultivation of delicate feelings and taste, but a rather austere and disciplined training program to develop "Aufmercksamkeit". The term occurs for the first time among the Hemsterhuis excerpts, where Novalis remarks that the education of the moral sense, as discussed above, could be achieved through the continued use of selected stimuli. As reason is sharpened through constant use of the mind and a concentration on its activity, so the moral sense—Novalis calls it "rational imagination" here—could be trained until it could make arbitrary use of the slightest and remotest stimulus and set the sense into a morally consistent activity (II, 377).

The notion continued to be on Hardenberg's mind. Among the fragments of 1798 he remarked that only a few have learned to give attention to everything that surrounds them, and noted for himself that according to C. Bonnet, attention was the mother of genius (II, 541).[11] Still in the same group of notes there is a longer discussion of "Aufmercksamkeit" and "Abstractionsfähigkeit" (II, 577 f.) in terms of the theory of magic. In posing himself the question of how an organism can cope with an array of simultaneously operating stimuli which impose upon it an ironclad rule of mechanism, Novalis found the answer in the development of "Aufmercksamkeit", a power which shifts, weighs, and channels external sensuous stimulation. On the most elementary level this may mean, for instance, a partial or complete ignoring and overcoming of pain, by directing the attention to some pleasing sound or sight; in general, the most beneficial impressions would receive attention. After an extended period of training a more sophisticated level would be reached, where it would become possible to distribute local pleasurable or painful stimulations over whole regions of the body, or to concentrate widely and thinly spread impressions in one area.[12]

Following the plan to present a "higher" view of specialized knowledge, Novalis gave even greater prominence to the term "Grad", which was to measure the degree of progress towards the "Graderhöhung der Menschheit" (III, 318). As a typically encyclopedic word, "Grad" was applied to a surprising range of phenomena to point out the hierarchic structure and ultimate unity of knowledge. Hence the expressions "Grade der Zeit" (III, 340), "Grade d[er] Kritik" (III, 343), "Grade der Wissenschaftlichkeit" (III, 347), "Grade des Willens" (III, 354), "Grade des Denkens" (III, 349) etc.; language appears as "Gedankenmeter" (III, 349), and philosophy as the highest degree of "Wissenschaftlichkeit" (III, 347). Life itself was "Gradbewegung" (III, 355), and thus the "Graderhöhung der Menschheit" represented a heightening of "Lebensfunktion" (III, 324) or the degree of existence (III, 343); in a wider sense the aim of the "Brouillon" was to raise the level of all nature: "Graderhöhung der Materie" (III, 179).

A few sketchy notes in the "Brouillon" show that Novalis intended to refine his thoughts on the qualitative improvement of matter, by following Eschenmayer and describing qualitative differences in terms of degrees in interacting forces. Every organism was a synthesis of "Grad und Quantitaet—Energie und Figur" (III, 341), whereby "Figur" was determined by "Grad", and this, in turn, was maintained by a universal life force, "Kraft", which Novalis associated with the "Weltseele": "Der Grad entsteht d[urch] innen modificirte Kraft. Ein Stoff kann nicht mit *Kraft* übersättigt seyn. Je mehr Kraft er besitzt— ruhende Kraft ist Vermögen—also je vermögender er ist, desto höher ist sein *Grad*. Alle Kraft gehört zur Welt Kraft. Die Kraft verhält sich zur Seele, wie die Seele zum Geist. Alle Berührung ist ein Anlaß zur Erregung der Einenden, systematisirenden Kr[aft]—i.e., der Weltseele—oder der Seele überhaupt" (III, 341). In this passage, as in much of the "Brouillon", the vocabulary, and the identification of the "Weltseele" with a "unifying and systematizing force", shows that this is taken in the sense of Plotinus rather than Schelling. "Kraft" itself is the emanating force which actually established the "chain of being" and ordered nature into a hierarchy, while "Stoff" is unformed matter upon which "Kraft" imprints the desired shape—"Figur". Novalis discusses here those imaginative "Stoffe und Kräfte" which the true physicist would have to use if he were to penetrate the secrets of nature. If we identify the "Weltseele" ("Seele überhaupt") with "Geist", then the concept of "Seele" is used here in accordance with other notes where the soul is defined as localized spirit: "... die Seele ist nichts, als gebundener, gehemmter, consonirter Geist."[13]

II. AN ESSAY ON MEDICINE

In the fall of 1798, only a few month after the first two volumes of Röschlaub's *Untersuchungen über Pathogenie* appeared, Novalis wrote critical comments on Röschlaub's ideas.[14] The *Untersuchungen* was not in his library, but his comments leave no doubt that he carefully read and considered it. That he highly respected Röschlaub's competence is shown by some notes he made during his final illness where he expressed the wish to turn to the doctor in Bamberg for consultation: "Ich werde, wenn ich erst mit Weigel gesprochen habe, umständlich an *Röschlaub* schreiben, Opium und Mandelwasser anschaffen. ... Wird es schlimmer, so verreis ich nach Leipzig, Bamberg oder Jena" (IV, 410). Death was, however, imminent and neither the letter nor the journey were accomplished; contrary to Dr. Leibbrand's assumption there was then no personal contact between Novalis and Röschlaub.[15]

Hardenberg made no excerpts or longer commentaries on the *Untersuchungen*, but his reaction to it may be reconstructed; as P. Kluckhohn noticed already, a remark in the "Brouillon" indicates that Novalis intended to write a review of the work in the *Journal* of Röschlaub's greatest foe, Ch. W. Hufeland. The outline of this review contains the following points: "1. Bemerck[ungen] üb[er] die Fundamentalsätze. 2. Bemerck[ungen] üb[er] d[ie] einzelnen zerstreuten Anwendungen. 3. Bemerkk[ungen] üb[er] die Anw[endung] d[es] Brownischen Systems überhaupt. 4. Über die Theorie der Potenzen. 5. Über die

Heilmethoden. 6. Was muß noch für die Medizin geschehn" (III, 377). Using this outline and correlating certain passages of the "Brouillon" with passages from Röschlaub's book, we may not only reconstruct the planned essay, but also obtain Novalis' general analysis of the German "Brownian movement": as the outline itself indicates, he did not differentiate between the various shades of the theory.

Notes 593-96 of the "Brouillon" contain a remark which is usually taken as a proof of Hardenberg's gradual alienation from Brown: "Nachgerade häufen sich immer mehr Gründe, die mich die Brownische Erregungstheorie nicht mehr in dem günstigen Lichte erblicken lassen, als ehedem" (III, 369, no. 593). Two points need to be clarified: 1. Novalis' own statement not withstanding, his early notes already show a hostility towards the mechanical bases of the theory of excitability, and the passage above means not a reversal but merely a shift in his critical opinion. 2. Although Novalis mentions the name of Brown, he actually argues with Röschlaub and the specific points of his criticism can only be understood in the context of Röschlaub's book.[16] Of the numerous cases where the reference is to Röschlaub's book (or some other German source) and not to Brown's *Elements* as it was assumed till now, I shall give here two examples only. In note no. 1148 Novalis asserted that irritability and sensibility were symptoms and not causes of diseases and continued: "Brown scheint also das Hauptverdienst zu haben—das wesentlichste, karakteristische Symptom der Kr[anckheit] bemerckt und sie darnach in *Beziehung auf Arzeneykunde*, (also schon *angewandte* Pathologie) geordnet zu haben" (III, 477). Novalis was probably unaware of the fact that irritability and sensibility were not used in the *Elements*. The second example concerns the polar terms "direct-indirect" and "external-internal", which were completely independent of each other in Brown's theory: the former ones were predicated to diseases, the latter to modes of stimulation. Here too, Novalis followed Röschlaub, in adopting his "Theorie der Potenzen" and making indirect and external all but synonymous. In general, no term in Novalis' medical vocabulary is unequivocally and directly related to the *Elements of Medicine*, and a reading of his notes is best facilitated by an acquaintance with the exchange of medical and philosophical ideas in Germany. If we add that 1) as far as we know Novalis made no notes or excerpts from the *Elements of Medicine*, and 2) the work was not found in Hardenberg's library, we may assume with reasonable certainty that he read neither the original nor a translation of it, and that his knowledge of it, as his knowledge of Plotinus and Plato, came through secondary sources. Under these conditions Röschlaub's work merits special attention.

The purpose of Röschlaub's book was: "... die von John Brown vorgetragenen Lehrsätze in Betreff der Pathogenie näher zu beleuchten, auseinander zu setzen, weiter zu verfolgen und zu ihrer Begründung etwas beyzutragen...."[17] As a consequence, Röschlaub tacitly defended the main philosophical contention of the *Elements of Medicine* and repeatedly asserted that the laws of mechanics were equally valid in the realm of living nature, that life was nothing but the ability to react to or accept impulses from the external world, and that without an external ignition the flame of life could not be kindled.[18] Since life was elicited from outside, the idea of a life force ("Lebenskraft"), be it Blumenbach's "Bildungstrieb" or Kielmeyer's multiplicity of forces, could not serve as an approach to the mystery of life. Instead of these forces—which Röschlaub defined as internal guidance to action[19]—the passive-receptive excitability was the principle of life, and, accordingly, the neuro-pathologists were right in assuming that the receptivity of the nervous system regulated the composition of fluids and through these the whole of the organism; in their attention to fluids the humoral pathologists were dealing with secondary phenomena, not with the cause itself.

Yet, for all the vehemence with which Röschlaub defended Brown and attacked his opponents, his medical philosophy was not orthodox. Although he accepted the primacy of external causation, he granted some importance to the body's ability to react, and regarded life as a dialectic interaction of the two components. Unlike Brown, he separated irritability from sensibility, by defining irritability as the muscles' capability to contract upon stimulation, and sensibility as the same property for the nerves. Decomposing excitability in another fashion, he conceived of a purely negative receptivity of which both sensibility and irritability were components, and a more active contractility ("Zusammenziehungsvermögen") through which the organism was able to answer the challenges of the world: "Untersuchen wir nach den Gesetzen unseres Vorstellungsvermögens diesen Begriff [Erregbarkeit], so finden wir ihn als einen aus zweyen verschiedenen zusammengesetzten Begriff: wir stellen uns nämlich a. die Fähigkeit (Empfänglichkeit, receptivitas) der organischen Masse vor, durch Eindrücke von außen affizirt zu werden. b. Das Vermögen, durch Selbstwirksamkeit bestimmte Handlungen hervorzubringen."[20]

It appears then that Röschlaub's principles were a blend of eighteenth-century mechanistic philosophy and idealistic "Naturphilosophie"—mechanistic perhaps by tradition and idealistic by inclination. As may be expected, the mechanistic views irritated Novalis and challenged him to a rebuttal. The basic issue may be formulated in terms of forces. How do they arise and what maintains them in action? The mechanists were interested only in the first of these questions and they answered it with the scheme of action and reaction. Brown and Röschlaub applied the formula to organisms, although the latter inconsistently defined force as "Handlung aus sich". Novalis ignored the mechanistic premises and accepted Röschlaub's definition. In the resultant theory force and matter could interact and even transform into each other; organic forces did not merely move matter mechanically, they formed, developed, and adopted it as an active catalyst of their own growth. Organic development itself tended simultaneously towards a qualitatively higher life and a perfect reflection of the macrocosm: "Org[anische] Kr[aft] ist Kraft, die sich selbst im Ideal eines Universums beabsichtigt" (III, 327); "Org[anische] Kraft ist also Kraft die das *Vermögen* zu bilden, sich zu assimiliren sucht—um sich selbst mittelst dieses correspondirenden *Gegenstandes*, gleichsam d[urch] Bildung ihres N[icht]I[chs], (Gradu, quantitate et Relatione), zu erhöhn, zu vermehren...."[21]

The main point of Novalis' criticism was that ultimately all motion and mechanical interaction will have to be understood in terms of this teleological development of organic forces. Hence his criticism of the theory of excitability and mechanism culminates in a note which promises nothing less than a "dethroning of the basic laws of Mechanics and of the Theory of Excitability" both of which are characterized with the phrase known from Kant and Eschenmayer: "Keine Bewegung ohne Sollicitation." Novalis' own theses against this are: "Alle Bewegung und Erregung entsteht nur d[urch] Bewegung und Erregung. Reitz und Beweglichkeit sind nur Verhältnisse von Bewegungen. Alles was erscheint z.B. Bew[egung] und Erreg[ung], war schon vorher da. Aller sog[enannter] Reitz stört die Bewegung und Erregung vielmehr—polarisirt sie—und nun wird sie, als gestörte Bewegung und Erregung sichtbar" (III, 388). Although Novalis did not follow Fichte in strictly separating matter from consciousness, these principles of his did exalt self-contained action, and thus he could remark with some justification that the new theory of excitability was compatible with the *Wissenschaftslehre* (III, 383).

The third heading of the review, "Bemerckungen über die Anwendung des Brownischen Systems überhaupt", suggests that this section would have dealt with the *a priori* aspects of Brown's medical theory and its relation to practice. Relevant to the topic are nos. 728, 777, 451, 511 and 502 of the "Brouillon". Following Röschlaub and Schelling who noted that excitability was an *a priori* concept of pure reason,[22] Novalis described Brown's method of cure as *a priori*, because it was a construction of pure logic rather than conclusion based on experience. As he remarked bitingly in the "Brouillon", pure empiricism was a hit-and-miss method which led the physician to illuminating insights once the cemetery was filled with subjects of unsuccessful experiments. To this, Brown's method was definitely preferable. Once again, however, Novalis' ideal was a dialectical "reconciliation of opposites", a synthesis in which, as he remarked of Goethe, the *a priori* constructs of consciousness would spontaneously meet the characteristics that the case history presented: "Der genialische Arzt wird von sich und dem Gegenstande zugleich, aber ohne gegenseitige Beschränkung—vielmehr mit gegenseitiger Vervollkommnung, bestimmt" (III, 331).

Brown's theory of medicine was both mathematical and poetical. Poetic, because it contained the "internal poetic—the so-called philosophical materials" (III, 351) which were enduring and impervious to change, and mathematical (more precisely: algebraic) because it purported to give the abstract rules into which data of the specific case would have to be fed if practical diagnoses and results were to be expected (III, 371 and 377). Indeed, Brown's theory had some mathematical features: 1. it used a collection of dual concepts such as sthenic and asthenic, direct and indirect, stimulation and excitability; 2. it claimed that only the quantity of stimulation mattered, due to which 3. all diseases fitted along a scale.

In short, the theory of excitability was an abstract science of life, and the method of the cure it recommended was only set by general guidelines.[23] In this respect the "idealist" philosophy of Fichte and the "dogmatic" physiology of Brown were on common grounds: if they were in polar opposition in what they said, they nevertheless agreed in the mode of approach to their subject matter, in the way they erected their ideal and abstract schemes to deal with reality.[24] Just as Fichte's Ego was "a Robinson—a scientific fiction—for an easier representation and development of the 'Wissenschaftslehre'" (III, 405), such concepts as "excitability", "sthenic", and "asthenic" were fictive aids to measure the state of health of an organism. Novalis well knew of course that Brown's theory was unsatisfactory both as an *a priori* system and as an aid in medical practice. But he believed that the shortcomings at either end were related to each other, so that the deficiencies in the opium treatment and the general pharmaceutical and therapeutical principles of Brown were due to their insufficient philosophical grounding.

The relationship between external and internal stimulation was a decisive feature in all theories of excitability. The issue would presumable have been discussed in Novalis' review under the heading "Theorie der Potenzen", although it is somewhat doubtful that he was aware of the differences that separated Röschlaub from Brown in this respect. These differences were actually quite significant, for Brown assumed that there were independent and primary internal stimuli, arising from "muscular contraction, sense, and the energy of the brain in thinking, and exciting passion and emotion",[25] while Röschlaub believed that internal stimuli were always induced by external ones. To be sure, the latter included not only physical impulses, but also thinking, the "operations of the soul", and the affections of the heart.[26] This point in Röschlaub's theory has been a concern of Novalis: "In dem *Sinn*, wie Röschlaub, die innern incitirenden Potenzen nimmt, müssen alle äußre Potenzen, wozu dann auch die Seele und der Geist gehört—*mittelst* der inneren incit[irenden] Pot[enzen] wircksam seyn" (III, 352). Indeed, as the identification of external with indirect, and internal with direct (II, 561) shows, Novalis was in agreement on this point with Röschlaub: external impulses become effective only indirectly, once they are transformed into internal stimulation. The theory appealed to Novalis, because it made no essential distinction between physiological and psychological impulses, and regarded the body, the sum of the internal stimulations, as the joint crystallization of the physical and the spiritual world.

The section entitled "Über die Heilmethoden" would have concerned the war between the various schools of medical philosophy, as notes immediately following the plan of the review indicate. The warring camps were, of course, the humoral pathologists and the neuro-pathologists, or, defined in terms of bedside practice, those who still believed in the relieving lancet and debilitating treatments, and those who followed Brown in believing in cures of fortification. Since Novalis saw the hallmark of the age in the asthenic constitution, he was siding more with the Brownians, although his position was equivocal and his judgements depended on the particular feature of the theory he had in mind at the moment. Thus, for instance, he observed that Brown embraced mechanistic views as an exaggerated gesture of revolt against the establishment, but he defined the neuro-pathologists elsewhere as "Idealisten, subjektive philosophische Mediziner", due to the importance they attributed to the nervous system, and to their methodological similarity to Fichte. The humoral pathologists, in turn, were "dogmatists" ("objektive philosophische Mediziner") inasmuch as they paid too much attention to material interactions. Yet they too had their point in basing their physiological analysis on fluids, the primeval form of life.

It is understandable therefore that the "Brouillon" should be dotted with calls for uniting the two schools, each of which had strengths and weaknesses:[27] "*Chemiker* und *Symptomatiker* und ihre nothwendige Vereinigung. Vollk[ommne] Chemie und vollkommne Symptomatik ergänzen sich gegenseitig. ... *Allg[emeine]* Sätze der Humoralpath[ologie] wie d[ie] allg[emeinen] Sätze der andern Pathol[ogie]" (III, 377); "Mech[anische]—chem[ische]— und zusammenges[etzte] oder synth[etische] Heilkunde" (III, 475). The unification was to be achieved by imposing the algebraic skeleton of Brown's medicine upon the specific data supplied by experience; in other words, "special historical pathology" was to be developed by observing individual organisms in terms of Brown's method (III, 351). Such a procedure would have reduced the rigidity inherent in the "dogmas", given a more exact account of the numeros factors in the environment and in the body itself,[28] and given recognition to the dialectical interchangeability of opposites. Novalis affirmed the last point in several concrete cases; for instance by stating that bloodletting might both be weakening and strengthening (III, 377), or that, in general, a body might be strengthened by weakening or vice versa (III, 371). Such self-coined terms as "Humoralsthenie" and "Humoralasthenie" (III, 311), point towards the synthesis that Novalis anticipated.

Presumably, the theme of the reconciliation of opposing schools would have led to the closing section of the essay, where Novalis would have expounded his own theory of medicine in terms of his general prognosis. The title "Was muß noch für die Medizin geschehn" indicates that medicine would have been considered here from a historical perspective, not according to the existing psychological and physiological conditions, but the development of dormant potentials which medicine was to help actively. From this point of view all existing theories, including Brown's, were lacking a sense of history. Medicine had to be reformed (III, 371) and made cognizant of the possibility that a rigorous training process could completely change the characteristics of the human body. Thus, for instance, a scientifically guided gradual increase in stimulation would not produce a sthenic disease,[29] but raise the body qualitatively in accordance with Hardenberg's "Graderhöhung der Menschheit". The following enthusiastic and visionary words, or words to the very same effect, would have surely formed the closing section of Hardenberg's essay:

> Wenn wir hier nach den Aussichten fragen, die die Menschheit jezt auf Befreyung ihrer körperlichen Übel hat—so wird man uns, zur Antwort, den Zustand der Heilkunde zeigen. Ihre *Ausbildung* und *Verbreitung* bestimmt das Gegengewicht der Last der körperlichen Übel, die uns drücken.
>
> Je mehr die Heilkunde Elementarwissenschaft jedes Menschen werden—je größere Fortschritte die gesammte Physick machen und die Heilkunde sie benutzen wird—Je inniger die gesammten Wissenschaften zur Beförderung ihres gemeinschaftlichen Interesse, des Wols der Menschheit, zusammentreten und die Philosophie zur Vorsitzerinn und Leiterinn ihrer Beschlüsse nehmen werden—desto leichter wird jener Druck, desto freyer die Brust des Menschengeschlechts werden.
>
> Jezt suche jeder Einzelne zur Beschleunigenden Annäherung dieser glücklichen Zeit das Übel an der Wurzel anzugreifen—er studire Medicin und beobachte und forsche—und erwarte mehr gründlichen Nutzen von der Aufklärung seines Kopfs, als von allen Tropfen und Extracten (III, 474 f.).

VI

The Case of *Die Lehrlinge zu Sais*

„... in deinem Geiste haben sich Poesie und Philosophie innig durchdrungen" (Schlegel: „An Novalis")

1. THE IMPORTANCE OF *DIE LEHRLINGE*

Although the subject matter of Hardenberg's notes and fragments prepares for the poetic works of his last years, one detects between the former and the latter a definite discrepancy which is manifest not only in mode of expression but also in point of view and creative intention. Since man's relationship to nature is reflected in the *Hymnen an die Nacht, Geistliche Lieder,* or *Heinrich von Ofterdingen* so differently that it would require both a different approach and a different context of study, and since Hardenberg's poetic temperament is the subject of my work only insofar as it relates to his philosophical and scientific thought, I can discuss here only that fictional work which is a transition, a curious blend, between his notebooks and the purer distillations of his poetic talent. More than any other work of Novalis, *Die Lehrlinge zu Sais* raises the question of the relationship between Hardenberg's philosophical and poetic achievements.

Indeed, this fragmentary novel was the bone of contention between two of Novalis' most perceptive early critics, Rudolf Haym and Wilhelm Dilthey. Dilthey, who believed that Novalis' natural philosophy was only a stage in the development of his poetic view of nature, held that a synthesis was indeed achieved in the novel through a *feeling* of unity and harmony with nature: "... und so öffnet sich auch nur dem Gefühl des Menschen das Wesen der Natur."[1] Haym, however, examined the work from a philosophical and scientific point of view and came to the conclusion that it was plagued by immaturity of thought: "Die Beziehung der Natur auf das Gemüth ist freilich, ... das Thema der ganzen Dichtung. Das jedoch ist gerade das Charakteristische, daß die Art und Weise dieser Beziehung schlechterdings unentschieden bleibt."[2] Since the issue between Haym and Dilthey remained suspended, one wonders why only few attempts have been made to comment upon the novel in the light of the improved and enlarged knowledge about Novalis.[3] The work deserves particular attention, not so much because of its literary merits—although it has highly poetic passages—but because it reveals something of the "two souls" in Hardenberg which were never reconciled. Although their clash was superseded in *Heinrich von Ofterdingen* or *Hymnen an die Nacht*, the "poetic synthesis" of these works does not include the empirical world and the realm of the sciences in the way in which the "Brouillon" and *Die Lehrlinge* had originally set out. My purpose here is to show that by being halfway between the notebooks and *Heinrich von Ofterdingen*, or, roughly speaking, between science and poetry, *Die Lehrlinge* possesses no center and no organic unity.

II. PLANS

Most works of Novalis are fragmentary. But the sketchiness of *Die Lehrlinge* is not due to lack of time, as might have been the case for *Heinrich von Ofterdingen*. In a letter dated February 23, 1800, Novalis thanked Tieck for acquainting him with Jakob Böhme and added: "Um so besser ist es, daß die 'Lehrlinge' ruhn—die jetzt auf eine ganz andere Art erscheinen sollen—Es soll ein echt-sinnbildlicher Naturroman werden. Erst muß 'Heinrich' fertig sein..."(IV, 331). Since the MS with marginal annotations is unfortunately lost, we cannot know for certain whether Novalis added anything to the novel after the date of this letter. However, since *Heinrich von Ofterdingen* also remained unfinished in spite of its priority, it seems very likely that we have now the version of February 1800 which does not correspond to the artistic intentions indicated in the letter.

What kind of changes would Novalis have made? While it is impossible to pinpoint this with any accuracy, the passage in the letter gives us some hints. The changes which were to make the novel into an "echt-sinnbildlicher Naturroman" were related somehow to the influence of Jakob Böhme. Now we know on the basis of recent datings[4] that probably all of the text was written in Freiberg, much of it probably at the same time as the "Brouillon" project. The original intention to give a symbolic treatment to nature is common to both, and only the form and the arrangement were to be different: the poetic and fictional form of *Die Lehrlinge* is already pointing towards the reawakening of Hardenberg's poetic forces. Evidently the planned and never executed changes would have carried the novel still further away from the "Brouillon" and from its original intentions. As the hyphenated expression "echt-sinnbildlich" suggests, Novalis was dissatisfied with his former attempts to treat nature symbolically and wished to find the true mode. Since the new direction is linked with the name of Jakob Böhme, we may assume that the final version would have surpassed the notebooks with its poetic and religious interpretation of nature. The unfinished sections suggest that on leaving Freiberg Novalis found it increasingly difficult—or boring—to deal with the problem of science in short prose remarks and finally decided that the subject needed a poetic form and a religious framework. Some of Novalis' earlier ideas, notably the Bible-project, had already anticipated such a form, but on the whole the notebooks written between 1797 and 1799 were directly related to his study of science. In *Die Lehrlinge* the manifestations of the empirical world—as indicated at the beginning with the wings, the eggshells, and the filings around the poles of the magnet—slowly receded and left behind a language which was neither concise enough to become a "Chiffernschrift", a forest of symbols, nor inspired with sufficient consistency to reach the hymnic tone of Hardenberg's later poetic works. One senses everywhere a friction between the will to formulate a philosophy of nature and the desire to give it a poetic expression: in the uneven style, the dialectic of the arguments, and the subtle shifts in narrative voice.

Two surviving outlines show that the progress of the novel also entailed a shift in perspective. The first, entitled "Die Naturlehre", probably preceded the writing of the second chapter by about a month; it contains the following outline:

> Doppelte Wege—vom Einzelnen—vom Ganzen—
> Von innen—von außen. Naturgenie. Mathematik.
> *Göthe. Schelling. Ritter. Die pneumatische Chemie. Das Mittelalter. Naturromane. Vortrag der Physik. Werner. Experimentiren.*
> Ob der Naturlehre *eine wahre Einheit* zum Grunde liegt (II, 669).

Clearly, this material for the second chapter was from Hardenberg's scientific notebooks, presented in a dialectic (von innen—von außen) that followed the pattern of his "Magic Idealism". References to J. W. Ritter's frog-leg experiments[5] and Schelling's "Naturphilosophie"[6] did indeed find their way into the chapter, but such bits of science are accidental in the text.

A second note, written much later but still before the mentioned letter to Tieck, suggests a very different content:

> *Verwandlung des Tempels zu Saïs*
>
> Erscheinung der Isis. Tod des Lehrers. Träume im Tempel. Werckstatt des Archaeus. Ankunft der griechischen Götter. Einweihung in die Geheimnisse. Bilds[äule] des Memnons. Reise zu den Pyramiden. Das *Kind* und sein Johannes. Der Messias der Natur. *Neues Testament*—und neue Natur—als *neues Jerusalem*" (III, 590).

It seems that the "Verwandlung" would have indeed changed the atmosphere, not by resolving the conflict between clashing views, but by transcending them. While the first outline concentrates on interpretations of nature, i.e., on ideas, the second delineates a poetic plot which leads to the mysteries of the godhead and leaves nature behind. Physics, chemistry, and mathematics are overshadowed by the mythical constructs of temples and pyramids; Goethe, Schelling, and Ritter give place to prophets and goddesses.[7]

III. "HYAZINTH UND ROSENBLÜTCHEN"

In the absence of unifying themes we have to focus on the components, in the hope that they reflect the general intentions. The second chapter includes the little tale of Hyazinth and Rosenblütchen, one of Hardenberg's most successful poetic creations; since he regarded the genre of "Märchen" as the canon of literature (III, 449), we may try to establish the design of the novel from the blueprint provided by the fairy-tale.

The first sketch for this tale appears in a well-known aphorism written in 1798, which states that to know the greatest mystery is to know oneself, and that, in turn, the "know thyself" is ultimate wisdom: "Einem gelang es—er hob den Schleyer der Göttin zu Saïs—Aber was sah er? er sah—Wunder des Wunders—Sich Selbst" (II, 584). This sketch is clearly in accordance with the often stated thesis of the notebooks that the knowledge of the microcosmic self is man's only way to explore the macrocosm. Such a preoccupation with the self is, however, narcissistic; in the actual fairy-tale the exploration of the self is intimately related to the love of another, and the veil of the goddess hides the image of the beloved.

Hyazinth, a healthy, handsome young boy, is estranged from his family and his "Schätzchen", Rosenblütchen, for he walks around lonely and dejected, talking to birds, animals, trees, and rocks without ever making himself understood. His strange disease originated with the visit of an old man, who returned the hospitality by telling Hyazinth about wonderful distant lands and customs. He left Hyazinth with an undecipherable book and in the hold of a spell that manifests itself in a mental derangement. One day, however, Hyazinth tells his parents that he met in the forest a strange old woman who advised him on how to recover. She burned the book and instructed the boy to leave his home with parental blessing; and so Hyazinth embarks upon an agitated journey through foreign lands in search of the Virgin Goddess. As his erratic and yet purposeful wandering progresses, both external nature and his own mind slowly mellow into a friendly mode, so that the disrupted communication between the youth and the universe is reestablished. When Hyazinth finds attunement with nature he also encounters the long-sought home of the goddess in sleep ("for only sleep was allowed to lead him into the realm of the holiest"), lifts the veil, and embraces his Rosenblütchen...

This little tale which has freshness and linguistic simplicity mirrors Hardenberg's philosophy without straining the fabric of the story itself. Thus Novalis' conception of history is reflected in the stages of Hyazinth's "Bildungsroman"; the initial state of naive love and harmony is followed by a fall and a period of unrest which lasts till the labours of love, lost and refound, establish a higher version of harmony. Rosenblütchen, the ultimate guiding force in Hyazinth's life, is the mediator ("Vermittlerin") of the divine sphere that Sophie represented in Novalis' own life. Significantly, the final revelation comes in a dream which is beyond sensuous experience.

But what are we to make of the old man and his book? The question is of some importance, for it has been frequently stated that they represent an unholy desire for empiricism and rational knowledge from which only love can deliver Hyazinth.[8] But upon taking a closer look at the old man one finds that his long beard, his deep-seated eyes with frightening bushy eyebrows, and the strange signs that adorn his majestic robe all exude an aura of mystery. His wisdom is communicable because his vivid travel accounts immediately catch the attention of the little boy, and his method is empirical for climbing with Hyazinth into the deep mining shafts he literally leads the boy into the mysterious bowels of the earth. His age, his wisdom, and his willingness to initiate his "apprentice", make him an attractive figure. If the jealous Rosenblütchen calls him "Hexenmeister", we have to remember that for Novalis the magician is the conjurer of wonderful effects, a forerunner of the future.

The name "Hexenmeister" inadvertently calls to mind Goethe's old sage from "Zauberlehrling". Since Novalis owned a copy of the *Musenalmanach zu 1798*, where the poem appeared for the first time, it could well be that he had Goethe's figure in mind when sketching his own "Hexenmeister". In any case, a comparison between Hyazinth, the apprentice of the tale, and sorcerer's apprentice in Goethe's poem is illuminating. Like the sorcerer's apprentice, Hyazinth attempts to emulate his mentor once the latter is gone, by taking the book, which is only the ossification of his art, and seeking the magic formula that would open nature for him. If Goethe's apprentice possesses a dangerous half-knowledge that can evoke magic powers but cannot master them, Hyazinth's naive attempt to imitate the old man is arrested at an even lower level, because his formulas, culled from a book that "nobody could read", were mere gibberish: "... und dann sprach er immer fort mit Tieren und Vögeln, mit Bäumen und Felsen, natürlich kein vernünftiges Wort, lauter närrisches Zeug zum Totlachen".[9]

Hyazinth has now acquired the taste for knowledge which carries him beyond that primitive and unadulterated world which he had enjoyed as a child. But he is still too inexperienced to find the right way, for, like Goethe's apprentice, he believes that it is enough to follow the bookish formula without grasping its real meaning. If his derangement signals failure, the corruption is not the old man's making; by taking to the script and forgetting that the old man showed him how to descend into underworld shafts, Hyazinth misunderstands the message and embraces the abstraction without empirical experience.

While Hyazinth is less successful in evoking the magic formula than the sorcerer's apprentice, his journey in the second part of the story takes him beyond the horizon of Goethe's simpleton, into a world where he can find for himself concrete wisdom. Only after the burning of the book does the real message of the deep shafts become revealed: like Goethe's Faust, Hyazinth has to find for himself the seat of the "Mutter der Dinge".

If this reading is correct, then the fairy-tale is not a refutation of empirical knowledge, but of pseudo-knowledge where acquaintance with the letter does not yield insight. The distinction is not between intuition and empiricism, but between independence and imitation; since half-knowledge has no rational foundation it might even be claimed that precisely irrationalism, undigested intuition, is shown to be in error. Although the story defines the limits of empirical and rational knowledge, the total vision does not amount to mysticism, but rather to something paralleling Dante's realism. Although Dante is guided through *Inferno* and *Purgatorio* by Virgil, who represents his rational thirst for knowledge, he is ultimately led by Beatrice's love, just as Hyazinth is both saved and guided by his love for Rosenblütchen. Just as Virgil withdraws to let Beatrice guide Dante through *Paradiso*, so the reunion with Rosenblütchen is consummated in a realm beyond the reach of rational powers—dream. The story of Hyazinth and Rosenblütchen represents a delicate but sound balance between the contending views evident already in Novalis' notebooks: empiricism and loving empathy, nature and consciousness are brought together through the unifying power of narration and language.

IV. "DER LEHRLING"

Themes and structures from the fairy-tale do appear in the rest of the novel, but no similar balance is achieved. In fact, if studied carefully, the common elements only accentuate the disunity of the novel. Those interpreters who do perceive a unity in it usually disregard the obvious parallel between the old man and Hyazinth on the one hand and teacher and apprentice on the other, and frequently reduce the teacher to a mere foil, a straw man. But the first chapter, although it is entitled "Der Lehrling", is mainly about the teacher and his philosophy, and the dialectic of confrontation between teacher and apprentice is based on both sides upon Hardenberg's notebooks. The following passage, for instance, clearly shows that the empirical method of the teacher is reminiscent both of the fairy-tale's old man and of Hardenberg's scientific method of analogizing: "Wie er größer ward, strich er umher, besah sich andre Länder, andre Meere, neue Lüfte, fremde Sterne, unbekannte Pflanzen, Tiere, Menschen, *stieg in Höhlen*.... Nun fand er überall Bekanntes wieder.... Er merkte bald auf die Verbindungen in allem, auf Begegnungen, Zusammentreffungen. Nun sah er bald nichts mehr allein" [italics mine] (I, 80).

Like the old man in the tale, the teacher cannot prescribe courses of action and the apprentice has to discover his own way. He is dissatisfied with the mere exploration of analogies in the external world, for he feels that everything leads back into the self and that the scattered objects in nature only suggest a road towards the deity whose image he carries within himself: "Mich freuen die wunderlichen Haufen und Figuren in den Sälen, allein mir ist, als wären sie nur Bilder, Hüllen, Zierden, versammelt um ein göttlich Wunderbild, und dieses liegt mir immer in Gedanken.... Es ist, als sollten sie den Weg mir zeigen, wo in tiefem Schlaf die Jungfrau steht, nach der mein Geist sich sehnt" (I, 81).

Among the structural similarities the tripartite arrangement is most obvious. As Striedter had already noted, the first chapter starts with an impersonally narrated section, continues with a long description of the teacher, and ends with a first person confession—all of which is a reflection of the tale. Similarly, it may be suggested that the circularity of the tale—Hyazinth leaves his home to find his Rosenblütchen in the distance—was also the plan for the novel: [der Lehrer will], "daß wir den eignen Weg verfolgen, weil jeder neue Weg durch neue Länder geht, und jeder endlich zu diesen Wohnungen, zu dieser heiligen Heimat wieder führet" (I, 82). Here, then, the teacher's message is clearly enunciated and the apprentice is spared Hyazinth's initial error. But if the teacher bears a resemblance to the old man and the latter represents the high wisdom of the tale, we have to direct greater attention to the words of the former and will have to abandon the usual notion that only the apprentice represents Novalis' own views. Teacher and apprentice are ironic inversions of each other existing side by side unsynthesized.

V. "DIE NATUR"

In the second chapter the narrative structure loosens further and, as will be shown, at certain points ironic play becomes the subject matter or the form of the narration. Far from exhibiting the unity which Striedter claimed for the first chapter (and by transfer for the second), this part shows fragmentation in form and content which is not improved by the insertion of the tale.

The section preceding the tale falls into two greater units, each of which contains several subdivisions. The first part (I, 82-87) is about the manifold ways in which man can establish a unity with nature, whereas in the second part (I, 87-91) man and nature are confronted and man's goal is defined as the overcoming of his opponent.

An unidentified narrator opens the first of these two parts with an essay that contrasts the unity of the Golden Age with the fragmentation of modern man. Poets and scientists are supposed to speak one language, but the latter communicate only with sick nature. When the issue is raised whether man is capable of improving his contact with nature, the monologue broadens into a discussion, and special attention is given to the views of some "sinnigere Seelen", who see in existing nature only great but neglected potentials (I, 86). Somewhat surprisingly, a nobler nature is to be built by taming and engineering as at the end of *Faust II* were streams are regulated, canals are dug, swamps are dried up, and gardens are cultivated. However, in describing these activities the prosaic narrative past tense subtly changes to the present and finally to a visionary future:

> [Allmählich fing das Herz der Natur wieder an] menschlich sich zu regen, ihre Phantasien wurden heitrer, sie ward wieder umgänglich, und antwortete dem freundlichen Frager gern, und so scheint allmählich die alte goldne Zeit zurückzukommen, in der sie den Menschen Freundin, Trösterin Priesterin und Wundertäterin war, als sie unter ihnen wohnte und ein himmlischer Umgang die Menschen zu Unsterblichen machte. Dann werden die Gestirne die Erde wieder besuchen.... dann legt die Sonne ihren strengen Zepter nieder.... Dann finden sich die alten verwaisten Familien, und jeder Tag sieht neue Begrüßungen, neue Umarmungen; dann kommen die ehemaligen Bewohner der Erde zu ihr zurück, in jedem Hügel regt sich neu erglimmende Asche,

überall lodern Flammen des Lebens empor, alte
Wohnstätten werden neu erbaut, alte Zeiten erneuert,
und die Geschichte wird zum Traum einer unendlichen, unabsehlichen Gegenwart (I, 86 f.).

What has happened here? Clearly, the final part of the passage is neither a recapitulation of what those "sinnigere Seelen" wished to do, nor an exaltation of engineering; the poet speaks here in a tenseless language of a space- and timeless vision which is beyond both the technological details of engineering and the sensuous experience of nature. Rhythm and wording are highly reminiscent of the central vision in *Hymnen an die Nacht*: "Zur Staubwolke wurde der Hügel... Jahrtausende zogen abwärts in die Ferne, wie Ungewitter" (I, 135). We are confronted here with a breaking point, not unique but typical for Novalis, at which a complex empirical reality yields to a poetic vision; instead of resolution we have a dissolution of conflicts. If the tone and setting in the hymns prepare us for a visionary climax, in the passage from *Die Lehrlinge* one is intellectually disturbed by the abrupt change and the inappropriate positioning, so that the final words remain unconvincing.

It could be argued that such discontinuities are part of Novalis' notion of "Romantisiren" were it not for a subsequent ironic inversion which seems to be accompanied a by change of narrator: "Wer dieses Stammes und dieses Glaubens ist ... geht in den Werkstätten der Künstler umher ..." Perhaps the tone is not meant to be disparaging here, but the detachment from the exalted narrator and the "sinnigere Seelen" is evident. Indeed, in the following section the visionary scene is all but repudiated when poetry is characterized by discipline, exercise, and attention, and an observing-collecting figure reappears: "... so sieht man einen künftigen Weltweisen in jenem, der allen natürlichen Dingen ohne Rast nachspürt, nachfrägt, auf alles achtet, jedes Merkwürdige zusammenträgt und froh ist, wenn er einer neuen Erscheinung, einer neuen Kraft und Kenntnis Meister und Besitzer geworden ist".[10] The first part ends then with a return to empiricism.

The second part of the first section is on the necessity of

overcoming nature; a protest is made against the pettiness of pedantic searching, questioning, and collecting, this time not in the name of poetry and inspiration but on behalf of reason. The argument has several shades. According to "some", nature is a horrendous mill of death, because every stimulation works towards the liquidation of human reason, which is the greatest enemy of nature. Some "more courageous" ones find man's battle against nature promising, because the heroes of science are willing martyrs for the benefit of mankind. Others again would completely withdraw from the battle and follow the inward leading path to a purer world. Next a "serious man" elucidates Fichte's[11] doctrine that nature is a mere impression of our self, because the meaning of the world is constituted in reason and the key to nature is man's own moral sense. No wonder that the confused apprentice is only saved from this barrage of conflicting opinions—most of which may be traced to Hardenberg's own notebooks—by the intervention of a jolly fellow who tells him the tale of Hyazinth and Rosenblütchen.

VI. THE TRAVELERS

According to current interpretations, the function of the tale in the chapter is to resolve the chaos preceding it and to prepare the way for the final section which supposedly gives the romantic view of nature in terms of the resolution in the tale. Since the form of this section is dialectic, it has been suggested that it is comparable to a musical composition which proceeds from variation to variation.[12] But in any good set of musical variations there is a common denominator, an initial proposition whose total meaning and inner richness is unfolded in the progression, so that the total composition forms an organic unity. The views presented in the final section of *Die Lehrlinge* neither form a dialogue nor do they constitute a systematic progression; thesis follows thesis without gradual enlightenment and deepening of sense.

True, the last section starts with a picture of harmony and peace lingering from the fairy-tale: the apprentices embrace each other and leave. But the "spirit of the place", consisting of the abandoned objects in the temple, is in itself divided, and, divided, it laments the even greater chasm that separates it from man: "O! daß der Mensch ... die innre Musik der Natur verstände und einen Sinn für äußere Harmonie hätte. ... Er kann nichts liegen lassen, tyrannisch trennt er uns und greift in lauter Dissonanzen herum" (I, 95). The voices conclude that mankind shall reunite with nature when emotions become once more the expression of humanity: "Das Denken ist nur ein Traum des Fühlens"—which to many interpreters is both the distillation of *Die Lehrlinge* and the essence of Hardenberg's thought. Yet this is only the view of the "spirit of the place" and the human answer in the novel is more complex. Travelers appear in search of a lost "Ursprache", and the rest of the chapter—save the last two paragraphs which are again devoted to the teacher—is taken up with their conversation. Four of them, three unnamed ones and a "beautiful youth",[13] participate in two rounds of speeches where the sequence and the views are meticulously maintained.

The first traveler claims that if man would devote his undivided attention to the sensations he receives, he could master them and use them according to his pleasure. If only part of his sensuous impressions would be utilized in such an arbitrary way, he could establish a reciprocal relationship with the sum of his sensations (that is: nature) and he would master the world while learning about it. True, the body's imaginative modification might separate it from the rest of nature, and the information received might become unreliable; but if as a result of careful self-observation one could decipher the process whereby sensations become thoughts, the unraveling of nature's "forest of symbols" would become easier, and man would eventually be capable of creating "Naturgedanken" and "Naturkompositionen" without external impressions. The first traveler's speech in the second round only confirms that this theory is identical with Novalis' "Magic Idealism" as formulated in the notebooks of 1798, for it asserts that in the highest form of life, reached through discipline and practice, knowledge and creation ("Hervorbringen und Wissen") should be in reciprocal relation: "... durch den Zusammenhang seiner Gedankenwelt in sich, und ihre Harmonie mit dem Universum, bildet sich von selbst ein Gedankensystem zur getreuen Abbildung und Formel des Universums" (I, 101).[14]

The short interjection by the second traveler represents a note of skepticism which largely cancels the effect of the first man's speech. According to the second man, nature is an incomprehensible agreement between infinitely different things, hence it cannot be pieced together into a coherent picture from external signs only. As in the case of the first traveler, one may find entries in Hardenberg's notebooks that correspond to this position (e.g., III, 662, no. 598).

The third traveler goes further than the first two in asserting the creative power of the mind: "... je willkürlicher das Netz gewebt ist, das der kühne Fischer auswirft, desto glücklicher ist der Fang"—which is the generalization of a remark Novalis made earlier about the medical theory of John Brown: "Je größer der Magus, desto willkührlicher sein Verfahren, sein Spruch, sein Mittel" (II, 546). Although this traveler does not deny the possibility of acquiring knowledge through philosophy, he believes that love will bring about the new golden age, not obedience to social duties. To reach his goal man will not only need to "improvise on nature as on a great instrument" —which seems to be the position of the first traveler—but he will also need an intuitive understanding of history, because "all things divine have a history" (I, 99).

The beautiful youth, who is fourth in the conversation, quite appropriately plays his tune on the lyre of Orpheus: only poets feel what nature could mean to man. Far from exaggerating, the poets themselves know not what powers they possess in taming and shaping the stones, trees, and beasts (I, 100). Accordingly, the beautiful youth disdains science. In contrast to the opening passage of the chapter where poets and scientists were said to speak the same language, the youth believes that scientists are lifeless beings. Such insensitive people as the chemists ("Scheidekünstler"—the choice of word is characteristic) should not be empowered to deal with the holiest and most enchanting phenomena of nature (I, 105). Rough minds that cannot comprehend the marvels enclosed in their test tubes shamelessly exploit phenomena which ought to be secrets of nature's lovers and of a higher mankind. Only poets should deal with fluids (I, 105). As if to counterbalance the last speech, the discussion of the travelers abruptly closes with the reappearance of the teacher. Instead of resolving their conflict he opens up new topics.

What kind of conclusions can one reach? Clearly, the variety of Hardenberg's notebooks appears also in *Die Lehrlinge*; the teacher, the apprentice, and the travelers expound views which are essentially Novalis' own, but the work is lacking in imaginative synthesis. In trying to establish some kind of order we may, perhaps, arrange the speeches of the four travelers in a dialectically ascending order, which would proceed from an initial emphasis on discipline and observation of detail to a final eloquent and rhythmical praise of mystic dissolution: "... so versinkt die glückliche Liebe gern in die endlose Tiefe" (I, 105). The arch between these extremes roughly corresponds to the span between Novalis' scientific training and his final poetic works. We may surmise that his newly-won love for Böhme would have shifted the emphasis of *Die Lehrlinge* from the earlier medico-scientific thoughts towards the figure of Orpheus among the travelers. But we have to agree with Haym that the surviving fragment is lacking in unity and we may regard the first sentence of the novel as an unintentional motto for its own diversity: "Mannigfache Wege gehen die Menschen".

VII

The Last Years

1. RELIGION AND POETRY

Novalis' departure from Freiberg on Whitsuntide 1799 meant important changes in his way of life, the direction of his studies, and the course of his professional career. Engaged to Julie von Charpentier, daughter of a professor at Freiberg, he hoped to find domestic bliss in marriage and a financial basis for it in the administration and supervision of the salt mines in Saxony. He entered service as an assessor at the end of the year, and soon afterwards, in April 1800, decided to apply for a vacant "Amtshauptmann" position. Although he managed to send off his test solution of a legal dispute in September, the appointment in December came too late: he spent the remaining months before his death on March 25, 1801, ailing and incapacitated.

Compared to the large mass of notes Novalis took in Freiberg, the notebook volume of the last years was understandably slender due to his professional duties, his renewed interest in poetry, and his later illness. He retained a philosophical interest in science and poetry, but no longer attempted to construct theoretical syntheses, and turned in both realms from the accumulation of knowledge to practical application, from "knowing" to "doing".[1] Since he was conscientious in carrying out the technical-scientific duties of his job and intensely poetic in his artistic vocation, the polarities of his temperament and character became more evident in the last two years of his life, and the relationship between his art and life took on a more enigmatic aspect.[2]

The plans for *Hymnen an die Nacht* go back to an earlier date, but only around the turn of 1799/1800 were the prolonged theoretical studies interrupted by a burst of creative energy that yielded the final version of the cycle and *Heinrich von Ofterdingen*.[3] The most prominent reason for this sudden onrush of creativity was Novalis' new-found friendship with Tieck, the only other poetically creative figure in the Romantic circle. The friendship, formed at their first encounter on July 17, 1799, "opened a new book" (IV, 294) in Novalis' life, and meant not merely a return to creative activity, but also a turn with respect to his old views and projects. Recalling his former philosophical and scientific studies he wrote to Tieck: "Unter Spekulanten war ich ganz Spekulation geworden" (IV, 330). Correspondingly, the first fruit of his reawakened poetic powers, *Heinrich von Ofterdingen*, was to be radically different in design from *Die Lehrlinge*. In conscious opposition to Goethe's *Wilhelm Meister*, where poetic aspirations were finally accommodated within everyday life, Novalis aimed at an "apotheosis of poetry" (IV, 330) and attempted to ascend from the material world to the concrete and yet abstract forms of the poetic imagination. As Novalis wrote to Schlegel, poetry was to have been born in the second part of the work (IV, 343), where the novel would have become metamorphosed into a "Märchen" (IV, 333). Since the "blue flower" became a symbol for the novel and for poetic romanticism in general, these intentions of Novalis were indeed understood by subsequent generations, who saw in the work not an encyclopedic effort comparable to the "Brouillon", but an attempt at pure poetry.

Changes in Hardenberg's philosophical and religious outlook may also be associated with Jakob Böhme.[4] Apart from the changes contemplated for *Die Lehrlinge*, Novalis also intended to write about Böhme as a poet and a philosopher of nature.[15] It seems that Novalis was not so much attracted by Böhme's quietism as by his poetic nature, his talent, and his particular way of life: Böhme's creative powers represented to him a "forceful spring" that "breaks forth, carries, forms and mixes" (IV, 331).

Paralleling the pattern of Novalis' last years, Böhme—philosopher, theologian, and poet—had written most of his works while tending his job as a simple cobbler.

While Hardenberg's religious convictions deepened and matured in his last years, their expression in poetry, the *Geistliche Lieder* became strikingly clear and simple. Perhaps both the deepening and the poetic clarity were related to a fine but perceptible shift from an analytical to an intuitional and communal affirmation of faith. As the quoted letter to Just reveals, his faith always issued from strongly held inner convictions rather than from literal interpretations of religious documents. The force of his personal creed, as well as a certain dislike for his father's emotional Herrnhuterism, delayed his surrender to the community;[6] but it seems that simultaneously to his marital and professional plans to blend more fully with the fabric of society he also reconsidered his religious communal attachment. As his brother Karl reports,[7] he immersed himself in the works of Zinzendorf, the founder of the Herrnhuter brotherhood,[8] and when his physical condition worsened, he gained relief and spiritual tranquility from this reaffirmation of his faith: ".... Wenn mich nicht körperliche Unruhe verwirrt, welches doch nicht häufig geschieht, so ist mein Gemüt hell und still. Religion ist der große Orient in uns, der selten getrübt wird. Ohne sie wäre ich unglücklich. So vereinigt sich alles in *einen* großen, friedlichen Gedanken, in *einen* stillen, ewigen Glauben..." (IV, 349 f.).

II. READINGS AND PROFESSIONAL WORK

As the poetic imagination and the religious convictions of Novalis became both more concrete and more metaphysical in the last years of his life, so his interest in science separated into speculative and practical concerns. But neither his work nor his thought became as dreamy and unsystematic as Olshausen described them:[9] the care and attention that Novalis showed in his professional activity testifies that he was both able and willing to deal with routine technical matters.

According to several recently discovered letters and documents Hardenberg was highly regarded for his professional competence.[10] In spite of his short stay in Freiberg, he had the honor to be selected by Werner to participate in a geological survey of Saxony, which aimed at the exploration of new resources and the investigation of certain theoretical problems. Novalis and his assistant, Friedrich Haupt, surveyed the region Gera-Borna-Zeitz-Leipzig in June 1800; the district report, completed and submitted by Haupt after Hardenberg's death, was placed among the best in Werner's final report on the entire project.[11] Further information on the scope of Hardenberg's interest in technical matters may be gained by looking at the list of books he read[12] or the letters and papers he wrote in his last years. Reading the reports and papers which were published for the first time in the new edition,[13] one is struck by their professionalism: they penetrate into concrete practical problems and seldom stray into philosophical and religious issues. For this reason they had little bearing on Hardenberg's philosophy or his views on poetry.

One observes the reverse tendency in Hardenberg's later notes on medicine, physiology, and chemistry. His readings contained many standard textbooks, journals, and reliable treatises in these fields, but, contrary to the earlier notebooks where one finds commentaries on and even excerpts from these, among the notes from his final years such references are scarce indeed.[14] This was not exclusively due to the renewed interest in poetry and religion and to the generally lean output of notes. Observations on science became more independent and abstract (i.e., not traceable to any particular reading), and those which were occasioned by scientific works departed from speculative and loosely written books of little scientific value.[15] Novalis' own remarks on these works became so speculative and unrelated that it is difficult to put them into a coherent system. While the earlier notebooks, particularly the "Brouillon", give frequent demonstration of Novalis' conviction that all aspects of life are organically interrelated and that, consequently, the consideration of any subject will lead to fundamental issues, in the final years the threads of thought from the particular to the universal, from the scientific to the poetic, and from the theoretical to the practical are less visible.

III. J. W. RITTER AND GALVANISM

The slow evolution in the understanding of electrical phenomena culminated in the eighteenth century in Galvani's experiments with frog legs, published in 1791. He placed two metals in contact with the muscles and nerves of the frog leg and made them twitch; but his interpretation of the phenomenon was erroneous, for he concluded that the acting current was an "animal electricity" residing in the tissues of the frog which was different from the electricity observed in other physical phenomena. The rival interpretation was made five years later by another Italian, Alessandro Volta, who correctly asserted that the current through the frog leg was due to the electrical potential difference between the two pieces of metal that formed a battery across the muscles and nerves of the frog. According to Volta, electricity and galvanism were the same phenomenon.

The tug-of-war between the rival theories in the last years of the century seemed to have wider philosophical implications and aroused great interest in Germany, particularly among adherents of the "Naturphilosophie" movement, who favored Galvani. Even before the publication of Volta's argument, C. H. Pfaff, the translator and editor of the *Elements of Medicine*, published a book on animal electricity and excitability,[16] in which he stated that Galvani's discovery proved the existence of a unique organic force of which all other forces in the organism were mere modifications. It seemed that galvanism brought the results of Haller, Blumenbach, and Brown to a common denominator.

In 1797 Alexander von Humboldt published a voluminous book about his experiments with muscles and nerves,[17] upholding the correctness of Galvani's conclusions and deducing from them the autonomy of the animal organism.[18] As Schelling remarked in the *Weltseele*, the "dignity" of Galvani's great discovery, jeopardized by Volta, was rescued (Sch, I, 623): once more the mechanistic and deterministic philosophies received a blow.

Humboldt gave in his book considerable space to a budding genius, Johann Wilhelm Ritter, who added his own remarks on the subject. In the fall of 1798 Ritter published his own book that made him famous: *Beweis, dass ein beständiger Galvanismus den Lebensprozess in dem Thierreich begleite*.[19] This reveals his two oddly incongruous talents, the inexhaustible patience in experimenting, and the genius to read visions into nature. Without taking sides in the Humboldt-Volta controversy, although envisioning an eventual synthesis between electric and galvanic phenomena resting on Volta's experiments, Ritter made a minute analysis of galvanic circuits and searched for the variables that determined their behavior. He found that the number of these factors was very large, but to his surprise he observed that all of them were affecting also organic life; hence he made his leap of faith and concluded that all organic life was constituted of a large collection of different galvanic circuits (cf. III, 952). Conforming to Brown's doctrine he surmised that the stimuli of the external world changed the behavior of galvanic circuits and that consequently the manipulation of life perhaps depended only on the proper knowledge of galvanism: "Der berauschende Weingeist modificirt die Action Galvanischer Ketten nicht unbeträchtlich, er aber ist es auch, der im thierischen Körper so thätig reizt.... Wie wenn sich alle Körper in Rücksicht ihres Verhaltens zum Galvanismus in Reihen ordneten, die parallel vielleicht liefen mit denen, in die sie eine vernünftige Materia medica theilt? ... Sollte es so dem Arzte einst noch möglich seyn am Studiertisch durch einige Versuche an der reizbaren Muskel- und Nervenfaser das Mittel aufzusuchen, was seinen Kranken retten soll?"[20] In the visionary ending of the book, which contrasts with the sober but execrably written main part of the argument, Ritter lumped together the sun, atoms, plants, animals, metals, stones, and other paraphernalia of the universe into a great "all-Tier"—Nature.

Novalis was exposed to the dispute on galvanism from so many sides that it is difficult to determine just where he first learned about it. Since the name galvanism appears already in the notebooks from 1798,[21] it seems now certain that the first impulse was not provided by Ritter. Novalis' wide acquaintance with Humboldt's works[22] and a vague reference in the "Brouillon" (III, 264) to "Bewegung der gereizten Muskelfaser" suggest that he had read Humboldt's treatise. In addition, Novalis owned a copy of Pfaff's book and he read articles both by and on Volta (III, 95).

But Hardenberg's excitement and enthusiasm concerning galvanism originated from his reading of Ritter's book probably not too long after its appearance. References to Ritter and his ideas appear in the "Brouillon" and the accompanying notebooks towards the end of 1798, and they run through the rest of his works. Although he was curious about the man, as he was about his work,[23] he probably got to know him only towards the end of November, 1799, when their lasting friendship was founded.[24]

Unfortunately it is extremely difficult to say something meaningful and consistent about Novalis' theory of galvanism or his friendship with Ritter, beyond these meager facts. Although we do not lack material, this does not congeal into a significant utterance. In the "Freiberger naturwissenschaftliche Studien" one finds a chart which develops one of Ritter's ideas (III, 83) and seems to establish a triadic pattern between galvanism, electricity, and chemistry. The idea recurs in the "Brouillon" (III, 597). In the same collection, a passage written against Brown's medicine contains a reference to Ritter, seemingly suggesting that his theory of galvanism could combat Brown's mechanistic physiology. This, however, is highly tenuous. The rest consists of very flimsy speculation in which it is asked whether galvanism was the agent in decomposition (III, 354), a producer of light (III, 471), or a phenomenon more universal even than Ritter believed it to be (III, 621).

It will have to be admitted that both from a scientific and philosophical point of view Novalis' notes on galvanism are the weakest among his notebooks, and this harsh judgment will only be slightly assuaged by adding that in those years very few people saw this issue clearly. Since the problem was solvable only through experiments and Novalis was no practicing physicist or chemist, he had to decide on the basis of his highly contradictory reading.[25] Not being able to add anything to the advancement of knowledge, he took the material as a starting point for speculation. One may remark in defense that every age has its fascination with those phenomena that promise to lead into the unknown and provide answers for fundamental questions.

But the notes on galvanism do reveal something about Novalis himself, even if they do not have an objective value. The disparaging remark in *Die Lehrlinge* that scientists only investigate "dead twitching remainders" (I, 84) suggests that Novalis was hardly impressed by the frog leg experiments themselves. Rather, in galvanism he saw a new hope of exploring that no-man's-land which lies between the material of the body and consciousness. He thought that if galvanism heightened the degree of existence of matter it might perhaps be regarded as the "higher consciousness of nature" (III, 603), or as "inner light" (III, 604). If the body was (as in a certain sense it is) a vast aggregate of galvanic circuits in which the mysterious stuff of life (electricity?) circulates, the phenomenon itself could be called the "inner light". He asked whether these closed circuits that ring the body could be the elemental forms in which nature attempted to double upon itself and achieve a consciousness of its own being. Understood in their widest sense, these circuits or chains organically linked the members of a body and seemed to build up an organic universe, an "all-Tier" (cf. III, 574), suggesting the existence of a physical "chain" of being. Finally, in Ritter's method of reading nature Novalis found what he thought was lacking in Werner's purely empirical method: Ritter, like the disciple in *Die Lehrlinge*, was reading the visible letters of nature, to decipher from them the secret of the "Weltseele" and the structure of inwardness: "Alle äußre Processe sollen als Symbole und lezte Wirkungen innerer Processe begreiflich werden" (III, 655).

IV. SENSIBILITY AND DISEASE

In the last years of Novalis' life his conception of disease expanded into a metaphysical and moral dilemma that brought the paradoxes of his philosophy into focus. Let us follow aspects of this transformation in concrete terms.

Once more it might be useful to start with a work by Schelling, his *Erster Entwurf eines Systems der Naturphilosophie*, which appeared in 1799. Although Schelling and Novalis were going in very different directions by this time, there is little reason to believe Th. Haering that Novalis did not read this work.[26] In fact, a critical remark in the last notebooks indicates that Novalis was concerned with Schelling's philosophy of nature, to which, for the first time, the title of this work referred to as "Naturphilosophie": "In der Schellingschen Nat[ur] Phil[osophie] wird ein beschränkter Begriff der Natur und der Phil[osophie] vorausgesezt. Was die Schell[ingsche] Nat[ur] Phil[osophie] eigentlich sey" (III, 666)?

While the *Erster Entwurf* retained the principle of duality and much of Schelling's earlier vocabulary, the structure of nature in this work was both simpler and more specific than in the *Weltseele*. The dualism of receptivity and activity, present in every organism, was denoted as "excitability", and this again was decomposed in a different manner into three components of unequal value: on the highest level was sensibility, the essence of life, below it irritability, the force directly responsible for activity and movement, and, finally, on the lowest level, there was the productive and reproductive force—Schelling's version of the "Bildungstrieb".[27] While irritability and sensibility were inversely proportional in the middle range of the evolutionary scale, beyond certain inversion points this relation ceased to be valid—a curious case of dialectics in Schelling's philosophy.

A surely unintended parody of this theory may be read in a passage immediately preceding Novalis' note on "Naturphilosophie", where he speculated that since plants are lower forms of organic life, their consumption should increase the body's reproductive force and should bring into balance a human body dominated by sensibility. The result is what may be called an "inverted" vegetarianism: "Alle Pflanzen verstärken im thierischen Körper den organischen Bildungstrieb und die Reproduktionskraft; vielleicht daß sie daher in den Erscheinungen der herrschenden Sensibilitaet ein mittleres Produkt, verstärkte Irritabilitaet befördern" (III, 665). Similarly, the principles of Schelling's theory suggested to Novalis that the consumption of minerals fortifies the "Bildungstrieb" and the chemical metabolism of the body, so that the level of sensibility may be reduced drastically, perhaps even beyond the inversion point and below the level of irritability (III, 665 f.).

We need not be concerned with the scientific accuracy of these half-humorous remarks, because their significance lies in what they tell us about Novalis' intentions: here too he is preoccupied with the reduction of excessive sensibility. As the early letters to Erasmus indicate, his incessant worry about this matter had a personal reason which only gained in importance during his final illness.[28] But this personal concern achieved a universal significance to him, once his paradoxical conception of sensibility became instrumental in shaping his theory of history: in his last years Novalis saw more and more clearly that sensibility was a dangerous yet ineluctable disease of man, destined to carry him towards the chiliastic vision.

What is the moral meaning and historical function of sensibility if the destiny of man is to become moral (III, 662)? Novalis' answer is a paradox: "Mit der Sensibilitaet und ihren Organen, den Nerven tritt Kranckheit in die Natur. Es ist damit Freyheit, Willkühr in die Natur gebracht und damit *Sünde*, Verstoß gegen den Willen der Natur, die Ursache alles Übels" (III, 657). Hence, as the "principium individuationis" sensibility represents that willful and sinful transgression of man's natural limitations which brings about his Fall but also opens his future, as in a more general sense all diseases are individualizations and deviations from natural and moral norms: "Alle Krankheiten gleichen der Sünde, darein; daß sie Transcendenzen sind. Unsere Krankh[eiten] sind alle Phaenomene erhöhter Sens[ibilität], die in höhere Kräfte übergehn will. Wie der Mensch Gott werden wollte, sündigte er. Kr[ankheiten] der Pflanzen sind Animalisationen. ... Krankh[eiten] der Steine—Vegetationen" (III, 662f.). Whether Man's Faustian sin of overreaching can finally be converted into a morally good end, or whether this refinement of his consciousness will have to be subordinated to a strict morality—this Novalis leaves unanswered.[29] What distinguishes his last thoughts on this topic from the earlier ones is a more determined effort to explore all the dark and questionable aspects of disease. And since he came to associate the physical deviation with the moral aberration of sin—a notion which was otherwise remarkably alien to Novalis—his understanding of Christianity suddenly became deeper and more dramatic. His faith in man's power and capability now matured through the recognition that although man is limited, precisely his physical and moral frailties are his means of understanding the ways of divine mercy: "Je hülfloser, desto empfänglicher für Moral und Religion."[30] Hence, his intention to explore all the dark regions of soul and body is paradoxically both within the framework of traditional Christian conceptions and prophetically anticipating the unorthodox struggles of Baudelaire, Rimbaud, Nietzsche, Gide, and many others, who, in diverse ways, investigated the "great sickness" in search of a new transcendental health (cf. III, 667). Holding simultaneously the Christian conception of mercy, the infinite perfectibility of man, and the necessity of exploring sin and disease, Novalis stands as a complex and unique figure at the threshold of modern literature.

V. EPILOGUE ON "ROMANTIC MEDICINE"

With Hardenberg's death in 1801, the German Romantic Movement lost its most valuable member, and the cohesion of the group slowly started to give way. But the odd history of "Romantic Medicine", initiated in Germany by some of the ideas of John Brown, was just in the making, and a whole generation of romantic doctors worked to integrate the disparate fields of philosophy, religion, art, and science in the sense of "Symphilosophieren." The lively interaction between scientists, poets, and philosophers was not quite as unfruitful as historians of medicine and science tend to portray it. One may think, for instance, of Christian Oersted's discovery that the magnetic needle gets deflected near a conductor of electric current—to which he was led largely through his romantic belief that electricity and magnetism were aspects of a single higher phenomenon—or the encyclopedic knowledge and achievement of Alexander von Humboldt. There were practicing physicians among the writers: Gotthilf Schubert, the author of *Ansichten von der Nachtseite der Naturwissenschaft*, Carl Gustav Carus, the versatile friend of Goethe, Justinus Kerner, whom we have encountered already as a patient of Weikard, F. G. Wetzel, the alleged author of the *Nachtwachen des Bonaventura*, and a host of minor figures. In turn, the "romantic doctors", many of them admirably portrayed in Ricarda Huch's *Die Romantik*,[31] were so deeply involved in the intellectual life of Germany that medical theories became significant in the "Weltanschauung" of the time. Although the complex cross-fertilization of religious, moral, artistic, political, and scientific questions probably yielded more fallacious than meaningful speculations, the period cannot be judged in terms of such simple tags as "irrationalism", "romanticism", or "reactionarism".

As R. Huch and later W. Milch (in a somewhat different formulation) had noted,[32] one may define several broad currents in "Romantic Medicine", and should separate the adherents of the "Naturphilosophie" movement from those who were nourished by "Sturm und Drang" and had no debt to the Kantian revolution in philosophy. The latter group comprised mainly followers of John Brown and Anton Mesmer. But while the last waves of the "Brownian movement" subsided towards the end of the first decade of the new century, Mesmerism enjoyed increasing popularity after its founder's death in 1815. Although Mesmer himself belonged to no particular philosophical movement, his intentions conformed to the general tendency of romantic science and even to some aspects of Novalis' philosophy, inasmuch as he hoped to identify and tap for the art of curing universal forces which went unrecognized until then. Far from being a mystic, he believed that the universe was pervaded by a fluid which established a reciprocal relationship between bodies under the laws of mechanics. Since he saw many analogies between the phenomenon of magnetism and the effect of this fluid, he called it "animal magnetism", and conducted a large number of experiments to determine the ways in which it affected the relationship between bodies. He did indeed get some startling results by unknowingly employing hypnotic treatment, but not being able to find the laws of the phenomenon he fell in disrepute among scientists. Nevertheless, his views and techniques slowly gained popularity, especially once they met with irrational currents, such as the belief in somnambulism.[33] His works were published in 1814[34] and his biography was written four decades later by Justinus Kerner, himself a Mesmerist.[35] Although the Mesmerist movement and Novalis' medical notes hold a few common ideas, the kinship is distant and one would do well to keep them apart: Novalis made only vague references to "animal magnetism", and he could scarcely have known much about it since Mesmerism was still little known then. Neither is there any evidence that later Mesmerists were acquainted with Novalis' medical theories.

Of Passavant, one of the most important romantic physicians, R. Huch remarked: "Sein Leben lang schwankte Passavant zwischen zwei Berufen, dem des Arztes, den er ausübte, und dem des Theologen, zu dem er neigte...."[36] What she says is true also of many others. According to Ringseis, all sciences, including medicine, have their principles in the books of revelation, which describe man and nature as fallen, incomplete, and dependent: "Vollkommenste Gesundheit mit der Möglichkeit der Trübung war einst im Paradiese; befestigt und ohne mögliche Trübung wird sie künftig sein nach der Wiederauferstehung; gegenwärtig aber ist vollkommene Gesundheit in keinem sichtbaren Theile des universellen Organismus."[37] In view of this sharp distinction between the innocent and healthy on the one hand, and the fallen and sick on the other, Ringseis insisted that the physiological laws of the healthy body were not applicable to pathological cases. Similar thoughts were entertained by Karl Windischmann, who shared with Ringseis an intense catholicism: diseases are independent organisms which change their constitutions with the passage of history, so that an intelligent cure would have to presuppose a knowledge of the "Zeitgeist". To Windischmann, the sensibility of modern constitutions was a sign that man had lost his former solidity of faith and had not yet achieved the assurance of a future synthesis. Since moral and bodily decay were inseparable in the fallen state, the external expression of moral weakness, disease, could only be cured by tending the soul. Windischmann was a friend of Friedrich Schlegel, and it may be that he knew something about Novalis' notion on sin and disease, but, once again, no evidence is available, and it seems more likely that Windischmann, a translator of Plotinus, had developed his ideas from the neo-Platonic tradition. As to Ringseis, he only tells us in his *Erinnerungen* that as a young man he was attracted to Novalis, and it seems plausible that his affection belonged more to the poet than to the philosopher and the scientist.[38]

A different sensibility links the religious convictions and the scientifically held ideas of the "Naturphilosophie" movement. Although most of the leading figures, including D. Kieser, H. Steffens, Fr. Hufeland, G. Schubert, I. P. V. Troxler, G. R. Treviranus, C. G. Carus, L. Oken, and J. Reil, were deeply religious, their natural philosophy was dominated by the concepts and the ideas of the young Schelling. Organism, dualism, polarity, sensibility, irritability, life force, and "Bildungstrieb" constituted the conceptual building blocks from which the various theories of "Naturphilosophie" were constructed, all of them having in common at least one principle, namely the postulate that the processes of the body be intimately linked with the oscillations of the soul. Kieser, for instance, believed that the increasing refinement of the human organism, that is the development of individuality and personality, dangerously increased the physical and the psychological tension between the self and the world, so that refinement would necessarily be accompanied by susceptibility to diseases.

Although these ideas are at several points in contact with Hardenberg's philosophy and psychology, there is no reason to assume that he was in any way responsible for the emergence of this movement. The correspondences may be traced back to Schelling, the founder of "Naturphilosophie", who was in the center of medical discussions for a long time after Hardenberg's death through his articles, his medical magazine, and his personal contacts.

Given only such vague correspondences it is surprising that

historians of medicine, who lay claim to a scientific temper they find lacking in romanticism itself, have built a rapidly swelling legend about Novalis' role in the shaping of "Romantic Medicine". This view was first expounded by E. Hirschfeld in an otherwise judicious and intelligent article.[39] Hirschfeld took an oddly double-pronged attitude with respect to Novalis: while he severely criticized his medical philosophy from the scientific point of view,[40] he raised him to an "Ideenführer" of "Romantic Medicine", and admired him for his psychological insights.[41] Bluth's dissertation, written largely in defense of Novalis, attempted to play down the first aspect of Hirschfeld's view by asserting that the "fragments" showed the unity of a systematizing mind which developed and transformed the current theories of stimulation in a highly independent way; unfortunately, Bluth laid equally great emphasis on supporting Hirschfeld in the contention that Novalis was a leader and moving force behind "Romantic Medicine", a view which he upheld partially with erroneous information, partially with arguments based on unsupported analogies.[42] With Bluth the legend of Novalis' influence became firmly established. P. Diepgen, who was the supervisor of Bluth's thesis, accepted all of his results and gave them wide publicity, first in a speech on "Novalis und die romantische Medizin", and later by incorporating the material in his history of medicine.[43] The more sympathetic evaluation of Hardenberg's medical views in W. Leibbrand's *Die spekulative Medizin der Romantik*, shows a similar uncritical indebtedness to Bluth's work,[44] especially where this was in support of Novalis' allegedly decisive influence on "Romantic Medicine".[45]

All of these evaluations from the point of view of medical history suffer from two major weaknesses: on the one hand their assessment of Novalis' comprehension of science is based on incomplete and often misleadingly arranged editions of his works, and on the other hand they make the mistake of claiming that Novalis' scientific notes, largely unpublished till the twentieth century, had a palpable influence on "Romantic Medicine". In reality, the two-volume Schlegel-Tieck editions,[46] the sole published works of Novalis during medical romanticism, contained few of his scientific notes. As a representative example, the 1815 edition contained *Heinrich von Ofterdingen* in the first volume and the rest of his poetry in the first third of the second volume. Only sixty pages of the remaining two thirds were devoted to "fragments" on "Philosophie und Physik". These were arranged in a rather haphazard fashion, thereby often giving rise to artificial obscurity. In the memoirs and autobiographies of the succeeding romantic generation there is equally little evidence to support Bluth's and Diepgen's claim. Apart from the above-mentioned reminiscences of Ringseis, Carl Gustav Carus makes a brief reference to Novalis, although only to his *Heinrich von Ofterdingen*,[47] while Gotthilf Schubert does not mention Novalis in his autobiography.[48] Of those who knew Novalis personally, H. Steffens was a disciple of Schelling, while Ritter died very early and his works gradually lost importance and popularity.[49]

One is left then with next to no palpable evidence concerning Novalis' effect on "Romantic Medicine". The transmission of his medical ideas could have of course followed subtler channels, inaccessible to positivistic investigations. If one wishes to find the root of the romantic movement in medicine, it seems much more reasonable, however, to turn to the great speculators of medicine, such as Mesmer, Brown, or Erasmus Darwin, to the dominating intellectual figures, such as Herder, Goethe, and Schelling, or to the holders of chairs of medicine at Jena, Leipzig, Halle, and Göttingen.

Notes

NOTES TO THE INTRODUCTION

[1] A remark by Bourget, as quoted by Irving Babbitt in *Rousseau and Romanticism*, 5th Meridian Books ed. (New York, 1960), p. 9.

[2] Thomas Mann, *Gesammelte Werke* (Frankfurt a. M., 1960), XI, 851.

[3] Novalis, the pen name adopted by Friedrich von Hardenberg, was used by his family as early as the thirteenth century, and was supposed to be stressed on the first syllable. To insist, as Heinz Ritter [*Der unbekannte Novalis* (Göttingen, 1967), p. 10] does, that the pen name be used only in connection with Hardenberg's last years and works seems somewhat pedantic and I will therefore use the two names interchangeably.

[4] G. W. F. Hegel, *Werke*, X/1 (Berlin, 1835), 205; H. Heine, „Die romantische Schule", bk. II, pt. IV, in *Sämtliche Werke* (Leipzig, 1887), III, 186; Thomas Carlyle, „Novalis" in *Critical and Miscellaneous Essays*, II (New York, 1899). In *Novalis und die französischen Symbolisten* (Stuttgart, 1963) W. Vordtriede elaborates on the associations between Novalis and symbolists. However, he fails to take notice of important translations in the *Nouvelle Revue Germanique* between 1831 and 1833 and consequently misses the possible link between Novalis and Nerval.

[5] *Novalis. Schriften*, ed. P. Kluckhohn and R. Samuel, III (Stuttgart, 1968), 578. All subsequent references will be made in the body of the text to the first three volumes of this edition still in progress (Stuttgart: I, 1960 and II, 1965), and the fourth volume of the first critical edition (Leipzig, 1929). References in the text will also be made to "Nachlese" = *Friedrich von Hardenberg (genannt Novalis). Eine Nachlese aus den Quellen des Familienarchivs herausgegeben von einem Mitglied der Familie*, 2nd ed. (Gotha, 1883); Sch= F. W. J. Schelling, *Werke*, ed. Manfred Schröter (München, 1927).

[6] The following works are indicative of the renewed interest in Hardenberg's science: Käte Hamburger, "Novalis und die Mathematik" in *Romantik-Forschungen* (Halle, 1929), reprinted in Hamburger's *Philosophie der Dichter*

(Stuttgart, 1966); Martin Dyck, *Novalis and Mathematics* (Chapel Hill, 1960); Theodor Haering, *Novalis als Philosoph* (Stuttgart, 1954).

7 Heinz Ritter (pp. 354 f.) writes that this picture disappeared. However, it survived in the archives of the East German town of Hettstedt, where, after some difficulties, I was permitted to see it in the summer of 1966. Recently it was transferred to the Municipal Museum in Weissenfels.

8 Carlyle, II, 15.

9 "[Die Berührung gewisser Fragmente mit Formulierungen anderer Denker] beweisen doch alle nur, wie Novalis Verwandtes aufnahm, wo er es fand; daß aber kein einziger dieser Einflüsse wirklich auch nur als 'Anreger' Novalisscher Gedanken bezeichnet werden darf" (Haering, p. 606).

10 Seen from another angle, this attitude does imply that the nature of the object itself is of secondary importance. This is what led Schelling to the famous remark: "Ich kann diese Frivolität gegen die Gegenstände nicht gut ertragen, an allen herum zu riechen, ohne Einen zu durchdringen" [G. L. Plitt, *Aus Schellings Leben, I* (Leipzig, 1869), 431 f.]. While Schelling's remark does contain an element of truth, it is unjust because in theory and in practice Novalis maintained deep attachments to things, ideas, or persons he had chosen from the sea of potentials available to him.

11 Such a contention is more applicable to Novalis' poetry than to his notebooks; it forms the basis of Bruce Haywood's hermeneutic interpretation in *Novalis. The Veil of Imagery* (Cambridge, Mass., 1959).

12 *Kritische Friedrich-Schlegel-Ausgabe*, II (Paderborn, 1967), 197.

13 This has been noted already by Anni Carlsson in *Die Fragmente des Novalis* (Basel, 1939), pp. 6 ff.

14 "Novalis and Plotin. Untersuchungen zu einer neuen Edition und Interpretation des 'Allgemeinen Brouillon'," *Jahrbuch des freien deutschen Hochstifts* (1963), 139-250. Further references to this article will be made with the author's name only.

15 W. Dilthey, *Das Erlebnis und die Dichtung*. 13th ed. (Göttingen, 1957), p. 324. The article appeared first in 1865 in the *Preußische Jahrbücher*.

16 *Friedrich von Hardenbergs (Novalis) Beziehungen zur Naturwissenschaft seiner Zeit* (Leipzig, 1905).

17 "Das Ergebnis der Untersuchung von Hardenbergs Beziehungen zur Naturwissenschaft seiner Zeit ist daher einerseits ein negatives. Es hat sich ergeben, daß er nicht soweit in die Erkenntnis der empirischen Tatsachen der Naturwissenschaften eindrang, um ihre Probleme selbständig erfassen und etwa weiter bilden zu können. Er war daher auch nicht imstande, eine philosophische Behandlung der Ergebnisse und Fragen der naturwissenschaftlichen Forschung seiner Zeit zu unternehmen. Wissenschaftliche Bedeutung haben darum weder seine naturwissenschaftlichen noch die naturphilosophischen Fragmente" (Olshausen, p. 75).

18 The most important of these are K. Th. Bluth, *Medizingeschichtliches bei Novalis* (Berlin, 1934) and Lydia Elisabeth Wagner, *The Scientific Interest of Friedrich von Hardenberg (Novalis)* (Ann Arbor, 1937).

19 R. Unger, *Herder, Novalis und Kleist. Studien über die Entwicklung des Todesproblems*

in Denken und Dichten vom Sturm und Drang zur Romantik (Frankfurt a.M., 1922) and W. Rehm, *Orpheus. Der Dichter und die Toten. Selbstdeutung und Totenkult bei Novalis, Hölderlin, Rilke* (Düsseldorf, 1950).

[20] A list of secondary literature relating to Novalis and Romantic Medicine is included in my bibliography. Among the titles listed, Hirschfeld gives a thorough although unsympathetic summary of Romantic Medicine and a detailed bibliography; Leibbrand is appreciative but often inaccurate and mushy; the essays by Fischer, Diepgen, and Schipperges, as well as the dissertations of Bluth (from which Diepgen draws) and Heller (mainly on Novalis' contact with physicians), are now inadequate in the light of the additional material available.

[21] Paul Diepgen, *Geschichte der Medizin*, II/1 (Berlin, 1951), 27.

[22] T. S. Kuhn, *The Structure of Scientific Revolutions* (Chicago, 1962), pp. 2 f.

[23] Ch. C. Gillispie, *The Edge of Objectivity* (Princeton, 1960), p. 199.

NOTES TO CHAPTER I
ASPECTS OF EIGHTEENTH-CENTURY SCIENCE

[1] This essay fragment, entitled *De Arte Medica*, is dated 1669 and printed in H. R. Fox Bourne's *The Life of John Locke* (New York, 1876), I, 222-27. According to K. Dewhurst [*John Locke* (London, 1963), p. 38], Locke merely recorded the dictation as secretary of Dr. Sydenham.

[2] On the relation between Locke's medical training and his mature philosophy see P. Romanell, *Journal of the History of Ideas*, XXV (1964), 107-16, and *Bulletin of the History of Medicine*, XXXII (1958), 293-321.

[3] "The Great Instauration" in *The New Organon and Related Writings*, ed. Fulton H. Anderson (New York, 1960), p. 12.

[4] Bacon, p. 11.

[5] G. W. v. Leibniz, *Selections*, ed. Philip Wiener (New York, 1951), p. 370.

[6] Leibniz, p. 534.

[7] Leibniz's objections against Stahl's theory that the anima of the body might change both the momentum and the direction of its motion are printed in *Clio Medica*, III (1968), 21-40.

[8] "A Dissertation on the Sensible and Irritable Parts of Animals", reprinted in *Bulletin of the Institute of the History of Medicine*, IV (1936), 658 f.

[9] *Lehrsätze aus der Physiologie des Menschen* (Wien, 1797).

[10] Cf. Novalis' definition: "Vernunft und Individuum in harmonischer Thätigkeit —ist Lebenskraft. Theorie der *Lebenskraft*" (II, 259). The last short sentence, meaning something like "I must think about the meaning and the function of 'Lebenskraft'", shows that in the early studies of Fichte, where the note occurs, Novalis was already groping for an organic view of nature.

[11] *Göttingisches Magazin der Wissenschaften und Literatur*, I/2 (1780), 249.

[12] „... daß schlechterdings Zeugung, Ernährung und Wiederersetzung im Grunde blosse Modificationen einer und eben derselben Kraft sind, die im ersten Fall baut, im andern unterhält, im dritten reparirt" (Blumenbach, p. 252).

[13] "Bei jedem lebendigen Geschöpf scheint der Cirkel organischer Kräfte ganz und vollkommen; nur, er ist bei jedem anders modificirt und vertheilet. Bei diesem

liegt er noch der *Vegetation* nahe und ist daher für die Fortpflanzung und Wiedererstattung seiner selbst so mächtig; bei andern nehmen diese Kräfte ab, je mehr sie in künstlichere Glieder, feinere Werkzeuge und Sinnen vertheilt werden. ... Ueber den mächtigen Kräften der Vegetation fangen die *lebendigen Muskelreize* zu wirken an ... Je mehr die Muskelkräfte in das Gebiet der Nerven treten, desto mehr werden auch sie in dieser Organisation gefangen und zu *Zwecken der Empfindung* überwältigt. Je mehr und feinere Nerven ein Thier hat, je mehr diese einander vielfach begegnen, künstlich verstärken und zu edlen Theilen und Sinnen verwandt werden, je größer und feiner endlich der Sammelplatz aller Empfindungen, das Gehirn ist: desto verständiger und feiner wird die Gattung dieser Organisationen." [*Herders Sämmtliche Werke*, ed. Bernhard Suphan, XIII (Berlin, 1887), 91-92.]

[14] The list (see IV, 471-75) contains also four other books by Herder.

[15] *Ueber die Verhältniße der organischen Kräfte unter einander in der Reihe der verschiedenen Organisationen, die Geseze und Folgen dieser Verhältniße* (Stuttgart, 1793). The essay is reprinted in *Sudhoffs Archiv*, XXIII (1930), 247-67. Two consecutive remarks in Novalis' notebooks are in direct reference to Kielmeyer's ideas: "Kielmeyers Idee vom Übergang einer Kraft in die Andre—(von ihrer Successiven und *Simultanen* Existenz.) (Synth[esis] d[er] *Antike* und *Moderne*)" "Reproduktionskraft ist organische *Elasticitaet*" (III, 432).

[16] The five forces in Kielmeyer's definition: "1. Sensibilität oder die Fähigkeit mit Eindrüken, die auf die Nerven oder sonst gemacht werden, gleichzeitig Vorstellungen zu erhalten, 2. Irritabilität oder die Fähigkeit mancher Organe, vorzüglich der Muskeln, auf Reize sich zusammenzuziehen, und Bewegungen hervorzubringen, 3. Reproductionskraft, oder die Fähigkeit der Organisationen, sich selbst ähnliche Wesen Theilweise oder im Ganzen nach- und anzubilden, 4. Sekretionskraft oder die Fähigkeit aus der Saftmasse dieser selbst unähnliche Materien von bestimmter Beschaffenheit wiederholt an bestimmten Orten abzusondern, 5. Propulsionskraft oder die Fähigkeit, die Flüssigkeiten in den vesten Theilen in bestimmter Ordnung zu bewegen und zu vertheilen" (Kielmeyer in *Sudhoff*, p. 251).

[17] Information about Cullen may be found in his biography by John Thomson, William Thomson, David Craigie, *An Account of the Life, Lectures, and Writings of William Cullen* (Edinburgh, 1859), and A. Kent, ed., *An Eighteenth Century Lectureship in Chemistry* (Glasgow, 1950).

[18] Brown is briefly mentioned in the Introduction of Ford Madox Ford's (Hueffer's) biography of his maternal grandfather, who was Dr. John Brown's grandson. See, *Ford Madox Brown* (London, 1896).

[19] London, 1780. References will be made to *The Works of Dr. John Brown*, ed. William Cullen Brown (London, 1804), which uses the author's own English translation of the *Elementa* and contains a biography by his son, the editor. There exists another English translation of the *Elementa* by Thomas Beddoes (London, 1795) which contains another biography of Brown, written by Beddoes, the father of the poet Thomas Beddoes.

[20] Brown, II, 125.

[21] Brown, II, 125. Direct references to Newton are found in several passages of Brown's works.

[22] Brown, II, 134.
[23] Brown, II, 138. By not probing into the meaning of "excitability" Brown thought to follow the example of Newton, who had left the ultimate nature of gravitation undefined. Whether, as Schelling and the more philosophically minded physicians believed, the concept ought to receive a philosophical *a priori* grounding became a major issue in Germany. Brown ignored Haller's distinction between irritability and sensibility.
[24] Brown, II, 135. Coleridge, who knew about Brown from his Manchester friend Beddoes, remarked in his notebook: "Strange Assertions, that we receive a given quantity of Incitability at our birth—yet that this is given out only in small quantities—and these small quantities can not be used suddenly without death—as in the case of those who die of fright or joy—however large the reservoir may be. As a Merchant who has a sudden run on him, stops, altho' his *capital* may exceed the Sum threefold—yet if all his ready Cash is exhausted, he must stop." [*The Notebooks of Samuel Taylor Coleridge*, ed. K. Coburn (New York, 1957), I, entry 388.]
[25] Brown, III, 41.
[26] Cf. Novalis: "Nach dem Brownischen System müssen die Abführenden Mittel schwächend und stärkend zugleich seyn—wenn schwächen—Vermehrung der Erregbark[eit]— und Stärken—Vermindern der Erregbarkeit bedeutet— und nach Brown kann es nichts anders bedeuten. Mir scheint bey vielen abführenden Mitteln die Stärkung, oder Erregung, beträchtlicher, als die Verminderung zu seyn" (II, 595).
[27] Brown, II, 230.
[28] Brown, II, 188.
[29] Coleridge, *Notebooks*, entry 389.
[30] *Journal de Physique*, XXXVI (1790), 139 ff. and 422 ff. The article was translated and published by Thomas Beddoes in *Observations on the Nature and Cure of Calculus* ... (London, 1793).
[31] Girtanner (1760-1800) studied medicine in Göttingen and later made a brief visit to Edinburgh where he learned about Brown's ideas. He returned to Göttingen in 1787 and starting in 1791 he published many volumes of news about the French Revolution (*Historische Nachrichten und politische Betrachtungen über die französische Revolution*). In the MS of the "Vermischte Bemerkungen", the early version of *Blüthenstaub*, there exist a crossed-out reference to Girtanner (II, 746) among remarks on the revolution, which suggests that Novalis was acquainted with this work. It seems likely that he did not know the article in the *Journal de Physique* since this was published earlier. There can be no doubt, however, that the article in question was widely known. Several scientific journals debated the issue, and in 1793 there appeared a book which was stimulated by it: J. U. G. Schaeffer, *Über Sensibilität als Lebensprincip* (Frankfurt).
[32] C. Girtanner, *Ausführliche Darstellung des Brownischen Systemes der praktischen Heilkunde*, II (Göttingen, 1798), 624.
[33] "Die Schlußart, auf welche Brown sein ganzes System gründet, ist die durch Analogie und Induktion" (Girtanner, II, 611).

[34] Coleridge, *Notebooks*, entry 389.
[35] A. Röschlaub, *Untersuchungen über Pathogenie*, 2nd. ed. (Frankfurt, 1800-1803), par. 444. Further references will be made to the pars. in this edition to facilitate comparisons with the first edition (Frankfurt, 1798-1800), the edition that Novalis read.
[36] Frankfurt, 1795.
[37] *Medizinisches-pracktisches Handbuch auf Brownische Grundsätze und Erfahrung gegründet* (Heilbronn, 1796), and *Magazin der verbesserten theoretischen und praktischen Arzneikunst* (Heilbronn, 1796-97).
[38] *Kerner's Werke*, ed. Raimund Pissin (Berlin, 1914), I, 114 f. Kerner himself became a leading figure in "Romantic Medicine" by adopting Mesmerism. That the practice of Brownian medicine often boiled down to the decision whether the disease at hand was sthenic or asthenic was ridiculed also in a farce by Kotzebue, entitled *Das neue Jahrhundert*, in which a "Dr. Reiz" and a" Dr. Potenz" are led to long disputations about a fake disease. As a reply, Röschlaub's magazine published a story about a hypochondriac cured with Brown's methods, making it obvious that the patient was Kotzebue. The latter then closed the feud by retracting.
[39] Marcus (1753-1816) was a patron of the theater at Bamberg and became a friend of E. T. A. Hoffmann during the latter's stay in the city.
[40] Further material on this issue may be found in G. L. Plitt's *Aus Schellings Leben* and R. Haym's *Die Romantische Schule*, photogr. reprod. of the 1870 ed. (Darmstadt, 1961), pp. 736 f.
[41] *Propyläen Ausgabe* (München and Berlin, 1909-32), XXXVIII, 244.
[42] *Propyläen Ausgabe*, XIV, 146. However, Goethe had also favorable comments on Brown; see letter to Schiller, March 19, 1802.
[43] "Es scheint besonders der Gedanke manchem Anhänger dieses Systems viel Vergnügen zu machen, eine Revolution in der Medizin zu bewirken. Diesen Herren habe ich nichts weiter zu sagen, als dieß: Im Reiche der Wahrheit sind nicht Revolutionen sondern Evolutionen der passende Weg zur Verbesserung" [*Journal*, IV (1797), 136].
[44] „Die ganze Medizin muß aus Erfahrung ausgehen und wieder auf Erfahrung, als Zweck, bezogen werden, der wahre Stoff, das Constituirende der Medizin, kann nichts als Erfahrung seyn, die Theorie dient ihr blos als Regulatif, muß aber immer bereit seyn, sich umzuändern und der Erfahrung anzuschmiegen, sobald sich diese ändert" (*Journal*, IV, 143).
[45] "Freyheit des Geistes ist von jeher die Wiege der Wahrheit, Sectengeist und Geistesdespotie ihr Grab gewesen.... Der glücklichste Zustand für die Wissenschaft ist unstreitig der, wenn gar kein Nahme, keine Auctorität herrschen, sondern eine allgemeine Freyheit, die Dinge zu nehmen und zu erklären, wie man will, vorausgesezt, daß man die Gesetze der gesunden Vernunft und die Erfahrung respectirt" (*Journal*, IV, 130 f.).
[46] See reference to an article by Girtanner which appeared in Hufeland's *Journal*: III, 39 and 841.

NOTES TO CHAPTER II
SOURCES AND IMPULSES

[1] R. Samuel, "Karl von Hardenbergs Biographie seines Bruders Novalis," *Euphorion*, LII (1958), 178. The account of Novalis' early life in Tieck's well-known biography (IV, 449-58) is a touched up version of this text. However, Tieck's "smoothing" of Karl's style is often misleading. He adds, for instance: "er war träumerisch still und verriet nur wenig [Karl: "keinen außerordentlichen"] Geist, er entfernte sich von andern Knaben..." Clearly, by adding these clichés Tieck wished to indicate Hardenberg's early poetic inclinations.

[2] "Es ist auffallend, daß auch die 'Bekenntnisse einer schönen Seele' mit der Erzählung einer ganz ähnlichen Verwandlung beginnen... und es scheint diese Fähigkeit, in frühestem Alter mit körperlichen Krankheitsprozessen seelische Vertiefungen sowie positive Entwicklungsbeschleunigungen zu erleben, sehr viele echte Mystiker auszuzeichnen. Es ist eine sehr frühe entscheidende Katharsis, die die Physis stark verändert und verfeinert und die Seele zum erstenmal auf sich aufmerken läßt" [K. J. Obenauer, *Hölderlin/Novalis* (Jena, 1925), p. 147.]

[3] There is a remote possibility that Novalis attended in Leipzig the lectures of Ernst Platner (1744-1818) who was professor of physiology with a bent for philosophy. According to notes in the "Brouillon", Novalis intended to use for his encyclopedic project the two best known works of Platner: *Neue Anthropologie für Aerzte und Weltweise* (Leipzig, 1790) and *Philosophische Aphorismen* (Leipzig, 1776-82); cf. III, 333 and 356. Indeed, Professor Mähl found that the last work led Novalis to a number of other books which were listed in Platner's bibliography, among them the important history of philosophy by Tiedemann (Mähl, pp. 147 and 151 f.; on Tiedemann, see below).

[4] IV, 47 f. Erasmus' hypochondria was the subject also of other letters by Novalis. See letters from March 1794 and January 20, 1797.

[5] "Fichtens prod[uctive] Einb[ildungs]Kr[aft] ist nichts, als durch Vernunft— durch *Idee* und *Glauben* und Willen erregter Sinn" (III, 435). See also III, 252, 408, and 412. Characteristically, Novalis describes the Fichtean concept with very personal terms: "Idee", "Glauben", and "Wille".

[6] That Novalis should consider Schiller's works as harmful strikes one as ironic, since it was Schiller who counseled against an indulgence in the imagination to the young Hardenberg. Incidentally, Schiller gave the same advice to Hölderlin, the only other poet in Hardenberg's generation who felt a strong need to restrain his imagination.

[7] The letter appeared in Hufeland's *Journal* (April 1798) and forms today the last section of *Streit der Facultäten* (Königsberg, 1798). Novalis' notebooks contain several additional critical remarks concerning this work of Kant (see Mähl, pp. 219 f.)

[8] II, 378. See also II, 552 and 589. An interesting analogy and contrast to these remarks is contained in an aphorism of G. Ch. Lichtenberg: "Mein Körper ist derjenige Theil der Welt, den meine Gedancken verändern können. Sogar

eingebildete Kranckheiten können würckliche werden. In der übrigen Welt können meine Hypothesen die Ordnung der Dinge nicht stöhren" [Georg Christoph Lichtenberg, *Aphorismen*, ed. A. Leitzmann, IV (Berlin, 1908), 201]. Lichtenberg believed in a limited power of hypochondria: he held that concrete physical maladies might be created by a hypochondrial disposition, but he did not believe that such spiritual powers can alter the world beyond the body. What interested Novalis in hypochondria was precisely the mode in which the subjective impression might be modified, and spiritual powers of an individual might assert themselves in the world at large. Hence his conviction: "Die Welt hat eine ursprüngliche Fähigkeit durch mich belebt zu werden..." (II, 554).

[9] It is a recurring difficulty in the understanding of Hardenberg that he denotes with one and the same word a concept of the existing world and its future transformed or elevated version. These two meanings are often fused into an ambiguous statement. In the "Brouillon", for instance, one finds the following remark: "PHYS[IOLOGIE]. Hypochondrie ist pathologisirende Fantasie—mit *Glauben* an die Realit[aet] ihrer Produktionen—Fantasmen verbunden" (III, 359). It would seem that this definition refers to the "untransformed" and negative kind of hypochondria, since Novalis rejected "pathological fantasy" in his letter to Erasmus and elsewhere. However, his definition of the creative genius is almost identical with hypochondria: "So ist also das Genie, das Vermögen von eingebildeten Gegenständen, wie von Wircklichen zu handeln, und sie auch, wie diese, zu behandeln" (II, 420).

[10] IV, 177. This passage clearly shows that Novalis did not naively expect instantaneous results from the sciences as Leta Jane Lewis contends in her article "Novalis and the Fichtean Absolute" [*German Quarterly*, XXXV (1962), 464-74]. Apart from the fact that at the time of Sophie's illness Novalis had no clear notion yet of "magic" and "produktive Einbildungskraft", this kind of argument establishes a misleading equation between experience and thought, because it suggests that Novalis adopted philosophical tenets for immediate practical use. As he himself remarked once, philosophy doesn't tell us how to bake bread.

[11] IV, 192. See also the letter to Schlegel from April 13, 1797.

[12] IV, 377. It is not clear to which work of Schelling Novalis refers here.

[13] IV, 379-98. The references are to: *Vom Ich als Princip der Philosophie oder über das Unbedingte im menschlichen Wissen* (Tübingen, 1795), "Philosophische Briefe über Dogmatismus und Kriticismus", *Philosophisches Journal* (1795), and *Ideen zu einer Philosophie der Natur* (Leipzig, 1797).

[14] On June 14, 1797 Novalis wrote to Schlegel: "Fichte ist der gefährlichste unter allen Denkern, die ich kenne. Er zaubert einen in seinem Kreise fest" (IV, 208).

[15] The literature on the relationship between Schelling and Novalis is extensive and very contradictory. Olshausen found Schelling's influence negligible because of Hardenberg's "mystic predisposition" (pp. 16 f.). Thereby he missed the link through Spinoza. Pixberg's positive conclusions rest on shaky foundations, for which they were criticized by Haering (pp. 605 f.) and Mähl. Bluth, Diepgen,

and Leibbrand erroneously assume that Novalis exerted a decisive influence on Schelling during his stay in Leipzig (1791-93).

[16] This was pointed out already by Professor Mähl (pp. 192 f.). Neither Professor Mähl nor Professor Samuel in his commentary emphasize sufficiently that in the *Philosophische Briefe* "intellektuale Anschauung" is not, properly speaking, part of Schelling's own philosophy, but rather a term with which he wishes to characterize Spinoza. Since the extent to which Schelling adopted Spinoza's view is not clear, the association is not so much between Novalis and Schelling as between Novalis and Spinoza.

[17] Tieck shows naivité when he mentions Hardenberg's study of Fichte and Spinoza in one breath: „In der Philosophie hatte er vorzüglich Spinoza und Fichte studiert; aber er suchte nachher eine eigne Bahn, die Philosophie mit der Religion zu vereinigen, und so wurden ihm, was wir von den Neuplatonikern besitzen, sowie die Schriften der Mystiker sehr wichtig" (IV, 457). One has to take exception to this statement on at least three accounts: 1. Novalis' study of Spinoza was by no means as extensive as his study of Fichte, and it is unlikely that he read the former in the original; 2. in spite of this, even before reading Schelling, Novalis found in Spinoza's philosophy a counterpart to Fichte's *Wissenschaftslehre*; 3. since he was attracted to the mystic and neo-Platonic strain in Spinoza's philosophy (he associated him with Zinzendorf!), this continued to be important to him even when he tried to find his own way.

[18] J. Fichte, *Ausgewählte Werke*, ed. F. Medicus (Darmstadt, 1962), I, 292.

[19] Sch, I, 696. The word "Weltseele" in this passage raises some questions about Novalis' use of it. Earlier it was assumed that he adopted the term from Schelling's work of the same title. Since Schelling's *Weltseele* did not appear until the spring of 1798 and since according to the newest dating Novalis had already used the term earlier, the editors of the new critical edition assumed that the concept caught Hardenberg's attention in Baader's *Beyträge zur Elementarphisiologie* which he had probably read as early as 1797 (cf. II, 513). Yet in Baader's work the word appears only in a rather innocuous footnote, while it is a central one in Schelling's *Ideen*, even if mentioned only once.

[20] S. Th. Sömmering, *Über das Organ der Seele, nebst einem Schreiben von I. Kant* (Königsberg, 1796). Eschenmayer's book was published in Tübingen, 1797.

[21] I. Kant, *Werke*, IV (Berlin, 1903), 468. Kant also uses "rein" for "eigentlich" and "angewandt" for "uneigentlich".

[22] Kant, IV, 470.

[23] "Die Rationalität der Principien wäre es demnach, welche die Kunst zur Wissenschaft erhöbe; Sieht man die Richtigkeit hievon ein, und vergleicht den gegenwärtigen Zustand der Wissenschaften damit, so wird man gestehen müssen, daß wir biß jezt weder in der Chemie noch in der Medicin ein System aufzuweisen haben, nirgends sind Principien, von welchen eine Deduction aus naturmetaphysischen Säzen versucht worden wäre, welches doch zum Behuf eines Systems gefordert wird.

Alles was wir haben, sind empirische Principien, aus der Erfahrung rückwärts gefolgert, die aber bloß eine komparative Allgemeinheit zulassen, es sind Hypothesen, in denen allemal eine Voraussezung angenommen wird, welche, ob sie gleich wahr seyn kann, dennoch eines weitern Beweises bedarf..." (Eschenmayer, pp. VIII-IX).

[24] "Die Dynamik belehrt uns, daß sich die Existenz der Materie blos unter der Annahme der Konkurrenz zweier ursprünglichen Kräfte denken lasse—diese Kräfte sind die Attractions- und Repulsionskraft" (Eschenmayer, p. 2). „... die Materie erfüllt nicht durch ihre bloße Existenz, sondern durch Kräfte einen Raum. Da nun die empirische Erfüllung des Raums unserer Anschauung unendlich verschieden gegeben ist, das Mannigfaltige einer Kraft aber blos in Graden bestehen kann, so hat man diese Verschiedenheiten auch als Grade anzusehen. Qualitäten sind daher Grade, und ein Grad Materie ist irgend ein Größen Verhältniß, in welchem die Attractions- und Repulsionskraft zu einander stehen. In diesem Punkte ist es, wo sich die dynamische Naturphilosophie von der mechanischen unterscheidet" (Eschenmayer, pp. 5 f.).

[25] "Am Ende deducirt sich ein solcher Dualismus aus der Nothwendigkeit des ursprünglichen Sezens und Gegensezens, welches Bedingungen sind, unter denen selbst die Möglichkeit unseres Bewusstseins steht" (Eschenmayer, p. 4). Although the book shows undeniable associations with Fichte's *Wissenschaftslehre* by employing these categories, the traces of Kant's philosophy, which are apparent even in the title ("Naturmetaphysik"—"Metaphysische Anfangsgründe"), are still more important.

[26] The mechanical and chemical foundations of Eschenmayer's theory are polemically discussed in the "Brouillon" (III, 246). It has not been noticed by the editors of the new critical edition that a note in the "Freiberger Studienhefte" (III, 45), which was later included (III, 428) and elaborated upon (III, 341) in the "Brouillon", may also be traced to Eschenmayer's book. They all deal with Eschenmayer's contention that the degree of a matter and its chemical interactions are determined by the relationship between the attractive and repulsive forces. Hence probably also Novalis' important expression, "Grad der Materie".

[27] "Daß seine Principien die Ersten seyn müssen, von welchen für die Arzneiwissenschaft auszugehen ist, und auf welche allein eine nosologische Ordnung gegründet werden kann, diß haben wir oben wenigstens erörtert.... So wenig sich dieses auch derjenige, der blos Arzt ist, eingestehen mag, so gewiß erkennt es der Naturphilosoph, der blos für Form und System der Naturwissenschaft arbeitet" (Eschenmayer, pp. 90-91).

[28] This led Professor Mähl to the suggestion that instead of reading the medical section of Eschenmayer's work Novalis turned to C. H. Pfaff's translation of the *Elements* (Kopenhagen, 1796) and made excerpts from the first part only after having read this book. In this way Novalis would have "discovered" Brown while reading Eschenmayer. Although Professor Mähl's assumption cannot be refuted factually, the repeated reading of Eschenmayer's book seems unlikely, and the marginal notes provide no evidence that Novalis actually read Brown's work itself. His extensive notes on medicine, physiology, and psychology, the use of medical terminology in his philosophy, and the large number of medical books in his library, all show that he read *about* Brown's theory, but nowhere do we find quotations or direct references that would conclusively prove that he read the *Elements* itself. As already the first remarks show, Novalis understood

and studied Brown within the framework of German medical and philosophical discussions; his sources were articles in Hufeland's *Journal* and *Bibliothek*, in Gren's *Journal*, or in Kausch's *Geist und Kritik*, and books by Röschlaub, Marcus, Mönch and others.

[29] Eschenmayer, p. 30. In Kant's formulation: "Lehrsatz 3. Zweites Gesetz der Mechanik. Alle Veränderung der Materie hat eine äußere Ursache. (Ein jeder Körper beharrt in seinem Zustande der Ruhe oder Bewegung, in derselben Richtung und mit derselben Geschwindigkeit, wenn er nicht durch eine äußere Ursache genöthigt wird, diesen Zustand zu verlassen.)" (p. 543).

[30] Fichte, III, 16.

[31] Fichte, III, 17.

[32] Eschenmayer, p. 53. Kant's definition: "Materie ist das Bewegliche im Raume" (p. 480).

[33] Haering, p. 515.

[34] Olshausen has his dates wrong (he did not know of the Eschenmayer excerpts) and he wrongly believes that Novalis had read Brown's work; he is nevertheless right in remarking that Novalis' acquaintance with Brown's theory coincides with his reading of Hemsterhuis' works. There is no evidence, however, that the ideas of Brown and Hemsterhuis were combined by him as Olshausen claims (p. 15). As the Eschenmayer excerpts show, Novalis immediately rejected the philosophical tenets of Brown, while Hemsterhuis left a deep and lasting impression on him.

[35] Upon Hemsterhuis' request Diderot wrote extensive commentaries on the former's *Lettre sur l'homme*. Although Diderot was at times highly critical of the work, he concluded by saying: "Il y a des idées très belles, très neuves et très fines" [*Lettre sur l'homme et ses rapports*, ed. Georges May (New Haven, 1964), p. 513]. Compared to Diderot's analytical notes Novalis' excerpts and commentaries show more enthusiasm, but they appear less critical and at times even naive.

[36] Cf. *Simon ou des facultés de l'âme* in *Oeuvres Philosophiques* (Paris, 1792), II, 233.

[37] "Ich habe jetzt seine ältere Abhandlung vom Wärmestoff gelesen – Av. 8f. welcher Geist? Ich denke an ihn zu schreiben. – Könnte er nicht zum „Athenäum" eingeladen werden? Vereinige Dich mit Baadern, Freund – Ihr könnt ungeheure Dinge leisten." Letter to Schlegel, November 7, 1798 (IV, 241).

[38] Letter to Schlegel, January 20, 1799 (IV, 261). On the same day he wrote to Karoline Schlegel and compared Baader with J. W. Ritter who was not only a speculative mind but also an experimentalist: "Ritter ist Ritter, und wir sind nur Knappen. Selbst Baader ist nur sein Dichter" (IV, 263).

[39] Baader, *Sämtliche Werke* (Leipzig, 1850-60; reprint: Aalen, 1963), III, 216.

[40] Baader, III, 220 f.

[41] "Die Möglichkeit aller Philosophie beruht darauf – daß sich die Intelligenz durch Selbstberührung eine Selbstgesezmäßige Bewegung – d.i. eine eigne Form der Thätigkeit, giebt. (Siehe Baaders Theorie der Gliedrung)" (II, 530). See also II, 540, no. 70.

[42] II, 582. Cf. Baader: "[Ich würde behaupten], dass die Materie, insofern sie aus

Grundkräften entsteht und in ihnen besteht, allerdings aus Monaden bestehe" (III, 234) — in answer to a passage in Kant's *Metaphysische Anfangsgründe*.
[43] Baader, III, 33.

NOTES TO CHAPTER III
THE ANTHROPOLOGY AND PHYSIOLOGY OF MAGIC

[1] My analysis will be based mainly on the following notes in Section VI of the new edition: nos. 105, 111, 112, 115, 117, 118, 119, 120, 125, 225, 233, 235, 247, 248, 249, and 256. A number of other passages from this section and the *Blüthenstaub* collection are also relevant. While these notes do form a unity, they remain ambiguous with respect to the proposed free association between mind and body. At times Novalis seems to uphold a theory of correspondences, while at others he advocates a manipulation or domination of nature. I believe that the second version forms the basis of Hardenberg's aesthetics, and I would, therefore, disagree with Professor Mähl who holds that in Novalis' mature philosophy and poetry the "theory of magic" is absent and only the "theory of correspondences" is upheld. The vocabulary and the field of attention changes (already in the "Brouillon"), but not the basic principle. See Mähl, *Die Idee des goldenen Zeitalters im Werk des Novalis* (Heidelberg, 1965), pp. 306 and 343.
[2] "Romantic Psychology and the Inner Senses: Coleridge" by Judson S. Lyon [*PMLA*, LXXXI (1966), 246-260] discusses this problem in connection with Coleridge and some of the other English romantics.
[3] II, 547. In II, 583, no. 247 even the idea of restauration of lost members is mentioned. In Hemsterhuis' *Simon* Socrates tells a Promethean myth about the lost senses of man which could be regenerated once the tyranny of reason is over.
[4] Recent research on this topic may be found in: *Psychopathology; A Source Book*, ed. Charles F. Reed, Irving E. Alexander, Sylvan S. Tomkins (Cambridge, Mass., 1963), especially "Schizophrenia: A New Approach. II. Result of a Year's Research," pp. 640-659; also: *Hallucinations*, ed. Louis Jolyon West (New York, 1962). On the effects of sensory deprivation see J. A. Vernon, *Inside the Black Room* (New York, 1964).
[5] See Heinz Ritter, *Novalis' Hymnen an die Nacht* (Heidelberg, 1930).
[6] I. Strohschneider-Kohrs, *Die romantische Ironie in Theorie und Gestaltung* (Tübingen, 1960), pp. 100 f. It is somewhat surprising that after having established the mystic unity of Hardenberg's thought Professor Strohschneider-Kohrs gives a detailed analysis of a little prose piece by Hardenberg — only to show its all-pervading irony.
[7] Strohschneider-Kohrs, p. 109. The phrase "indifferente Einheit von Welt und Ich" was coined by Hugo Kuhn in "Poetische Synthesis," *Zeitschrift für philosophische Forschung*, V (1950), 161-178 and 358-384.
[8] II, 551 f. In the "Brouillon": "Wir verstehn natürlich alles Fremde nur durch Selbst*fremdmachung — Selbstveränderung —* Selbstbeobachtung" (III, 429).
[9] This idea appears in Hemsterhuis' *Sur les désirs* and, in slightly different form, in Baader's *Beiträge* (III, 217).

[10] "Mein Körper würde mir nicht specifisch vom Ganzen verschieden—sondern nur als eine Variation desselben vorkommen. Meine Erkenntniß des Ganze[n] würde also den Character der Analogie haben—diese würde sich aber auf das innigste und unmittelbarste auf die directe und *absolute* Erkenntniß des Gliedes beziehn" (II, 551). Cf. also II, 650, no. 485. The analogy between microcosm and macrocosm is a central idea in the works of Paracelsus; his name occurs in Hardenberg's notebooks, but probably only in connection with the reading of Tiedemann's *Geist der spekulativen Philosophie*.

[11] II, 589. In the "Brouillon": "Denken ist Wollen oder Wollen—Denken" (III, 464). "Das ächte Denken erscheint, wie ein Machen—und ist auch solches" (III, 404).

[12] In these early notes there is little difference between Schelling's and Novalis' use of the "Weltseele". Novalis saw in it an idea of the whole which permeates every particle and secures the necessary harmony (II, 551). The self was a "Weltglied", whereby Novalis defined the meaning of "Glied" as "... eine Variation des Ganzen—es besteht aus denselben Elementen—die nur auf eine verschiedne und d[urch] d[ie] Gesetze des Ganzen bestimmte Weise in denselben geordnet sind" (II, 552).

[13] B. Croce, *Aesthetic*, transl. D. Ainslie, 2nd ed., (London, 1922), p. 277. Mentions of the "lex continui" and "lex parsimoniae" (II, 670 and III, 419) might be references to Kant's Introduction in *Critique of Judgement*.

[14] W. H. Wackenroder, *Werke und Briefe* (Heidelberg, 1967), p. 13.

[15] *Poetical Works of Wordsworth*, ed. T. Hutchinson (London, 1960), pp. 735 and 738.

[16] These differences may be traced to Hardenberg's Kantian and Fichtean schooling and to his greater concern for science. The quoted note continues by saying that the non-artist is yet incapable of producing ideas without external solicitation for he seems to suffer under the yoke of mechanics, namely "that all changes presuppose an external cause". The last phrase, adopted almost word for word from Eschenmayer, shows how inseparable Hardenberg's thoughts on science and poetry are.

[17] II, 575. Novalis originally compared poetry with painting, and only later substituted music for poetry.

[18] A similar analogy is made between external and indirect stimuli in Röschlaub's *Untersuchungen*. See ch. V below. Since the first volume of Röschlaub's book appeared in 1798 and the note in question was written in May of that year, it may be related to the reading of this book, See notes on II, pp. 561, 594, 598 and III, 352.

[19] Cf. *Die Lehrlinge* (I, 104) and Baader, III, 226.

[20] "Eben darum geht auch alle Umbildung und Assimilation, alle Zeugung und Zerstörung, durch die Mittelstufe des Flüssigen.—Letzteres ist gleichsam der zartere Schleier am Gewande der Mutter Isis..." (Baader, III, 226).

[21] III, 327. It is curious to observe that the English adjectival compounds (e.g., "indirectly asthenic") acquire a certain substantiality by being turned into nouns (e.g., "indirecte Sthenie").

²² "Das Schwächungs und AbtödtungsSystem der strengen Moralisten und strengen Asceten ist nichts, als das bekannte, bisherige Heilungssystem in der Medicin. Ihm entgegen muß man ein Brownisches Stärkungssystem setzen, wie dem leztern" (II, 602).
²³ II, 573. Whether Novalis means that drama is a mixture of two sthenic or of sthenic and asthenic symptoms is not quite clear. In the "Brouillon": "Alle Leidenschaften endigen sich, wie ein *Trauerspiel*. Alles Einseitige endigt sich mit Tod..." (III, 306).
²⁴ II, 563. Novalis cites the example of Hamlet, who is asthenic at the outset (passive and introverted) but asserts himself at the end of the drama. No doubt, his scheme would also fit the epitome of romantic "Trauerspiel", *Tristan und Isolde*, where the subject is "Selbstauflösung des Triebes" (II, 562). It starts with an excess of excitement and ends with a passive, asthenic dissolution of form and life.
²⁵ II, 616. For a further example see II, 649, no. 479.
²⁶ Mähl, p. 142.
²⁷ F. Schlegel, II, 155.
²⁸ The letter to Schlegel from December 26, 1797 which also mentions Brown and medicine communicates about a "Traktat vom Lichte" for which Novalis had some material available. Professor Samuel suggests that the fragments from Teplitz might be related to this project (see II, 517), while H. Ritter in his *Der unbekannte Novalis* has recently claimed that the "Traktat" found expression in the hymns. The common medical background of the fragments and the hymns shows that probably both of them are right.

NOTES TO CHAPTER IV
IDEAS FOR AN ENCYCLOPEDIA

¹ I shall not deal with these notebooks separately, but will include them in my discussion of the "Brouillon".
² One should keep in mind the grandiose ambitions of the "Brouillon" and that Novalis later criticized the prosaic nature of Goethe's *Wilhelm Meister*.
³ About the "Brouillon" and the French encyclopedia see III, 300 and Mähl, pp. 210 f.
⁴ "Jedes Stück meines Buchs, das in äußerst verschiedner Manier geschrieben seyn kann—In Fragmenten—Briefen—Gedichten—wiss[enschaftlich] strengen Aufsätzen etc.—Einem oder einigen meiner Freunde dedicirt" (III, 450).
⁵ The disagreement with Schlegel's famous *Athenaeum* fragment no. 116 (Schlegel, II, 182 f.) may be indicated by saying that Schlegel hoped to give a modern definition to literature, while Novalis was more directly concerned with the artistic reconstitution of life itself. About Novalis' criticism of the *Athenaeum* fragment see: II, 623.
⁶ Leipzig, 1774. An English translation of this book is now available: *On the External Characters of Minerals*, transl. Albert V. Carozzi (Urbana, 1962).
⁷ "Im Classificiren und definiren etc. will ich mich an Werners System und an den Wissenschaften üben" (III, 363). See also III, 367 (no. 580), and 394 (no. 670).

8 III, 358. Also: "Werners Beschr[eibungen] sind zu individuell – zu sehr auf die individuelle Stufe, die er vor sich hatte, gerichtet" (III, 375).

9 „Die Basis aller Wissenschaften und Künste muß eine W[issenschaft] und Kunst seyn – die man der Algéber vergleichen kann" (III, 257); „Die höchste Elementarwissenschaft ist diejenige, die schlechterdings kein *bestimmtes* Obj[ect] – sondern ein reines N. behandelt" (III, 257).

10 Johann Heinrich Lambert, *Neues Organon* (Leipzig, 1764). Photomechanically reproduced as vols. I-II in Lambert's *Philosophische Schriften* (Hildesheim, 1965).

11 From the Introduction to the *Neues Organon* by Hans-Werner Arndt: *Philosophische Schriften*, I, x.

12 "Allerdings ist das absichtslose Zusammentreffen unsrer biblischen Projekte eines der auffallendsten Zeichen und Wunder unsres Einverständnisses und unsrer Mißverständnisse" (IV, 247).

13 "Comme l'organe du tact développe à l'homme individu l'univers en tant que tangible, comme l'ouïe & l'air lui développent l'univers en tant que sonore, comme la vue & la lumiere lui développent l'univers en tant que visible; ce qu'il appelle coeur ou conscience, & la société avec des Etres homogenes, lui développent l'univers en tant que moral" (*Lettre sur l'homme*, ed. May, p. 226).

14 *Lettre sur l'homme*, ed. May, p. 416.

15 I disagree here with Professor Samuel who suggested that the extraterrestial examination of man (cf. II, 616) constitutes the meaning of the phrase (II, 517). "Moral astronomy" seems to be, rather, a special case of what Dilthey called "Realpsychologie" in Novalis' philosophy, i.e., a science of the interior dimension.

16 To A. W. Schlegel: "Mit Schelling bin ich sehr Freund geworden. Wir haben einige köstliche Stunden symphilosophiert" (IV, 218). To Friedrich: "Er hat mich zum Briefwechsel eingeladen. Diese Tage über werde ich auch an ihn schreiben. Er hat mir sehr gefallen – ächte Universaltendenz in ihm – wahre Strahlenkraft – von Einem Punkt in die Unendlichkeit hinaus" (IV, 220). The correspondence probably never started: neither letters nor other indicators survived.

17 See IV, 233, 238, 241, and 263. Whether, as Professor Samuel believes, Novalis' sixth "Dialog" is directed against Schelling is open to question, because the remarks are not very applicable to Schelling's "Naturphilosophie". Cf. II, 658 f. and 669-71.

18 See *Friedrich Schlegel und Novalis*, ed. M. Preitz (Darmstadt, 1957), pp. 83, 84, 93.

19 Upon the possibility of rivalry Novalis touched only once and even then with tact: "Schelling könnte in der Kraft Dein Rival sein; er übertrifft Dich vielleicht an Bestimmtheit aber wie eng ist seine Sphäre gegen die Deinige" (IV, 208).

20 „Seine Denkungsart scheint mir zu jenem fragmentarischen Wesen, wo man die Natur gleichsam auf witzigen Einfällen zu ertappen sucht und alles nur auf ein regelloses Zusammenhäufen solcher Einfälle hinausläuft, kurz: auf Schlegelianismus der Naturwissenschaft zu führen…" (IV, 463).

21 Cf. Mähl, pp. 188 f. A reference to Plotinus' concept is to be found, for instance, in the following note: "Über d[as] irrdische Individuum – das himmlische Individuum und ihre Verhältnisse./ (Gott ist die Weltseele der *Ideal*welt)" (III, 445).

²² Thirteenth Letter in the *Ästhetische Erziehung*: Schiller, *Sämtliche Werke*, V (München, 1959), 608.
²³ Still an other relevant passage from Novalis: "Die Natur soll moralisch werden. Wir sind ihre *Erzieher*—ihre moralischen *Tangenten*—ihre moralischen Reitze" (III, 252).
²⁴ Fourteenth Letter: Schiller, V, 612 f.

NOTES TO CHAPTER V
SENSIBILITY AND MEDICINE

¹ P. Trahard, *Les maîtres de la sensibilité française au XVIII⁰ siècle*, I (Paris, 1931), p. 7.
² There has been recent discussion whether the designation "Age of Sensibility" could be applied to the pre-romantic age in English literature. See N. Frye, "Towards defining an Age of Sensibility" in *Fables of Identity* (New York, 1963), and *From Sensibility to Romanticism*, ed. Frederick Whiley Hilles (New York, 1965).
³ All English quotations were taken from the OED which gives seven different meanings of the word.
⁴ Novalis was probably not familiar with Haller's classic report [he planned to read his book on physiology (III, 585)], but he must have read about sensibility in Herder's *Ideen* and the medical works of Hufeland, Ith, Schaeffer, and Stark. All these authors use the term, although the meaning they attach to it does not coincide with that in Novalis' notebooks. More relevant are Kielmeyer's *Rede*, where sensibility was the highest of the five organic forces, and Röschlaub's *Untersuchungen*, where it designated the contractility of nerves.
⁵ According to Schelling, both stimuli and excitability were negative conditions for life: "Der Schottländer Joh. Brown läßt zwar das thierische Leben aus zwei Faktoren (der thierischen Erregbarkeit und den erregenden Potenzen, exciting powers) entspringen, was allerdings mit unserm positiven und negativen Princip des Lebens übereinzustimmen scheint; wenn man aber nachsieht, was Brown unter den erregenden Potenzen versteht, so findet man, daß er darunter Principien begreift, die unsrer Meinung nach schon zu den negativen Bedingungen des Lebens gehören, denen also die Dignität positiver Ursachen des Lebens nicht zugeschrieben werden kann" (I, 573); "Erregbarkeit ist ein synthetischer Begriff, er drückt ein Mannichfaltiges negativer Principien aus…" (I, 574).
⁶ III, 113 and 850. The following confused and confusing "Brouillon" note ought to be read in the light of this theory: "Schelling geht nur von dem *Irritabilitätsphaenomèn* der Welt aus—er legt den *Muskel* zum Grunde.—Wo bleibt der *Nerv*—die Adern—das Blut—und die *Haut*—der *Zellstoff*. Warum geht er, der Chymiker, nicht vom *Process* aus—von dem Phaenomèn der Berührung—der *Kette*?" (III, 470). Novalis had some justification in claiming that Schelling placed too much emphasis upon irritablity; but, as the passage from Schelling clearly shows, irritability was precisely the oxygen capacity of *nerves* (in this he deviated from Haller and Röschlaub) and therefore Novalis' accusation that Schelling neglected the nerves seems unfounded. Similarly, it

cannot be said that Schelling was a chemist, since he expressly repudiated the physiological and pathological theories of the humoral pathologists.

[7] The only note which does not fit this interpretation is an earlier one, from the summer of 1798. Using "Reitzbarkeit" for "Irritabilität" (these were interchanged in later notes too), Novalis states here that "Reitzbarkeit" (and not "Sensibilität") is inversely proportional to capacity: "Je *geringer die Capacitaet ist*, desto schneller die Wirkung des Reitzes – desto empfindlicher der Stoff oder das *Erregbare* – (desto leichter entzündbar.) Reitzbarkeit und Capacitaet stehn in umgekehrten Verhältnisse. C[apacitaet] und E[rregbarkeit] stehn im Verhältnisse, wie O[xigène] und Phlogiston" (II, 555). The mix-up may be a slip of the pen (when reworking his notes Novalis crossed this one out). Anyway, the remark was probably written before reading Schelling's *Weltseele*.

[8] "Aufnahmefähigkeit für Reize", Bluth's definition of "Capacität", actually describes "Erregbarkeit". A body with a large reservoir of excitability is indeed capable of receiving much stimulation, but only a body with high capacity is capable of receiving the stimuli without becoming overstimulated. Interpreting Novalis' statement "Die Erregbarkeit ist Repulsivkraft – die Capacitaet – Attractionskraft" (III, 276), Bluth associated the attractive force with capacity: "Die Kapazität vermag den Reiz gleichsam zu sammeln, aufzusaugen, an sich zu ziehen, weshalb auch... von einer Attraktionskraft gesprochen wird, die in ihm wirksam sei" (Bluth, p. 35). But for Novalis the attractive force was the gravitational force, the force of stability (the attractive force on earth *is* the gravitational force) which prevents the positive force from compelling objects to an unceasing motion towards an infinitely remote goal.

[9] Schelling was careful to define "Weltseele" as a mere stimulating and coordinating principle: "Davon freilich kann nicht die Rede seyn, daß dieses Princip die todten Kräfte der Materie im lebenden Körper aufhebe, wohl aber, daß es 1. diesen todten Kräften eine Richtung gebe, die sie, sich selbst überlassen, in einer freien ungestörten Bildung, nicht genommen hätten; 2. daß es den Conflikt dieser Kräfte, die sich selbst überlassen, sich bald in Gleichgewicht und Ruhe versetzt hätten, immer neu anfache und continuirlich unterhalte" (Sch. I, 636).

[10] Haering, who contemptuously dismissed all influences on Novalis, misinterpreted the meaning of "sensibility" by not being acquainted with the background: "[Unter den positiven Aspekten von Browns Lehre] war es die starke Betonung des ständigen Zusammenwirkens von Reizbarkeit (Irritabilität) und Sensibilität, die ihn anzog, wobei erstere die vorwiegend passiv-rezeptive ('objektive'), letztere die vorwiegend aktiv-'subjektive' Seite der Ichfunktion betonen soll" (p. 515). Apart from the error of attributing the terms to Brown, Haering makes a mistake in terming irritability active and sensibility passive. According to Novalis both irritability and sensibility have active and passive, positive and negative components.

[11] See also II, 560 (no. 164) and 570 (no. 208).

[12] "Aufmercksamkeit" seems to have been widely used in the fight against mechanistic theories. In arguing against Hartley's association theory, Coleridge wrote in the *Biographia Literaria*: "But the will itself by confining and intensi-

fying the attention may arbitrarily give vividness or distinctness to any object whatsoever..." (ch. VII).

In Schiller's first medical dissertation, entitled *Philosophie der Physiologie*, the parallel to Novalis is even stronger: "Die Seele hat einen tätigen Einfluß auf das Denkorgan. Sie kann die materiellen Ideen stärker machen und nach Willkür darauf haften, und somit macht sie auch die geistigen Ideen stärker. Dies ist das Werk der Aufmerksamkeit. Sie hat also Macht auf die Stärke der Beweggründe; ja sie selbst ist es, die sich Beweggründe macht.... Alle Moralität des Menschen hat ihren Grund in der Aufmerksamkeit, d.h. im tätigen Einfluß der Seele auf die materiellen Ideen im Denkorgan" (Schiller, V, 265 f.).

[13] III, 317. See also II, 546. Novalis deviates from Schelling inasmuch as he makes "Kraft" the shaping force of the physical world; Schelling followed Leibniz and saw no possibility for interaction between spiritual and physical forces (Sch, I, 700). This view was criticized by Novalis in the earlier notes on the *Weltseele* (III, 114).

[14] Novalis was probably not acquainted with the third volume (Frankfurt, 1800).

[15] Leibbrand, p. 229.

[16] In the group of notes under discussion (nos. 593-596) the following points testify to Röschlaub's influence:
 a. only Röschlaub made a distinction between "Stoff" and "Kraft",
 b. the terms "Wärmestoff" and "elektrischer Stoff" were not used by Brown,
 c. the passage: "Die Luft ist so gut *Organ* des Menschen, wie das Blut. Die Trennung des Körpers von der Welt ist, wie die der Seele vom *Körper*" (III, 370) is a direct reference to pars. 1424-25 in Röschlaub's book, where it was asserted that the air in the inner cavities of the body was not part of internal stimulation (see the discussion below of Röschlaub's "Theorie der Potenzen"),
 d. Novalis explicitly refers to Röschlaub's contention that oxygen reduces excitement and is therefore a negative stimulus.

[17] Röschlaub, § 53.

[18] „Der Grund der Wirklichkeit des Lebens liegt in einer äußeren Ursache. Und hier ist das allgemeine Gesetz der Mechanik auch in der lebenden Natur bestätigt: Jede Bewegung (Veränderung der Materie) hat eine äußere Ursache" (§ 442).

[19] "Kraft ist Grund der Wirklichkeit der Handlung aus sich" (§ 236).

[20] Röschlaub, § 287.

[21] Novalis, III, 327. Röschlaub's name in the first sentence indicates that these remarks were made in direct response to his book. Nevertheless, the idea of organic development, as well as the use of such terms as "Bildung ihres Werkzeugs" and "Korrespondierender Gegenstand", shows that the position is consistent with Hardenberg's earlier physiological and psychological theories.

[22] „Erregbarkeit, als die innerliche Bedingniß zur Möglichkeit des Lebens, ist kein Gegenstand möglicher Wahrnehmung, ist Begriff, a priori..." (Röschlaub, § 444).

[23] "Die ganze Lehre von den speciellen Kr[anckheiten] und ihrer Kur gehört in die specielle Lebenslehre — die Erregungsth[eorie] gehört in die theoretische

Lebenslehre..." (III, 324). The view that the theory of excitability was not merely a method of cure but a theory of life (III, 419) was expressed already in Röschlaub's book: "Die meisten Betrachtungen betreffen die Erscheinungen des Lebens ohne Rücksicht auf Wohlbefinden und Gesundheit" (§ 22).

24 "Fichte ist, wie Brown zu Wercke gegangen—nur noch universeller und absoluter" (II, 546). „Browns Theorie handelt (wie die *Fichtische*), vom *physiologischen Ideal*... Er stellt auch nur das Ideal der *Heilmethode* auf" (III, 409).

25 Brown, II, 134 f.

26 Röschlaub, §§ 1424 and 1425.

27 Novalis owned a book by an anonymous author on this particular issue: *Praeliminarien zum medizinischen Frieden, oder Vereinigungspunkte zwischen Brown und seinen Gegnern* (Leipzig, 1798).

28 "Relativitaet der Ausdrücke, stärkend, schwächend, entzündlich etc. Trüglichkeit der *Symptome* bey Individuen—Der Arzt muß sich hier oft nach der Indikation der *Zeit*—des Orts—der Epidemie etc. richten—und über die einzelnen Symptome weg sehn" (III, 475).

29 III, 327. The note starts with a specific reference to Röschlaub's theory of diseases.

NOTES TO CHAPTER VI
THE CASE OF *Die Lehrlinge zu Sais*

1 Dilthey, p. 324.

2 Haym, p. 348.

3 Only in a few recent studies has the work been treated in any detail. In *Novalis, Die Lehrlinge zu Sais; Versuch einer Erläuterung* (Winterthur, 1954), H. Bollinger paraphrases the text with the help of Novalis' notebooks, but refrains from any analysis. J. Striedter's „Die Komposition der 'Lehrlinge zu Sais'" [*Der Deutschunterricht*, VII/2 (1955), 5-23] is a thorough, although overstated study of the novel's structural unity. I was unable to consult the typewritten dissertation of H. D. Schmid, *Friedrich von Hardenberg (Novalis) und Abraham Gottlob Werner* (Tübingen, 1952), which is supposed to contain a discussion of *Die Lehrlinge* (see I, 592).

4 According to Professor Mähl (pp. 205 f.), ch. I was written at the beginning of 1798, ch. II at the turn of 1798 and 1799, the sketch entitled "Naturlehre" immediately before ch. II, while the tale dates from the summer or the fall of 1798.

5 See for instance the negative comment on scientists: "Unter ihren Händen starb die freundliche Natur, und ließ nur tote, zuckende Reste zurück..." (I, 84).

6 Schelling's famous postulate from the *Weltseele*, "Die Natur soll der sichtbare Geist, der Geist die unsichtbare Natur seyn", is echoed, for instance, by one of the travelers in Novalis' novel: "Die Natur wäre nicht die Natur, wenn sie keinen Geist hätte..." (I, 99).

7 Striedter showed with great skill that the first chapter is arranged in a tightly knit triadic pattern which proceeds from the general to the specific and from the

impersonal to the personal. While he makes a convincing case for the structural unity of the first chapter, his analogical argument for the second is weaker. There is in fact a very strong discontinuity between these two chapters, and the "Verwandlung" outline suggests that a similar discontinuity would have appeared in the novel's progression towards "higher realms".

[8] For anti-empiricist interpretations see, for instance, Luitgard Albrecht, *Der magische Idealismus in Novalis' Märchentheorie und Märchendichtung* (Hamburg, 1948), p. 85 and the commentary in the revised critical edition: I, 74.

[9] I, 91. In my view this passage describes the state of interrupted communication after the old man's visit, not the primitive happiness that preceded it. The condition where Hyazinth was "fröhlich und lustig... wie keiner" is a few years back in the past, and his present "närrisches Zeug zum Totlachen" is as unintelligible to trees and animals as it is to man.

[10] So far only Professor Mähl took notice of this visionary "dann" passage and even he misses the subsequent ironic inversion. His interpretation of the whole section preceding the fairy-tale is somewhat inconsistent, because he regards the opinions voiced there as alien to Novalis' own, but at times, as in the case of the "dann" passage, he admits that the poet himself is the speaker. (See Mähl, *Die Idee*, pp. 356 f.)

[11] As Professor Mähl pointed out (see reference in note 10), Novalis is directly referring here to passages in Fichte's *Einige Vorlesungen über die Bestimmung des Gelehrten*. Cf. Fichte, I, 250 f.

[12] See Striedter, p. 15 and also R. Samuel in I, 75.

[13] It is not clear from the context whether this youth is one of the travelers or not.

[14] See for instance the following passage from the notebooks: "Ich würde meinen Sinn, oder Körper, theils durch sich selbst, theils durch die Idee des Ganzen – durch seinen Geist – die Weltseele bestimmt finden und zwar beydes als unzertrennlich vereinigt.... Mein Körper würde mir nicht specifisch vom Ganzen verschieden – sondern nur als eine Variation desselben vorkommen" (II, 551). To this many more relevant quotations from the notebooks could be added. Hence it is erroneous and misleading to trace the passage from the novel to Schiller's "Spieltrieb", as F. Hiebel did. See *Novalis* (Chapel Hill, 1954), p. 57. In general, Hiebel's book vastly underrates the scientific background of *Die Lehrlinge* by relating it to Hardenberg's studies of Plato and Plotinus (p. 55). It is now evident that Novalis read neither Plato nor Plotinus.

NOTES TO CHAPTER VII
THE LAST YEARS

[1] The following two passages reflect this change from "learning" and "knowing" to "doing" very clearly: "Die Philosophie ruht jetzt bei mir nur im Bücherschranke. Ich bin froh, daß ich durch diese Spitzberge der reinen Vernunft durch bin und wieder im bunten erquickenden Lande der Sinne mit Leib und Seele wohne" (IV, 329); "Ich habe viele Jahre nicht daran gekonnt einen größeren Plan mit Geduld auszuführen, und nun seh ich mit Vergnügen diese Schwierigkeit

hinter mir. Eignes Arbeiten bildet in der Tat mehr, als wiederholtes Lesen. Beim Selbstangriff findet man erst die eigentlichen Schwierigkeiten und lernt die Kunst schätzen" (IV, 335).

[2] One of the most puzzling documents in this respect is a letter that was erroneously assigned to the beginning of 1800 in the 1929 critical edition, but actually belongs to the first days of Hardenberg's stay in Freiberg [cf. G. Schulz, "Ein neuer Brief von Novalis," *Deutsche Vierteljahrsschrift*, XXXV (1961), 216-223]. Novalis wrote to Rahel Just: "Die Schriftstellerei ist eine Nebensache—Sie beurteilen mich wohl billig nach der Hauptsache—dem praktischen Leben.... Ich behandle meine Schriftstellerei als ein Bildungsmittel—ich lerne etwas mit Sorgfalt durchdenken und bearbeiten—das ist alles, was ich verlange.... Nach meiner Meinung muß man zur vollendeten Bildung manche Stufe übersteigen. Hofmeister, Professor, Handwerker sollte man eine Zeitlang werden wie Schriftsteller. Sogar das Bedientenfach könnte nicht schaden—dafür möchte der Schauspieler wegbleiben, der manche Bedenklichkeiten erregt" (p. 217). There is some danger in reading such documents as literally as Professor Schulz does in his commentary: "Einmal zeigt sich hier deutlich die Schlichtheit und Einfachheit von Hardenbergs Wesen, zum anderen aber auch, wie er ganz bewußt die Gefahren des romantischen Subjektivismus—wie sie sich später etwa in dem Schauspielertum eines Roquairol verkörpern—erkannt hat und zu vermeiden trachtet" (p. 223). The letter can hardly be read as proof of Novalis' simplicity. For once the quoted passage contains a barely hidden irony: the educational value of acting may safely be ignored once the process of education becomes a continuous change of professions, that is, a changing of roles in life. Novalis might have had the education and acting career of Wilhelm Meister in mind here, in which case he only repeats the idea of the novel; if to, one has to remember that his later answer to this novel, his *Heinrich von Ofterdingen*, was precisely an affirmation of art in face of the "practical life" mentioned in the letter. Besides, in such letters his style and views often take on fine changes according to the personality of the addressee—a sign of his mimetic talents which found a philosophical expression in the supreme versatility advocated by Magic Idealism. An awareness of the dangers inherent in "subjectivism" is, of course, not only not incompatible with indulging in it, but even to be expected, since all forms of "romantic subjectivism", including that of Roquairol, are characterized by a high degree of self-awareness. If not a reference to *Wilhelm Meister*, the suspicion concerning acting may well be Novalis' reflection on his own nature.

[3] The third of the six *Hymnen an die Nacht*, the so-called "Urhymne", was probably written in the summer of 1797, while early versions of hymns 1, 2, 4, and 5 might lead back to the year at Freiberg (see H. Ritter, *Der unbekannte Novalis*, pp. 94 f.). But the final version was written around Christmas 1799 (the revised prose version in January 1800), i.e., after *Die Lehrlinge*, and the differences in content and form are in my opinion much too great for a meaningful analogy between the two works (cf. Ritter, p. 96). The initial impulse of *Die Lehrlinge* is, rather, related to the "Brouillon". The first plans for *Ofterdingen* were probably made in the summer of 1799, i.e., after the year at Freiberg (see Ritter, pp. 183 ff.).

[4] W. Feilchenfeld [*Der Einfluss Jacob Böhmes auf Novalis* (Berlin, 1922)] claims that an early indirect influence of Böhme was mediated by Lavater (pp. 36 ff.), which is possible although there is no evidence to substantiate it.

[5] "Abh[andlung] über Jac[ob] Boehme—Seinen Werth, als Dichter. Über dichterische Ansichten der Natur überhaupt" (III, 646). It is interesting that both this note and the reference to Böhme in the almost simultaneously written letter to Tieck (IV, 329) is in the immediate vicinity of an attack on Goethe's *Wilhelm Meister*. Apparently Böhme's mystic and poetic nature appeared to Novalis as the counterpart to Goethe's "'Candide' against poetry" (IV, 331).

[6] Surprisingly little attention has been paid so far to Novalis' religious unorthodoxy and independence. In several of his remarks one may detect an ironic detachment with respect to organized religion and orthodox sentiments. About Matthias Claudius' religious and conservative "Urians Nachricht von der neuen Aufklärung" he wrote to Schlegel: "Vom Urian hab ich nur das Lied in der Zeitung gelesen, worüber mein Alter besonders sein Fest hatte" (IV, 165). As late as 1799 he noted for himself: "Sonderbarer alter *Schul* und *Erziehungsgeist* im Herrnhuthismus— bes[onders] meines Vaters" (III, 557). The difference in religious views was surely a source of tension between Novalis and his father, and very likely Novalis had his father in mind when he wrote that the Herrnhuters annihilate reason (II, 548). The last notebooks contain a polemical remark about the "Kindergeist" of the Herrnhuters and a planned "proclamation" to them. Schlegel's indignant remark, recalling that on the first day of his visit to the Hardenbergs Novalis' "Herrnhuterei" greatly annoyed him (IV, 420), should therefore be read in the proper light, taking into account that Novalis' behavior at home was probably conditioned by the prevailing atmosphere of piety.

One should, however, separate Novalis' aversion to sectarianism from his consistent philosophical defense of mysticism, which is evident, for instance, in his quarrel with Kant. According to Professor Mähl's finding (pp. 219 f.), passages in the "Brouillon" represent a polemic on mysticism against Kant's *Streit der Facultäten*.

[7] "Während... seiner Krankheit las er viel von geistlichen Schriften außer der Bibel besonders die Schriften von Zinzendorf und Lavater, die er... geliebt hatte..." (Samuel, "Karls Biographie", p. 181). Both Just and Tieck inserted this sentence in their respective biographies (cf. IV, 434 and 455). The interest in the works of Lavater had, however, a "scientific" angle too, for Novalis studied physiognomy and interpreted it as "Metrik des Innern und seiner Verhältnisse" (III, 639). Next to Lavater's *Physiognomische Fragmente* (see reference in a letter from 1797: IV, 199) he probably read the book by La Sue (see III, 284 and Appendix IV) and, above all, books by the Dutch artist, physician, and physiognomist Peter Camper (1722-89). References to Camper (III, 172, 282, 403, and 439) indicate that here too, Novalis was interested in the relationship between exterior appearance and interior makeup, physiology and psychology. Camper's medical and geographical "mapping" of the face was to Novalis a step towards "interior metrics".

8 Zinzendorf's *Deutsche Gedichte* and two Herrnhuter songbooks were in Novalis' library.
9 Olshausen, p. 67.
10 See G. Schulz, "Die Berufslaufbahn Friedrich von Hardenbergs (Novalis)," *Jahrbuch der deutschen Schillergesellschaft*, VII (1963), 253-312 — especially pp. 297, 309, and 310.
11 Schulz, pp. 291 f.
12 Information about Hardenberg's readings in these last years may be gathered from the inventory of his library (IV, 470-81), and a notebook list which, among other things, contains a plan for purchasing or reading books (III, 754). Several books on this second list were later found in his library. Both lists contain a great many technical books and journals on mining and geology.
13 Section XIII in Vol. III, entitled "Technische Aufzeichnungen und Schriften aus der Berufstätigkeit", contains mostly unpublished material. Many additional papers are lost or still hidden in archives.
14 Specifically mentioned are Jeremias Benjamin Richter the physicist (III, 574), Haller (III, 585), and Hufeland (III, 613).

As the note on books (III, 754) indicates, Novalis intended to purchase or read the fourth volume of K. Sprengel's *Versuch einer pragmatischen Geschichte der Arzneikunde* (Halle, 1799); he read the first three volumes of this soberly written work earlier, and, as Professor Mähl discovered, he culled from it important information on mysticism and magic by ignoring Sprengel's rational tone (see Mähl, pp. 167-70).

The library inventory — which of course contains books that Novalis read earlier — shows that Novalis was particularly well read in medicine; it contains, among other things, Sömmering's five volumes on anatomy, textbooks on pharmacy by Ch. G. Selle, S. F. Hermbstädt, and K. Mönch, an issue of the Edinburgh Dispensatory, J. Ith's book on physiology, and several volumes on pathology, among which was a handbook by D. J. Ch. Stark, the family physician who had also treated Sophie. There was also the monumental *System einer vollständigen medicinischen Polizey* by J. P. Frank, the first great work on public health and preventive medicine. To the last work there are references in the notebooks (see II, 464 and III, 313 f.).

In chemistry Novalis was familiar with Lavoisier's *Traité élémentaire de chimie* (III, 51) and owned several other serious books. He took extensive notes on Laplace's *Exposition du Système du Monde* (German translation 1797) during his stay at Freiberg (III, 69 ff.), and he also read a history of physics by Murhard (II, 647). For complete list and titles see Appendix IV.

There can be no doubt that Novalis continued to read solid scientific works even in those fields that were not related to his profession. In many earlier studies this fact was either ignored or distorted. A good example for this is L. Kleeberg's article "Studien zu Novalis. (Novalis und Eckartshausen)," [*Euphorion*, XXIII (1921), 603-39], where it is suggested that Hardenberg's ideas were closely related to certain works by K. Eckartshausen on mysticism and magic: *Mistische Nächte oder der Schlüssel zu den Geheimnissen des Wunderbaren* and *Auflösung der höheren Geheimnisse der Magie* (München, 1788-91). If, however, one gets suspicious about the rather vague analogies of Kleeberg and inspects the various lists of Hardenberg's readings, one finds Eckartshausen represented only by books which were on scientific topics, partly relating to Brown's theory of medicine (titles 92 and 93 in the inventory). [There is actually some confusion about these books. The inventory lists three works, and the critical edition of 1929 gives the complete titles of these according to Heinsius and Kayser. I inspected, however, a book which is not listed in either bibliography, bearing the combined title of nos. 92 and 93 in the inventory: *Ideen über das affirmative Princip des Lebens, und das negative Princip des Todes, zur Bestättigung des Brownischen Systems*. Since this volume was published in Leipzig (1798) and the listed ones in München and Frankfurt, it seems more likely that Novalis owned the former. This rather inconsequential book tried to show that all constructs of nature consisted of fire, light, and heat, the first being the excitable, the second the stimulus producer, and the third the interaction of the two (p. 43).]

[15] It is still in doubt whether Novalis read the works of the neo-Platonist and Paracelsian scientists Johann Baptist van Helmont and Robert Fludd. A notebook entry (III, 86) and a subsequent letter to Karoline Schlegel (IV, 237 f., Sept. 1798) indicate that he intended to. He asked A. W. Schlegel to borrow the works from the Royal Saxon Library, for he felt he needed them for his own important ideas on cosmogony. Several of the "Brouillon" notes carry cosmogony in their title, but they can neither be pieced together into a coherent whole nor directly be linked with the works of van Helmont and Fludd.

[16] *Über thierische Electricität und Reizbarkeit* (Leipzig, 1795).

[17] *Versuche über die gereizte Muskel- und Nervenfaser* (Berlin, 1797).

[18] "Ich fange von der Erscheinung des Galvanismus an, weil ich durch die Art, wie ich diese Versuche anstellte, unwidersprechlich erweisen zu können glaube, daß der Stimulus in diesem wunderbaren Phänomen größentheils von den belebten Organen selbst ausgeht, und daß diese sich dabei keinesweges bloß leidend, etwa als elektroskopische Substanzen, verhalten" (Humboldt, p. 2).

[19] Weimar, 1798. Novalis owned a copy of this book.

[20] Ritter, *Beweis*, pp. 162-63.

[21] "Der Geist galvanisirt die Seele mittelst der gröbern Sinne" (II, 545); "Die Chymie ist schon Galvanism — Galvanism der leblosen Natur" (II, 644).

[22] In the new critical edition a newly published section (III, 195-200) contains Novalis' notes on various articles and books by Humboldt. The latter was a student of Werner and attended the academy a few years before Novalis.

[23] Novalis inquired at the Schlegels about Ritter even before he came to know him personally. One gets a vivid picture of Ritter's fanatic zeal from Karoline's answer: "Er wohnt in Belvedere und schickt viel Frösche herüber, von welchen dort Überfluß und hier Mangel ist. Zuweilen begleitet er sie selbst, allein ich sah ihn noch nie, und die andern versichern mir, er würde auch nicht drei Worte mit mir reden können und mögen. Er hat nur *einen* Sinn, soviel ich merke. Der soll eminent sein, aber der höchste, den man für seine Wissenschaft haben kann, ist es doch wohl nicht — der höchste besteht aus vielen" (IV, 267).

[24] The first encounter between the two men is nostalgically recorded in Ritter's

Fragmente aus dem Nachlasse eines jungen Physikers. Novalis' high regard for Ritter may, for example, be seen in his letters to Karoline Schlegel (IV, 263) and Miltitz (IV, 327).

[25] The notebooks of the last years do contain some vague references to experiments with Novalis' fiancèe and other members of his family (III, 602 and 614). The first of these was apparently a plan to perform some Mesmerist (animal magnetism) experiments, the second refers to these again and to some primitive experiments on galvanism. None of these notes suggest any serious experimentation; in fact, we know of no experimental work done by Novalis.

[26] Haering, p. 606.

[27] Schelling assumed that a similar tripartite arrangement, comprising magnetism, electricity, and chemical interactions, existed in the inorganic realm. Extensive speculations on these phenomena in Novalis' notebooks, [e.g., "Sollte Elektr[icitaet] wieder in Galv[anism] übergehn?" (III, 665)] are surely related to the reading of Schelling's work. It is very likely that the sudden renewed interest in oxydation was also under Schelling's influence, although the speculative excursions are unmistakably Novalis' own. In one note oxygen is defined as "UniversalArzeneymittel" and oxydation is identified with fifteen different processes, such as "Auflösung", "Lichtbindung", "Verminderung der Kohäsion", "Demagnetisation", and "Verminderung der Acusticität" (III, 658). Immediately following, the process is described as a "diminishing of the personality" and is attributed to the corrosive action of the devil (III, 659). Surprisingly, these meditations on oxygen culminate in a remark which contains a profound scientific truth: "Der Trieb unsrer Elemente geht auf Desoxyd[ation]. Das Leben ist eine erzwungne Oxydation" (III, 687). Thomas Mann unknowingly used reminiscences of Brown's theory when he later quoted this remark that fitted so well his sense of irony and drama.

[28] Novalis' diet during his illness could be related to his odd thoughts on the use of eating vegetables. According to Tieck's report: "Er selbst war auf seine Diät noch aufmerksamer als sonst, er trank wenig oder keinen Wein, genoß fast keine Fleischspeisen und nährte sich hauptsächlich von Milch und Vegetabilien. ... ich suchte daher seine Gewonheit zu bestreiten, weil ich seine Entwöhnung von Wein und stärkenden Nahrungsmitteln für irrig und falsche Ängstlichkeit hielt" (IV, 454).

[29] For instance, the above quoted note on sensibility and disease (III, 657) goes on to say: "Der sittliche Mensch muß auch eine freye Natur haben — eine gegenstrebende, eine zu erziehende, eine eigenthümliche Natur" — it remains unclear whether the "freye Natur" is identical with sensibility, or has to be developed to curb it.

[30] III, 667. This could be the meaning of that "new conception of morality" to which there are three references in these notebooks.

[31] Devoting the last chapter of her book to medical doctors, Ricarda Huch was probably the first to associate the trend in medicine with the literary movement.

[32] See Huch (Tübingen, 1951), p. 608 and W. Milch, "Zum Problem der Krankheit in der Dichtung der deutschen Romantik," *Sudhoffs Archiv*, XXIII (1930), 213-35.

³³ Among the literary records of these interests one may find E. T. A. Hoffmann's *Der Magnetiseur*, J. Kerner's *Die Seherin von Prevorst*, and, above all, the works of Kleist (e.g., *Das Kätchen von Heilbronn, Prinz Friedrich von Homburg*) where somnambulism plays an important role.
³⁴ *Mesmerismus*, ed. K. Ch. Wolfart (Berlin, 1814).
³⁵ *Franz Anton Mesmer aus Schwaben* (Frankfurt a. M., 1856).
³⁶ Huch, p. 602.
³⁷ J. N. Ringseis, *System der Medizin* as summarized in his *Erinnerungen*, ed. E. Ringseis (Regensburg, 1886-94), III, 427.
³⁸ Ringseis, *Erinnerungen*, I, 67-68:"...mächtig aber wirkte auch der Verkehr mit christlich Gesinnten, theils persönlich, theils in ihren Werken.... Vor Allem seien hier genannt: ... die an Glanz und Wirkung dem Blitze vergleichbaren Abhandlungen Franz Baader's, des Ersten, welcher die Philosophie wieder auf Bahnen der Objektivität lenkte und christianisirte; G. H. Schubert's Schriften, vorzüglich die über 'die Nachtseite der Natur', sodann Tieck, Novalis, die beiden Schlegel, überhaupt die Romantiker, von denen zwar ein Theil noch sehr im Unklaren schwamm, mancher aber doch schon das Ufer gewonnen hatte, wie z.B. der zum Katholizismus übergetretene Friedrich Schlegel." Ringseis was a student of Röschlaub and wrote his dissertation on Brown, hence he had direct access to the sources of romantic medicine.
³⁹ E. Hirschfeld, "Romantische Medizin," *Kyklos*, III (1930), 1-89.
⁴⁰ "Aber es ist ebenso nutzlos, aus Novalis' Fragmenten ein medizinisches System herauszustellen wie es zu kritisieren – die Bedeutung dieser wirklich unvergleichlichen Aphorismen liegt für das Thema der Medizin in einer ganz anderen Richtung" (Hirschfeld, p. 23); "Um es noch einmal zu betonen, all diese und ähnliche Stellen zu vielen medizinischen Themen (Fieber, Entzündung, spezielle Therapie usw.) lassen sich höchstens mit großer Vorsicht in ein subjektiv-gedankliches Philosophieren ihres Verfassers einbauen, bedeuten aber nur in der Perspektive dieses analogisierenden und exemplifizierenden Geistes etwas, objektiv fast nichts" (Hirschfeld, p. 24).
⁴¹ "Unbestrittener Protagonist aber und Psychagog des romantischen Kreises ist Novalis, Ideenführer der romantischen Medizin auch er" (Hirschfeld, p. 21).
⁴² Although the dissertation was published in 1934, it made use of the old and very incomplete Minor edition of Novalis' works. Bluth not only assumed, without giving evidence, that Novalis influenced Ringseis, Windischmann, Volz, Stark, and Kieser, but also claimed that Novalis personally knew Schelling during his studies in Leipzig and that Schelling's early "Naturphilosophie" was indebted to Novalis. His final conclusion: "Auch Albrecht von Haller und Andreas Gryphius waren Dichter, aber sie waren gleichzeitig Ärzte. Novalis hat nur als Dichter auf die zeitgenössische Medizin eingewirkt. Damit ist ein höchst merkwürdiger Fall aufgewiesen, in dem wissenschaftliche Berufsmedizin aus den Bezirken der Dichtung beeinflußt worden ist" (p. 54).
⁴³ Diepgen's speech is included in the collection of his essays, *Medizin und Kultur* (Stuttgart, 1938). The following are representative passages: "Novalis ist die Quelle, aus der leitende Sätze der romantischen Medizin geschöpft sind. Von ihm, dem Dichter, gehen gerade die merkwürdigen Anschauungen aus, die uns

manche Naturforscher und Ärzte jener geistigen Strömung schwer verstehen lassen, Anschauungen, die man auf den ersten Blick nur mit weltfremder Unkritik und von allen Göttern verlassener Phantastik erklären möchte" (p. 243). "Novalis dachte nicht Kausal" (p. 244). For Diepgen's view in his history of medicine, see pp. 10 f. of my Introduction.

[44] Obviously echoing Bluth, Leibbrand writes: "Wo und wann hatte je ein Dichter ärztliche Lehrsätze mitgestaltet, dem medizinischen Denken seiner Zeit Gehalt und Gestalt gegeben? Rabelais hatte die Heilkunde seiner Zeit geistvoll verspottet. Nach der Romantik hat Zola die Abstammungslehre und den Degenerationsgedanken Morels romanhaft verwertet, die physiologischen Theorien Claude Bernards verwendet. Dennoch ist all dies nicht mit der Romantik vergleichbar. Der Einfluß des Dichters Novalis war anderer Art.... Wichtig bleiben die Folgen, die sich aus Novalis' Gedanken für die Berufsärzte ziehen lassen" [*Die spekulative Medizin der Romantik* (Hamburg, 1956), p. 227 and p. 232].

[45] Following Bluth, Leibbrand mistakenly claims that Schelling knew Novalis in Leipzig, and, as mentioned, he writes that Röschlaub was a personal friend of Novalis.

[46] Appeared at Reimer in Berlin in 1802, 1805, 1815, 1826, and 1837.

[47] In *Lebenserinnerungen und Denkwürdigkeiten*, II (Leipzig, 1866), 317.

[48] *Der Erwerb aus einem vergangenen und die Erwartung von einem zukünftigen Leben* (Erlangen, 1854-56).

[49] In spite of his hostility during Novalis' lifetime Steffens draws in *Was ich erlebte*, an excessively affectionate picture of Hardenberg, and vaguely mentions that the "poetically religious" words of Novalis were "wonderful and promising oracles" to many natural scientists of his age—which tells us nothing useful.

Appendix I. Disease Chart According to Brown

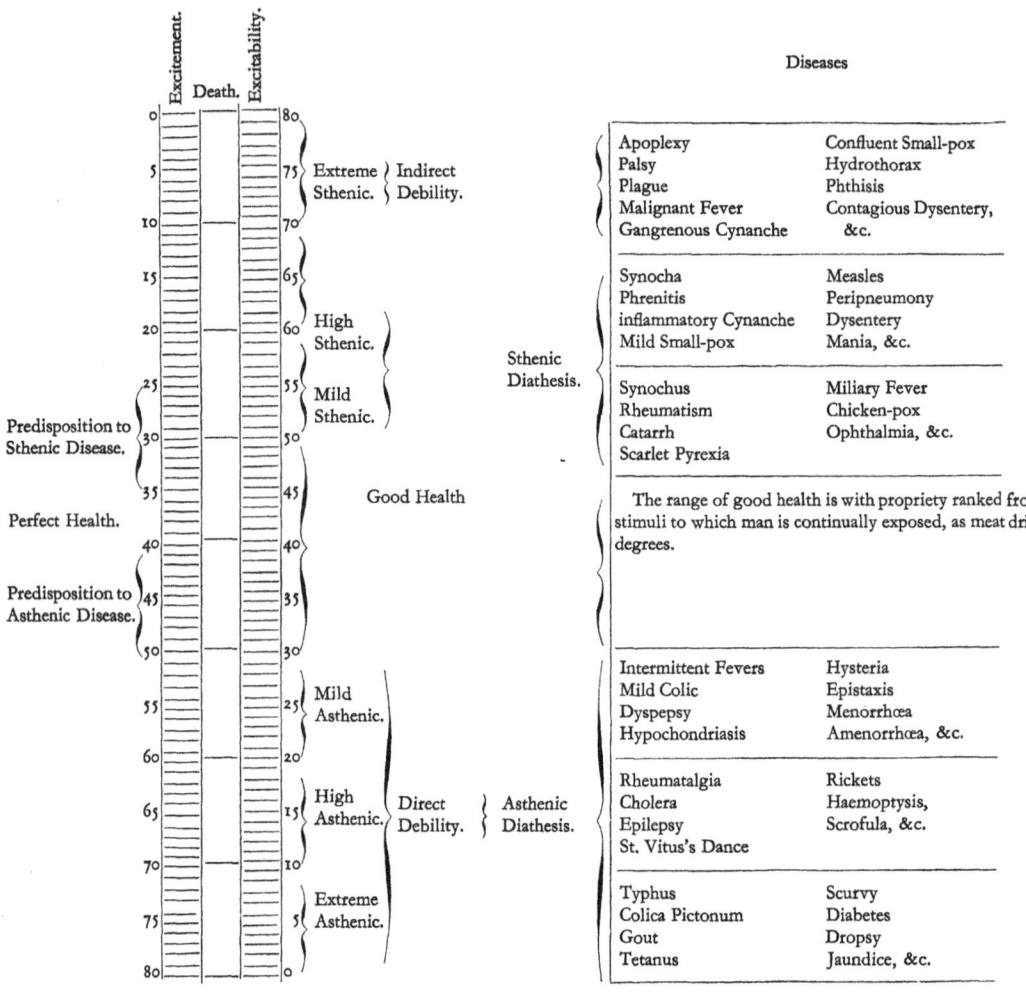

FROM: THE ELEMENTS OF MEDICINE
(PHILADELPHIA, 1806)

Note: The columns of excitement and excitability are erroneously interchanged in this edition.

TABLE OF EXCITEMENT AND EXCITABILITY

Causes (Noxious)	Causes (Immediate)	Cure
Excessive action of powerful stimuli; as heat, exercise, food, abundance of blood, violent passions of the mind, contagion, and the like.	Indirect debility	The indication of cure is to support the excitement. The remedies are powerful stimuli, as electricity, opium, aether, spirituous, liquors, wine, musk, cinchona bark, snake root, camphor, rich soups, and the like.
The same as above, but not to that excess which induces indirect debility; yet acting with greater force than in the next range of disease.	Greatly increased excitement	The indication of cure is to diminish the excitement; which is to be effected by avoiding powerful stimuli, and employing slight or defective stimuli, as lying cool in bed, tranquillity of mind, bleeding, purging, spare diet, and the like.
The same as above, but not acting with that force which induces high sthenic diathesis; yet greater than in the state of health.	Less increased excitement	The indication of cure is, as above, to diminish the excitement, but with more moderation.

thirty to fifty degrees in the scale; for perfect health, which consists in the middle point solely, or forty degrees, rarely occurs; in consequence of the variation of the and the passions of the mind; which sometimes act with more power, sometimes with less, so that the excitement commonly fluctuates between thirty and fifty

Causes (Noxious)	Causes (Immediate)	Cure
A deficiency of the stimuli necessary to the maintenance of good health; and an improper application powers, which, though stimulant, do not stimulate a sufficient degree.	Diminished excitement, or Direct debility	The indication of cure is to increase the excitement. The remedies are powerful stimuli, such as exhibited for the cure of indirect debility, but with this difference, that here it is necessary to begin with a small degree of stimulus, and increase it gradually.
Defective stimuli alone; as cold, diet sparing and not of good quality, fear, and the like.		The indication of cure is here the same as above, but stimuli must be applied somewhat more cautiously.
Defective stimuli alone		The indication of cure is the same here also, but still greater caution is necessary in the application of stimuli.

TO
JOHN BROWN, M. D.
THIS TABLE IS DEDICATED, AS A TESTIMONY OF RESPECT,
BY HIS FRIEND AND PUPIL,
SAMUEL LYNCH

Appendix II

Brown's Disease Chart in German

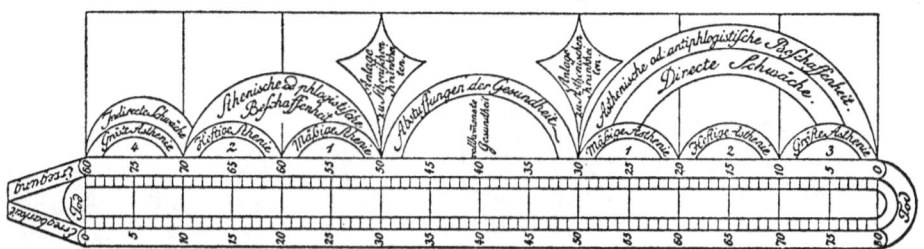

From Pfaff's translation (1804 edition); reproduced from P. Diepgen, *Geschichte der Medizin*, II, pt. i.

Appendix III

A Diagram of Diseases from Novalis (ms. 53/96)

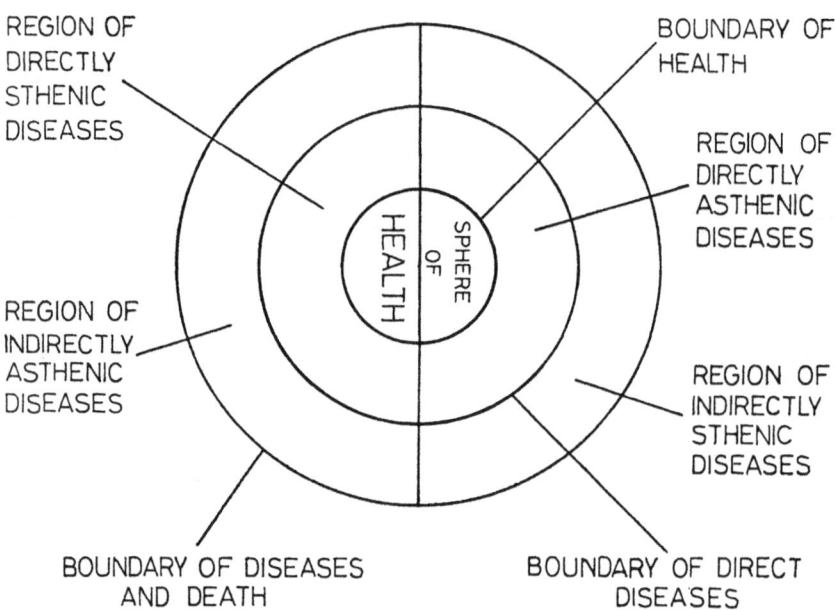

Appendix IV

List of Scientific Books Read by Novalis

The following list is only tentative. Numbers behind the references show that the work was in Hardenberg's library and is listed under that number in the critical edition of 1929 (IV, 476-81). I put a question mark if it is doubtful that Novalis read the work. For journals that continued publication well beyond his death I only indicate the initial date. I chose those editions of books which were probably used by Novalis, but frequently I was able to consult other editions only. Since the list is intended only for surveying and judging the range of Hardenberg's reading, I used mostly short titles. Complete but cumbersome titles are given when the auxiliary information is important. Some of the entries are also included in the BIBLIOGRAPHY.

Allgemeines Journal der Chemie, ed. A. N. Scherer. Leipzig & Berlin, 1798-1803.
Almanach oder Taschenbuch für Scheidekünstler und Apotheker, ed. Johann Friedrich August Göttling et al. 1780-1800 (50).
Annalen der Physik, ed. F. A. K. Gren (1797-1799) and L. W. Gilbert. (1799-) Halle, 1797-1800 (20)
Annales de Chimie, ed de Morveau et al. Paris, 1789-1800 (73).
Archiv für die theoretische Chemie, ed. Alexander Nik. Scherer. Jena, 1800-1802.
Baader, Franz Xaver von. *Beiträge zur Elementar-Phisiologie.* Hamburg, 1797. (87)
— *Ueber das pythagoräische Quadrat in der Natur oder die vier Weltgegenden.* Tübingen, 1798. (86)
— *Vom Wärmestoff, seiner Vertheilung, Bindung und Entbindung, vorzüglich beim Brennen der Körper.* Wien, 1786.
Blumenbach, Johann Friedrich. *Über den Bildungstrieb und das Zeugungsgeschäfte.* Göttingen, 1781. (?)
Bonnet, C. *Philosophische Palingenesie*, transl. J. C. Lavater. Zürich, 1770.
Bürja, Abel. *Lehrbuch der Astronomie.* 5 vols. Berlin, 1794-1806. (47)
Camper, Peter. *Sämmtliche Kleinere Schriften die Arzney-, Wundarzneykunst und Naturgeschichte betreffend*, transl. J. F. M. Herbell. 3 vols. Leipzig, 1784-1790.
— *Vorlesungen über den Ausdruck der verschiedenen Leidenschaften durch die Gesichtszüge; über die bewunderungswürdige Ähnlichkeit im Bau des Menschen, der vierfüssigen Thiere,*

der Vögel und Fische..., ed. A. G. Camper, transl. G. Schaz. Berlin, 1793. (?)
— *Abhandlung über den natürlichen Unterschied der Gesichtszüge in Menschen verschiedener Gegenden und verschiedenen Alters*; ..., ed. A. G. Camper, transl. S. Th. Sömmering. Berlin, 1792. (?)
Chaptal, J. A. *Anfangsgründe der Chemie*, transl. Franz Wolf, preface and notations S. F. Hermbstädt. 4 vols. Königsberg, 1791-1804. (116)
Chladni, Ernst F. F. *Entdeckungen über die Theorie des Klanges*. Leipzig, 1787. (81)
Crell, Lorenz Flor., ed. *Chemische Annalen für die Freunde der Naturlehre, Arzneygelahrtheit, Haushaltungskunst und Manufacturen*. Helmstädt, 1784-1800. (1)
Darwin, Erasmus. *Zoonomie, oder Gesetze des organischen Lebens...*, transl. J. D. Brandis. 2 vols. Hannover, 1795.
Diderot, D., J. d'Alembert, eds. *Encyclopédie*. 35 vols. Bern, 1781.
Eckartshausen, Karl von. *Die neuesten Entdeckungen über Licht, Wärme und Feuer, für Liebhaber der Physik und Chemie*. München, 1798. (88)
— *Ideen über das affirmative Princip des Lebens, und das negative Princip des Todes, zur Bestättigung des Brownischen Systems*. Leipzig, 1798. (92-93)
Emmerling, Ludwig August. *Lehrbuch der Mineralogie*. 3 vols. Gießen, 1793-1797. (118)
Eschenmayer, Carl August. *Säze aus der Natur-Metaphysik auf chemische und medicinische Gegenstände angewandt*. Tübingen, 1797.
— *Versuch, die Gesetze magnetischer Erscheinungen aus Sätzen der Naturmetaphysik zu entwickeln*. Tübingen, 1797.
Frank, Johann Peter. *System einer vollständigen medicinischen Polizey*. 4 vols. Mannheim, 1779-1788. (4)
Gehler, J. S. T. *Physikalisches Wörterbuch*. 4 vols, Leipzig, 1787-91.
Geist und Kritik der medicinischen und chirurgischen Zeitschriften Deutschlands für Ärzte und Wundärzte, ed. J. J. Kausch. Leipzig, 1798. (8)
Gellert, Christ. Ehregott. *Die Probierkunst*. Leipzig, 1755. 2nd ed. Leipzig, 1773. (79)
Göttling, Joh. Friedr. Aug. *Handbuch der theoretischen und praktischen Chemie*. 3 vols. Jena, 1798-1801. (?)
Gren, Fr. Albr. K. *Grundriß der Naturlehre*. Halle, 1787. (53)
— *Systematisches Handbuch der gesammten Chemie*. 3 vols. Halle 1787-1790. 2nd ed. 1794. (57)
— ed. *Journal der Physik*, Halle, 1790-
Gruner, Christian Gottfried. *Physiologische und pathologische Zeichenlehre*, 3rd ed. Jena, 1801. (7)
Hahnemann, Samuel, transl. [with notations], *Neues Edinburger Dispensatorium*. 2 vols. Leipzig, 1797-1798. (16)
Heidmann, Joh. Anton. *Vollständige auf Versuche und Vernunftschlüsse gegründete Theorie der Elektricität*. 2 vols. Wien, 1799-1803. (117)
Hemsterhuis, Franciscus. *Oeuvres philosophiques*. 2 vols. Paris, 1792.
Herder, Joh. Gottfr. *Ideen zur Philosophie der Geschichte der Menschheit*. 4 vols. Riga & Leipzig, 1784-1791.
Hermbstädt, S. F. *Grundriss der theoretischen und experimentellen Pharmacie*. 2 vols. Berlin, 1792-1793. (13)

Hufeland, Christ. Wilh., ed. *Bibliothek der practischen Heilkunde.* Jena & Berlin, 1799- (?)
— *Die Kunst, das menschliche Leben zu verlängern.* 2 vols. Jena, 1796.
— *Ideen über Pathogenie.* Jena, 1795. (?)
— ed. *Journal der practischen Arzneykunde und Wundarzneykunst.* Jena & Berlin, 1795-
Humboldt, Friedrich Heinr. Alexander von. *Versuche über die chemische Zerlegung des Luftkreises und über einige andere Gegenstände der Naturlehre.* Braunschweig, 1799. (115)
— *Über die unterirdischen Gasarten und die Mittel ihren Nachtheil zu vermindern.* Braunschweig, 1799. (119)
— *Aphorismen aus der chemischen Physiologie der Pflanzen,* transl. from the Latin by Gotthelf Fischer. Leipzig, 1794.
— *Versuche über die gereizte Muskel- und Nervenfaser nebst Vermuthungen über den chemischen Process des Lebens in der Thier- und Pflanzenwelt.* 2 vols. Posen & Berlin, 1797. (?)
Ith, Johann. *Versuch einer Anthropologie, oder Philosophie des Menschen nach seinen körperlichen Anlagen.* 2 vols. Bern, 1794-1795. (14)
Jacobson, Joh. Karl Gottfried. *Technologisches Compendium nach den drei Naturreichen.* Elbing, 1788. (105)
— *Technologisches Wörterbuch oder alphabetische Erklärung aller nützlichen mechanischen Künste, Manufakturen, Fabriken und Handwerker...* 4 vols. Berlin, 1781-84. Vols. 5-8 were continued by G. E. Rosenthal: Stettin, 1793-1795.
Journal der Pharmacie fuer Aerzte, Apotheker und Chemisten, ed. J. B. von Trommsdorff. Leipzig, 1794-1800.
Journal de Pharmacie. Paris, 1797-99.
Journal de Physique, de Chimie et d'Histoire Naturelle et des arts..., ed. J. C. La Métherie. Paris, 1794-1800.
Kant, Immanuel. *Metaphysische Anfangsgründe der Naturwissenschaft.* Riga, 1786. (124)
— „Von der Macht des Gemüths durch den bloßen Vorsatz seiner krankhaften Gefühle Meister zu sein. Ein Antwortschreiben an Hrn. Hofr. und Prof. Hufeland," in *Der Streit der Facultäten.* Königsberg, 1798.
Kausch's medicinische und chirurgische Erfahrungen in Briefen an Girtanner, Hufeland, Loder, Quarin, Richter usw... Leipzig, 1798.
Kielmeyer, Karl Friedr. von. *Ueber die Verhältniße der organischen Kräfte unter einander in der Reihe der verschiedenen Organisationen, die Geseze und Folgen dieser Verhältniße.* Stuttgart, 1793. (89)
Klaproth, Martin Heinr., ed. *Beiträge zur chemischen Kenntniß der Mineralkörper.* 5 vols. Berlin, 1795-1810.
Krug, Wilh. Traugott. *Versuch einer Systematischen Enzyklopädie der Wissenschaften.* 2 vols. Leipzig, 1796-1797.
Lagrange-Bouillon, C. J. B. *Handbuch der Chemie,* transl. D. Jäger. 2 vols. Leipzig 1801-1802 (55)
Lambert, Johann Heinrich. *Neues Organon.* 2 vols. Leipzig, 1764.
Laplace, Pierre Simon. *Darstellung des Weltsystems,* transl. J. K. F. Hauff. 2 vols. Frankfurt, 1797. (54)

Lavoisier, Antoine Laurent. *Traité élémentaire de chimie*. Paris, 1789.
Macquer, Peter Josef. *Chymisches Wörterbuch oder Allgemeine Begriffe der Chymie*, transl. J. G. Leonhardi. 6 vols. Leipzig, 1781-1783. (122)
Magazin für die Wundarzneiwissenschaft, ed. J. Arnemann. Göttingen, 1797-
Marcus, Adalbert Friedrich. *Prüfung des Brownischen Systems der Heilkunde*. 4 issues. Weimar, 1797-1799. (18)
Medicinisch chirurgisches Journal, ed. J. K. Tode, Leipzig, 1794-
Medicinische Commentarien von einer Gesellschaft der Aerzte zu Edinburgh, transl. O. A. F. A. Diel. Altenburg, 1774-97.
Mönch, Conrad. *Systematische Lehre von denen gebräuchlichsten einfachen und zusammengesetzten Arzney-Mitteln*. 3rd ed. Marburg, 1795. (3)
Murhard, Friedr. Wilh. Aug. *Geschichte der Physik*. Göttingen, 1798-1799.
Nudow, Heinr. *Aphorismen zur Erkenntniß der Menschennatur im lebenden gesunden Zustande*. Riga, 1791; *im lebenden kranken Zustande*. Riga, 1792. (11)
Palm, Joh. Jak. *Versuch einer medizinischen Handbibliothek*. Erlangen, 1788. (5)
Pfaff, Christ. Heinrich. *Über thierische Electricität und Reizbarkeit*. Leipzig, 1795. (59)
Platner, Er. *Neue Anthropologie für Aerzte und Weltweise*. Leipzig, 1790. (?)
— *Philosophische Aphorismen nebst einigen Anleitungen zur philosophischen Geschichte*. Leipzig, 1776-1782.
Praeliminarien zum medizinischen Frieden, oder Vereinigungspunkte zwischen Brown und seinen Gegnern. Anon. Leipzig, 1798. (9)
Prochaska, Georg. *Lehrsätze aus der Physiologie des Menschen*. 2 vols. Wien, 1797. (17)
Reil, Joh. Ch., ed. *Archiv für die Physiologie*. Halle, 1795-
Richter, Jeremias Benj. *Anfangsgründe der Stöchiometrie oder Meßkunst chemischer Elemente*. 3 vols. Breslau, 1792-1793. (63)
— *Über die neuern Gegenstände in der Chemie*. 11 issues. Breslau, 1791-1802. (64)
Ritter, Joh. Wilh. *Beweis, dass ein beständiger Galvanismus den Lebensprocess in dem Thierreich begleite*. Weimar, 1798. (120)
— *Beiträge zur nähern Kenntniß des Galvanismus und der Resultate seiner Untersuchung*. 2 vols. Jena, 1800-1805.
Römer, J. J. ed. *Annalen der Arzneymittellehre*. Leipzig, 1798-
Röschlaub, Andreas. *Magazin zur Vervollkommnung der theoretischen und praktischen Heilkunde*. Frankfurt, 1799-1800.
— *Untersuchungen über Pathogenie*. 3 vols. Frankfurt, 1798-1800.
Rüdiger, Joh. Geo. Gottl. *Physische Ketzereien oder Versuche eine leichtere Erklärungsart in die Naturlehre einzuführen*. Leipzig, 1798. (94)
Schaeffer, Joh. Ulrich G. *Versuche aus der theoretischen Arzneykunde*. 2 vols. Nürnberg, 1782-1784. (?)
Schelling, Friedrich J. W. *Erster Entwurf eines Systems der Naturphilosophie*. Jena & Leipzig, 1799. (?)
— *Ideen zu einer Philosophie der Natur*. Leipzig, 1797.
„Philosophische Briefe über Dogmatismus und Kriticismus," *Philosophisches Journal*, 1795.
— *Von der Weltseele*. Hamburg, 1798. (77)
— *Vom Ich als Princip der Philosophie oder über das Unbedingte im menschlichen Wissen*. Tübingen, 1795.

Scherer, Alexander Nikol. *Grundzüge der neuern chemischen Theorie.* Jena, 1795. (19)
— *Nachträge zur neuern chemischen Theorie. Nebst Nachrichten von Lavoisiers Leben.* Jena, 1796. (114)
Schmidt Joh. Joach. *Psychologie, Versuch über die psychologische Behandlung der Krankheiten des Organs der Seele.* Hamburg, 1797.
Schrader, Joh. Gottl. Friedr. *Versuch einer neuen Theorie der Elektricität.* Altona, 1797. (90)
Selle, Chr. G. *Medicina clinica oder Handbuch der medicinischen Praxis.* 3rd ed. Berlin, 1786. (15)
Sömmering, Sam. Thom. *Über das Organ der Seele.* Königsberg, 1796. (12)
— *Vom Baue des menschlichen Körpers.* 4 vols. Frankfurt, 1791-1796.
Sprengel, Kurt von. *Versuch einer pragmatischen Geschichte der Arzneikunde.* 5 vols. Halle. 1792-1803. (6)
— *Handbuch der Pathologie.* 3 vols. Leipzig, 1795-1797.
Stark, Joh. Christ. *Handbuch zur Kenntniss und Heilung innerer Krankheiten des menschlichen Körpers, vorzüglich aus eigenen Beobachtungen und Erfahrungen am Krankenbette gezogen.* 2 vols. Jena. 1799-1800.
La Sue, Jean Jos. *Grundlinien zur Physiognomik aller lebenden Körper vom Menschen bis zur Pflanze.* Leipzig, 1798. (?)
Tiedemann, Dietrich. *Geist der spekulativen Philosophie.* 6 vols. Marburg, 1791-1797.
Weikard, M. A. *Entwurf einer einfachern Arzeneykunst oder Erläuterung und Bestätigung der Brownischen Arzeneylehre.* Frankfurt a. Main, 1795. (?)
— *Magazin der verbesserten theoretischen und praktischen Arzneikunst für Freunde und Feinde der neuen Lehre.* Vol. I, pts. 1-4. Heilbronn, 1796-1797. (?)
— *Medizinisches-pracktisches Handbuch auf Brownische Grundsätze und Erfahrung gegründet.* Heilbronn, 1796. (?)
Werner, A. G. *Von den äußerlichen Kennzeichen der Foßilien.* Wien, 1785.
Windischmann, K. J. *Versuch über die Medicin.* Ulm, 1797. (?)

Bibliography

I. PRIMARY SOURCES

Baader, Franz Xaver von. *Sämtliche Werke.* 15 vols. Leipzig 1850-60. Reprint: Aalen, 1963.
Brown, John. *The Works of Dr. John Brown with a Biography by W. C. Brown.* 2 vols. London, 1804.
Fichte, J. G. *Ausgewählte Werke,* ed. F. Medicus. 6 vols. Darmstadt, 1962.
Hardenberg, Friedrich von. *Eine Nachlese aus den Quellen des Familienarchivs herausgegeben von einem Mitglied der Familie.* 2nd ed. Gotha, 1883.
— *Novalis. Der handschriftliche Nachlaß des Dichters. Versteigerungskatolog,* ed. R. Samuel. Berlin, 1930.
— *Schriften,* ed. P. Kluckhohn, R. Samuel. 4 vols. Leipzig, 1929.
— *Schriften,* ed. P. Kluckhohn, R. Samuel. 5 vols. Vol. I (1960); vol. II (1965); vol. III (1968); vols. IV and V to appear.
Hemsterhuis, F. *Oeuvres philosophiques.* 2 vols. Paris, 1792.
Kant, Immanuel. *Werke.* 9 vols. Berlin, 1902-1923.
Preitz, Max, ed. *Friedrich Schlegel und Novalis. Biographie einer Romantikerfreundschaft in ihren Briefen.* Darmstadt, 1957.
Schelling, F. J. W. *Werke,* ed. Manfred Schröter. 12 vols. München, 1927.
— *Briefe und Dokumente,* ed. H. Fuhrmans. vol. I, Bonn, 1962.

II. SECONDARY LITERATURE ON NOVALIS

Albrecht, Luitgard. *Der magische Idealismus in Novalis' Märchentheorie und Märchendichtung.* Hamburg, 1948.
Bluth, Karl Theodor. *Philosophische Probleme in den Aphorismen Hardenbergs.* Jena, 1914.
— *Medizingeschichtliches bei Novalis.* Berlin, 1934.
Bollinger, Heinz. *Novalis, Die Lehrlinge zu Sais; Versuch einer Erläuterung.* Winterthur, 1954.
Bollnow, Otto Friedrich. "Der 'Weg nach innen' bei Novalis," in *Unruhe und Geborgenheit im Weltbild neuerer Dichter.* Stuttgart, 1953.
Bonarius, Gerhard. *Zum magischen Realismus bei Keats und Novalis.* Gießen, 1950.

Calvez, J.-Y. "L'âge d'or. Essai sur le destin de la 'belle âme' chez Novalis et Hegel," *Etudes Germaniques*, IX (1954), 112-127.
Carlsson, Anni. *Die Fragmente des Novalis*. Basel, 1939.
Carlyle, Thomas. "Novalis," in *Critical and Miscellaneous Essays*, II. New York, 1899.
Diepgen, Paul. "Novalis und die romantische Medizin," in *Medizin und Kultur*. Stuttgart, 1938.
Dilthey, Wilhelm. "Novalis," in *Das Erlebnis und die Dichtung*. Leipzig, 1906.
Dyck, Martin. *Novalis and Mathematics*. University of North Carolina Studies in the Germanic Languages and Literatures. Chapel Hill, 1960.
Feilchenfeld, W. *Der Einfluss Jacob Böhmes auf Novalis*, Berlin, 1922.
Fischer, Hans. "Die Krankheitsauffassung Friedrich von Hardenbergs (Novalis)," in *Arzt und Humanismus*. Zürich & Stuttgart, 1962.
Friedell, Egon. *Novalis als Philosoph*. München, 1904.
Haering, Theodor. *Novalis als Philosoph*. Stuttgart, 1954.
Hamburger, Käte. "Novalis und die Mathematik," in *Philosophie der Dichter*. Stuttgart, 1966.
Harrold, Charles Frederick. "Carlyle and Novalis," *Studies in Philology*, XXVII (1930), 47-63.
Haussmann, J. F. "Die deutsche Kritik über Novalis von 1850-1900," *Journal of English and Germanic Philology*, XII (1913), 211-244.
— "German Estimates of Novalis from 1800 to 1850," *Modern Philology*, IX (1911-1912), 399-415.
Haywood, Bruce. *Novalis. The Veil of Imagery*. Cambridge, Mass., 1959.
Hederer, Edgar. *Novalis*. Wien, 1949.
Heilborn, Ernst. *Novalis, der Romantiker*. Berlin, 1901.
Heller, Eitel-Fritz. "Die Ursprünge der Krankheitsanschauungen bei Novalis und seine persönlichen Beziehungen zur romantischen Medizin," unpubl. med. diss. University of Leipzig, 1945.
Hiebel, F. *Novalis*. Chapel Hill, 1954.
Kleeberg, Ludwig. "Studien zu Novalis. (Novalis und Eckartshausen)," *Euphorion*, XXIII (1921), 603-639.
Kluckhohn, Paul. "Schillers Wirkung auf Friedrich von Hardenberg (Novalis)," *Dichtung und Volkstum*, XXXV (1934), 507-514.
Kormann, F. "Zur Novalisfrage," *Schopenhauer-Jahrbuch*, XXXVIII (1957), 133-136.
Kreft, Jürgen. "Die Entstehung der dialektischen Geschichtsmetaphysik aus den Gestalten des utopischen Bewußtseins bei Novalis," *Deutsche Vierteljahrsschrift*, XXXIX (1965), 213-245.
Kuhn, Hugo. "Poetische Synthesis," *Zeitschrift für philosophische Forschung*, V (1950), 161-178, 358-384.
Lewis, Leta, J. "Novalis and the Fichtean Absolute," *German Quarterly*, XXXV (1962), 464-474.
Mähl, Hans-Joachim. *Die Idee des goldenen Zeitalters im Werk des Novalis*. Heidelberg, 1965.
— "Novalis und Plotin," *Jahrbuch des freien deutschen Hochstifts* (1963), 139-250.
— "Novalis' Wilhelm-Meister-Studien des Jahres 1797," *Neophilologus*, XXXXVII (1963), 286-305.

- "Novalis-Zitate in Goethes Gesprächen? Corrigenda zu Friedrich Wilhelm Riemers *Mitteilungen über Goethe*," *Euphorion*, LIX (1965), 150-159.
Maeterlinck, Maurice. *Le Trésor des Humbles*. Paris, 1904.
Malsch, W. *"Europa", Poetische Rede des Novalis*. Stuttgart, 1965.
Müller-Seidel, Walter. "Probleme neuerer Novalis-Forschung," *Germanisch-Romanische Monatsschrift*, XXXIV (1953), 274-292.
Neubauer, John. "Stimulation Theory of Medicine in the Fragments of Friedrich von Hardenberg," diss. Northwestern University, 1965.
- "Dr. John Brown (1735-1788) and Early German Romanticism," *Journal of the History of Ideas*, XXVIII (1967), 367-382.
Novalis *(Friedrich von Hardenberg). The Novices of Sais*. Transl. R. Manheim, pref. Stephen Spender, with drawings by Paul Klee. New York, 1949.
Obenauer, K. J. *Hölderlin/Novalis*. Jena, 1925.
Olshausen, Waldemar. *Friedrich von Hardenbergs (Novalis) Beziehungen zur Naturwissenschaft seiner Zeit*. Leipzig, 1905.
Peacock, R. "Novalis and Schopenhauer," *German Studies Presented to L. A. Willoughby* (Oxford, 1952), 133-143.
Pixberg, Hermann. *Novalis als Naturphilosoph*. Gütersloh, 1928.
Reed, Eugene E. "Novalis' *Heinrich von Ofterdingen* as *Gesamtkunstwerk*," *Philological Quarterly*, XXXIII (1954), 200-211.
Rehder, Helmut. "Novalis and Shakespeare," *PMLA*, LXIII (1948), 604-624.
Rehm, Walter. *Orpheus. Der Dichter und die Toten. Selbstdeutung und Totenkult bei Novalis, Hölderlin, Rilke*. Düsseldorf, 1950.
Reiss, H. S. "The Concept of the Aesthetic State in the Work of Schiller and Novalis," *Publications of the English Goethe Society*, new ser. V, xxvi (1957), 26-51.
Ritter, Heinz. *Der unbekannte Novalis*. Göttingen, 1967.
- *Novalis' Hymnen an die Nacht. Ihre Deutung nach Inhalt und Aufbau auf textkritischer Grundlage*. Heidelberg, 1930.
- "Die Datierung der 'Hymnen an die Nacht'," *Euphorion*, LII (1958), 114-141.
Samuel, Richard. "Novellenentwürfe und Aufzeichnungen Friedrich von Hardenbergs," *Jahrbuch der deutschen Schillergesellschaft*, V (1961), 187-195.
- "Karl von Hardenbergs Biographie seines Bruders Novalis," *Euphorion*, LII (1958), 174-182.
- "Zur Geschichte des Nachlasses Friedrich von Hardenbergs (Novalis)," *Jahrbuch der deutschen Schillergesellschaft*, II (1958), 301-347.
- "Der berufliche Werdegang Friedrich von Hardenbergs," *Deutsche Vierteljahrsschrift*, Buchreihe, No. 16: *Romantik-Forschungen* (Halle 1929), 83-112.
Schanze, Helmut. *Romantik und Aufklärung; Untersuchungen zu Friedrich Schlegel und Novalis*. Nürnberg, 1966.
- "'Dualismus unsrer Symphilosophie'. Zum Verhältnis Novalis–Friedrich Schlegel," *Jahrbuch des freien deutschen Hochstifts* (1966), 309-335.
Schipperges, Heinrich. "Grundzüge einer 'polarischen' Medizin bei Novalis," *Antaios*, VII (1965), 196-207.
Schulz, Gerhard. "Die Berufslaufbahn Friedrich von Hardenbergs (Novalis)," *Jahrbuch der deutschen Schillergesellschaft*, VII (1963), 253-312.

— "Ein neuer Brief von Novalis," *Deutsche Vierteljahrsschrift*, XXXV (1961), 216-223.
Simon, Heinrich. *Der magische Idealismus. Studien zur Philosophie des Novalis.* Heidelberg, 1906.
Spenlé, E. "Schiller et Novalis," *Revue Germanique*, I (1905), 535-554.
Striedter, J. "Die Komposition der 'Lehrlinge zu Sais,'" *Der Deutschunterricht*, VII/2 (1955), 5-23.
Unger, R. *Herder, Novalis und Kleist.* Frankfurt a. Main, 1922. Reprint: Darmstadt, 1968.
Vordtriede, Werner. *Novalis und die französischen Symbolisten.* Stuttgart, 1963.
Wagner, Lydia Elisabeth. *The Scientific Interest of Friedrich von Hardenberg (Novalis).* Ann Arbor, 1937.
Wasmuth, E. "Novalis. Beitrag zu einer 'Physik in höherem Stile'," *Neue Schweizer Rundschau*, XVIII (1950/51), 531-546.
Worbs, Erich. "Novalis und der schlesische Physiker Johann Wilhelm Ritter," *Aurora: Eichendorff Almanach*, XXIII (1963), 85-92.
Zimmermann, Eléonore M. "*Heinrich von Ofterdingen*: A Striving towards Unity," *Germanic Review*, XXXI (1956), 269-275.

III. PHILOSOPHY, SCIENCE, AND ROMANTICISM

Babitt, Irving. *Rousseau and Romanticism.* Boston, 1919.
Bacon, Francis. *The New Organon and Related Writings*, ed. F. H. Anderson. New York, 1960.
Balss, H. "Eine Rede Karl Friedrich Kielmeyers," *Sudhoffs Archiv*, XXIII (1930), 247-267.
— "Kielmeyer als Biologe," *Sudhoffs Archiv*, XXIII (1930), 268-288.
Baumgardt, David. *Franz von Baader und die philosophische Romantik.* Halle, 1927.
Bell, Arthur E. *Newtonian Science.* London, 1961.
Berendes, Julius. "Medizin in der Zeit der Romantik," *Jahrbuch des Marburger Universitätsbundes*, II (1963), 1-14.
Bietak, Wilhelm, ed. *Romantische Wissenschaft.* Leipzig, 1940.
Borden, Friedrich. "Die deutsche Romantik und die Wissenschaft," *Archiv für Kulturgeschichte*, XXI,i (Leipzig & Berlin, 1931), 44-80.
Bourne, H. R. Fox. *The Life of John Locke.* 2 vols. New York, 1876.
Bréhier, Émile. *Schelling.* Paris, 1912.
Brown, John. *Elements of Medicine.* London, 1788.
— *The Elements of Medicine*, transl. from the Latin by Thomas Beddoes. With a biographical preface by T. Beddoes. London, 1795.
Buttersack, F. "Karl Friedrich Kielmeyer (1765-1844)," *Sudhoffs Archiv*, XXIII (1930), 236-246.
Carus, Carl G. *Lebenserinnerungen und Denkwürdigkeiten.* 4 vols. Leipzig, 1865-1866.
Cassirer, Ernst. *The Philosophy of the Enlightenment*, transl. F. C. A. Koelln, J. P. Pettegrove. Boston, 1955.

Coleridge, S. T. *The Notebooks of Samuel Taylor Coleridge*, ed K. Coburn. 2 vols. New York, 1957-62.
Comrie, John Dixon. *History of Scottish Medicine to 1860*. London, 1927.
Croce, Benedetto. *Aesthetic*, transl. D. Ainslie. 2nd ed. London, 1922.
Dewhurst. K. *John Locke (1632-1704), Physician and Philosopher*. London, 1963.
Diepgen, Paul. *Deutsche Medizin vor hundert Jahren*. Freiburg im Breisg., 1923.
— *Geschichte der Medizin*. 2 vols. Berlin, 1949-1955.
— *Medizin und Kultur. Gesammelte Aufsätze*. Stuttgart, 1938.
Eis, Gerhard. "Irrealer Magnetismus in der vorromantischen Fachliteratur," *Medizinische Monatsschrift*, XVIII (1964), 66-69.
From Sensibility to Romanticism, ed. Frederick Whiley Hilles. New York, 1965.
Frye, Northrop. *Fables of Identity*. New York, 1963.
Garrison, Fielding H. *An Introduction to the History of Medicine*. 4th ed. Philadelphia & London, 1929.
Gillispie, Charles Coulston. *The Edge of Objectivity*. Princeton, 1960.
Girtanner, Ch. *Ausführliche Darstellung des Brownischen Systemes der praktischen Heilkunde, nebst einer vollständigen Literatur und einer Kritik desselben*. 2 vols. Göttingen, 1797-1798.
Glass, Bentley. *Science and Ethical Values*. Chapel Hill, 1965.
Gode von Aesch, Alexander. *Natural Science in German Romanticism*. New York, 1941.
Goethe, Johann Wolfgang von. *Werke*. Propyläen Ausgabe. 45 vols. München and Berlin, 1909-32.
Guthrie, Douglas. *A History of Medicine*. London & New York, 1945.
Haeser, Heinrich. *Grundriss der Geschichte der Medicin*. Jena, 1884.
Haller, Albrecht von. "A Dissertation on the Sensible and Irritable Parts of Animals," intr. O. Temkin. *Bulletin of the Institute of the History of Medicine*, IV (1936), 651-699.
Hallucinations, ed. Louis Jolyon West. New York, 1962.
Hamburger, Käte. *Thomas Mann und die Romantik*. Berlin, 1932.
Haym, Rudolf. *Die Romantische Schule*. Berlin 1870. Photographic reproduction: Darmstadt, 1961.
Hegel, G. W. F. *Werke*. Jubiläumsausgabe. 20 vols. Berlin, 1832-1840. Photographic reproduction: Stuttgart, 1928.
Heine, Heinrich. *Sämtliche Werke*. 4 vols. Leipzig, 1887.
Heisenberg, Werner, *Das Naturbild der heutigen Physik*. Hamburg, 1955.
Herder, Johann Gottfried. *Sämmtliche Werke*, ed. Bernhard Suphan. 33 vols. Berlin, 1877-1913.
Hirsch, August. *Geschichte der medicinischen Wissenschaften in Deutschland*. München, 1893.
Hirschel, Bernhard. *Geschichte des Brown'schen Systems und der Erregungstheorie*. Dresden, 1846.
Hirschfeld, Ernst. "Romantische Medizin," *Kyklos*, III (1930), 1-89.
Huch, Ricarda. *Blüthezeit der Romantik*. Leipzig, 1899.
Hueffer, Ford Madox. *Ford Madox Brown*. London, 1896.

Hunter, Richard A. and I. Macalpine. *Three Hundred Years of Psychiatry*, 1535-1860. London, 1963.
d'Irsay, Stephen. "Der philosophische Hintergrund der Nervenphysiologie im 17. und 18. Jahrhundert," *Sudhoffs Archiv*, XX (1928), 181-197.
— "Scientific Thought and Enlightenment," *Kyklos*, III (1930), 136-146.
Kent, A., ed. *An Eighteenth Century Lectureship in Chemistry*. Glasgow, 1950.
Kerner, Justinus. *Werke*, ed. Raimund Pissin. 2 vols. Berlin, 1914.
Knittermeyer, Hinrich. *Schelling und die romantische Schule*. München, 1929.
Korff, H. A. *Geist der Goethezeit*. 6th ed. 4 vols. Leipzig, 1964.
Kotzebue, August. "Das neue Jahrhundert. Eine Posse in einem Aufzuge," (1800) in *Theater von Kotzebue*, X. Wien & Leipzig, 1840, 205-252.
Kuhn, Thomas S. *The Structure of Scientific Revolutions*. Chicago, 1962.
Leibbrand, Werner. *Die spekulative Medizin der Romantik*. Hamburg, 1956.
Leibniz, G. W. v. *Selections*, ed. Philip Wiener. New York, 1951.
Lichtenberg, Georg Ch. *Aphorismen*, ed. A. Leitzmann. 5 vols. Berlin, 1902-1908.
Lyon, Judson S. "Romantic Psychology and the Inner Senses: Coleridge," *PMLA*, LXXXI (1966), 246-260.
Mann, Thomas. *Gesammelte Werke*. 12 vols. Frankfurt a. M., 1960.
May, Georges, ed. *François Hemsterhuis; Lettre sur l'homme et ses rapports avec le commentaire inédit de Diderot*. New Haven, 1964.
Medicus, Fritz. *J. G. Fichte*. Berlin, 1905.
Mesmerismus, ed. K. Ch. Wolfart. Berlin, 1814.
Milch, Werner. "Zum Problem der Krankheit in der Dichtung der deutschen Romantik," *Sudhoffs Archiv*, XXIII (1930), 213-235.
Meyer-Abich, A., ed. *Biologie der Goethezeit*. Stuttgart, 1949.
Nagel, Ernest. *The Structure of Science*. New York, 1961.
Nohl, Johannes. "Franz von Baader, der Philosoph der Romantik (1765 bis 1841)," *Euphorion*, XIX (1912), 612-633.
Obenauer, K. J. *August Ludwig Hülsen. Seine Schriften und seine Beziehungen zur Romantik*. Erlangen, 1910.
Ostwald, Wilhelm. "Johann Wilhelm Ritter," in *Abhandlungen und Vorträge allgemeinen Inhaltes*. Leipzig, 1904.
Plitt, Gustav L. *Aus Schellings Leben*. 3 vols. Leipzig, 1869-70.
Poritzky, J. E. *Franz Hemsterhuis*. Berlin, 1926.
Praz, Mario. *The Romantic Agony*. 2nd ed. Oxford, 1951.
Psychopathology, ed. Charles F. Reed, Irving E. Alexander, Sylvan S. Tomkins. Cambridge, Mass., 1963.
Ringseis, Johann Nepomuk. *Erinnerungen*, ed. Emilie Ringseis. 4 vols. Regensburg, 1886-1894.
Ritter, Johann Wilhelm. *Das electrische System der Körper*. Leipzig, 1805.
— *Die Physik als Kunst. Ein Versuch, die Tendenz der Physik aus ihrer Geschichte zu deuten*. München, 1806.
— *Fragmente aus dem Nachlasse eines jungen Physikers*. 2 vols. Heidelberg, 1810.
Romanell, Patrick. "Locke and Sydenham: A Fragment on Smallpox (1670)," *Bulletin of the History of Medicine*, XXXII (1958), 293-321.

- "Some Medico-Philosophical Excerpts from the Mellon Collection of Locke Papers," *Journal of the History of Ideas*, XXV (1964), 107-116.
Schaeffer, Joh. Ul. G. *Über Sensibilität als Lebensprincip in der organischen Natur.* Frankfurt, 1793.
Schiller, Friedrich. *Sämtliche Werke.* 5 vols. München, 1958-1959.
Schimank, Hans. "Johann Wilhelm Ritter: der Begründer der wissenschaftlichen Elektrochemie," *Deutsches Museum*, V (1933), 175-203.
Schlegel, Friedrich. *Kritische Friedrich-Schlegel-Ausgabe.* Ed. Ernst Behler, Jean-Jacques Anstett, and Hans Eichner, 22 vols. Paderborn, 1958-
Schmidt, Peter. "Gesundheit und Krankheit in romantischer Medizin und Erzählkunst," *Jahrbuch des freien deutschen Hochstifts* (1966), 197-288.
Schrödinger, E. *Mind and Matter.* Cambridge, Engl., 1958.
Schubert, Gotthilf, H. v. *Der Erwerb aus einem vergangenen und die Erwartung von einem zukünftigen Leben.* 5 vols. Erlangen, 1854-1856.
Speyer, C. Fr. and Marc Speyer. *Dr. A. F. Marcus nach seinem Leben und Wirken geschildert.* Bamberg & Leipzig, 1817.
Stein, Robert. "Naturwissenschaftliche Romantiker," *Sudhoffs Archiv*, XV (1923), 121-125.
Strohschneider-Kohrs, Ingrid. *Die romantische Ironie in Theorie und Gestaltung.* Tübingen, 1960.
Thomson, John, William Thomson, and David Craigie. *An Account of the Life, Lectures, and Writings of William Cullen.* 2 vols. Edinburgh, 1859.
Toulmin, Stephen. *The Philosophy of Science.* New York, 1953.
Trahard, Pierre. *Les maîtres de la sensibilité française au XVIII° siècle.* 4 vols. Paris, 1931-1933.
- *La sensibilité revolutionnaire.* Paris, 1936.
Vernon, J. A. *Inside the Black Room.* New York, 1964.
Wackenroder, W. H. *Werke und Briefe.* Heidelberg, 1967.
Weikard, M. A. *Denkwürdigkeiten aus der Lebensgeschichte des Kaiserl. Russischen Etatsrath M. A. Weikard.* Frankfurt & Leipzig, 1802.
Wellek, René. *A History of Modern Criticism*: 1750-1950. Vol II: *The Romantic Age.* New Haven, 1955.
- *Concepts of Criticism.* New Haven, 1963.
- *Immanuel Kant in England, 1793-1838.* Princeton, 1931.
Whitehead Alfred N. *Science and the Modern World.* New York, 1925.
Withington, Edward Theodore. *Medical History from the Earliest Times.* London, 1894.
Wordsworth, William. *Poetical Works of Wordsworth*, ed. T. Hutchinson. London, 1960.
Wundt, Max. *Johann Gottlieb Fichte.* Stuttgart, 1927.

Index

References in the INDEX are to both Text and Notes. In general, only names are given, but in some cases references to specific works are included under the author's name. Page numbers which refer to the Notes are followed by chapter (Roman) and note (Arabic) numbers in parentheses.

Albrecht, Luitgard 163 (VI, 8)

Baader, Franz Xaver von 41, 52, 54-56, 71, 152 (II, 19), 154-155 (II, 37-42; III, 9), 169 (VII, 38)

Bacon, Francis 17

Baudelaire, Pierre Charles 6, 138

Beddoes, Thomas 147 (I, 19), 148 (I, 24, 30)

Bernard, Claude 170 (VII, 44)

Blake, William 2, 12

Blumenbach, Johann Friedrich 21, 22, 26, 29, 106, 132

Bluth, Karl Theodor 142, 143, 145 (Intro., 18), 146 (Intro., 20), 151 f. (II, 15), 160 (V, 8), 169 (VII, 42), 170 (VII, 44-45)

Böhme, Jakob 114, 115, 127, 129, 130, 165 (VII, 4-5)

Boerhave, Hermann 19 f.

Bollinger, Heinz 162 (VI, 3)

Bonnet, Charles 102

Brown, Ford Madox 23

Brown, John 23-30, 49-52, 59, 61, 71, 73, 77, 100, 105-111, 126, 132, 133, 134, 138, 139, 143, 148 (I, 22-26, 31-33), 149 (I, 37-38, 42), 153 f. (II, 28, 34), 157 (III, 22), 159 (V, 5), 160 (V, 10), 162 (V, 24), 167 (VII, 14)

Byron, George Gordon 95

Camper, Peter 165 (VII, 7)

Carlsson, Anni 145 (Intro., 13)

Carlyle, Thomas 6

Carus, Carl G. 139, 141, 143

Charpentier, Julie 128

Claudius, Matthias 165 (VII, 6)

Coleridge, Samuel Taylor 1, 26, 27, 148 (I, 24), 155 (III, 2), 160 f. (V, 12)

Croce, Benedetto 67

Cullen, William 23, 147 (I, 17)

d'Alembert, Jean le Rond 80

Dante, Alighieri 53, 120

Darwin, Erasmus 143

Descartes, René 17 f., 42, 66

Dewhurst, Kenneth 146 (I, 1)

Diderot, Denis 53, 80, 154 (II, 35)

Diepgen, Paul 10 f., 142, 143, 146 (Intro., 20), 151 f. (II, 15), 169 f. (VII, 43)

Dilthey, Wilhelm 9 f., 113, 114, 158 (IV, 15)

Dyck, Martin 145 (Intro., 6)

Eckartshausen, Karl von 166 f. (VII, 14)

Eschenmayer, Carl August 43, 46, 48-52, 59, 99, 103, 108, 152 f. (II, 23-28)

Feilchenfeld, Werner 165 (VII, 4)

Fichte, Johann Gottlieb 13, 14, 15, 34, 35, 38, 39, 40, 41, 44, 46, 47, 48, 49, 50 f., 61, 63, 65, 66, 71, 83-85, 87, 88, 108, 109, 110, 124, 146 (I, 10), 150 (II, 5), 151 (II, 10, 14), 152 (II, 17), 153 (II, 25), 162 (V, 24)

Fischer, Hans 146 (Intro., 20)

Flaubert, Gustave 6

Fludd, Robert 167 (VII, 15)

Ford, Ford Madox 23, 147 (I, 18)

Frank, Johann Peter 166 (VII, 14)

Freud, Sigmund 2, 36

Frye, Northrop 159 (V, 2)

Fülleborn, Georg Gustav 80

Galvani, Luigi 132

Gide, André 138

Gillispie, Charles Coulston 11

Girtanner, Christoph 26 f., 97, 148 (I, 31), 149 (I, 46)

Goethe, Johann Wolfgang von 2, 12, 21, 26, 29, 53, 58, 69, 78-79, 82, 108, 116, 117, 139, 143, 149 (I, 42), 165 (VII, 5)
Faust 2, 81, 119, 122
Wilhelm Meister 32, 129, 157 (IV, 2), 164 (VII, 2), 165 (VII, 5)
"Zauberlehrling" 118 f.

Gren, Friedrich Albert Karl 154 (II, 28)

Gryphius, Andreas 169 (VII, 42)

Haering, Theodor 6, 34, 52, 136, 145 (Intro., 6, 9), 151 (II, 15), 160 (V, 10)

Haller, Albrecht von 18, 20-23, 95, 100, 132, 148 (I, 23), 159 (V, 4, 6), 166 (VII, 14), 169 (VII, 42)

Hamburger, Käte 12, 144 (Intro., 6)

Hardenberg, Erasmus 33, 34, 38, 61, 96, 137, 150 (II, 4), 151 (II, 9)

Hardenberg, Karl 31, 68, 130, 150 (II, 1)

Hartley, David 160 (V, 12)

Haupt, Friedrich 131

Havenstein, Eduard 8

Haym, Rudolf 113 f., 127

Haywood, Bruce 145 (Intro., 11)

Hegel, Georg Wilhelm Friedrich 3, 63, 67, 73

Heine, Heinrich 3

Heller, Eitel-Fritz 146 (Intro., 20)

Hemsterhuis, Franciscus 46, 52-54, 61, 88-90, 92, 96, 100, 102, 154 (II, 34-35), 155 (III, 3, 9)

Herder, Johann Gottfried 22, 26, 32, 53, 143, 159 (V, 4)

Hermbstädt, Sigismund Friedrich 166 (VII, 14)

Hiebel, Frederick W. 163 (VI, 14)

Hirschfeld, Ernst 142, 146 (Intro., 20)

Hölderlin, Friedrich 73, 150 (II, 6)

Hoffmann, Ernst Theodor Amadeus 3, 169 (VII, 33)

Hoffmann, Friedrich 19

Huch, Ricarda 139, 140, 168 (VII, 31)

Hufeland, Christian Wilhelm von 29 f., 36, 104, 154 (II, 28), 159 (V, 4), 166 (VII, 14)

Hufeland, Friedrich 141

Humboldt, Friedrich Heinrich Alexander von 132-34, 139, 167 (VII, 18, 22)

Ith, Johann 159 (V, 4)

Jacobson, Johann Karl Gottfried 80

Johnson, Samuel 95

Just, August Cölestin 37, 38, 87, 130

Kafka, Franz 6

Kant, Immanuel 12, 18, 27, 35, 36, 40, 42-48, 52, 56, 60, 65, 77, 83, 85, 86, 90, 99, 108, 150 (II, 7), 152 (II, 21), 153 (II, 25), 154 (II, 29, 32), 165 (VII, 6)
  Kritik der reinen Vernunft 2
  Kritik der Urteilskraft 67, 156 (III, 13)
  Metaphysische Anfangsgründe der Naturwissenschaft 43, 46-47, 50, 52, 155 (II, 42)

Kausch, Johann Josef 154 (II, 28)

Keats, John 1, 2, 34, 68

Kerner, Justinus 27 f., 139, 140, 149 (I, 38), 169 (VII, 33)

Kielmeyer, Karl Friedrich von 22 f., 26, 97, 106, 147 (I, 15-16), 159 (V, 4)

Kieser, Dietrich 141, 169 (VII, 42)

Kleeberg, Ludwig 166 f. (VII, 14)

Kleist, Heinrich von 2, 62, 169 (VII, 33)

Kluckhohn, Paul 8, 104

Kotzebue, August von 149 (I, 38)

Krug, Wilhelm Traugott 80

Kühn, Sophie von 4, 6, 33, 35, 38, 59, 151 (II, 10), 166 (VII, 14)

Kuhn, Hugo 62, 155 (III, 7)

Kuhn, Thomas S. 11

Lambert, Johann Heinrich 85-86

Lamettrie, Julien Offroy de 20, 100

Laplace, Pierre Simon 166 (VII, 14)

Lavater, Johann Kaspar 165 (VII, 4)

Lavoisier, Antoine Laurent 166 (VII, 14)

Leibbrand, Werner 104, 142, 146 (Intro., 20), 152 (II, 15), 170 (VII, 44-45)

Leibniz, Gottfried Wilhelm von 17 ff., 42, 46, 55, 66, 86, 146 (I, 7), 161 (V, 13)

Lewis, Leta Jane 151 (II, 10)

Lichtenberg, Georg Christoph 150 f. (II, 8)

Linné, Carl 82

Locke, John 16 f., 24, 29, 85

Luther, Martin 86

Lyon, Judson S. 155 (III, 2)

Mähl, Hans-Joachim, 9, 85, 93, 150 (II, 3), 151 (II, 15), 152 (II, 16), 153 (II, 28), 155 (III, 1), 162 (VI, 4), 163 (VI, 10-11), 165 (VII, 6), 166 (VII, 14)

Maeterlinck, Maurice 3

Mandelsloh, Fridericke 5

Mann, Thomas, 2, 6, 168 (VII, 27)

Marcus, Adalbert Friedrich 28, 154 (II, 28)

Medicus, Fritz C. 21

Mesmer, Franz Anton 139 f., 143

Milch, Werner, 139

Minor, Jacob 8

Mönch, Conrad 154 (II, 28), 166 (VII, 14)

Mohamed 86

Morel, August Benedikt A 170 (VII, 44)

Murhard, Friedrich W. A. 166 (VII, 14)

Napoleon Bonaparte 26

Newton, Isaac 2, 12, 17, 18, 24 45 48, 50, 51, 147 (I, 21), 148 (I, 23)

Nietzsche, Friedrich 138

Novalis, *Blüthenstaub* 7, 8, 61, 76, 77, 148 (I, 31)
    Die Christenheit oder Europa 7
    Die Lehrlinge zu Sais 7, 14, 65, 83, 113-127, 129 135, 164 (VII, 3)
    Geistliche Lieder 7, 113, 130
    Glauben und Liebe 7, 8, 12, 76
    Heinrich von Ofterdingen 7, 14, 83, 113, 114, 129, 143, 164 (VII, 2, 3)
    Hymnen an die Nacht 2, 7, 61, 75, 113, 114, 123, 129, 164 (VII, 3)

Obenauer, Karl Justus 32

Oerstedt, Hans Christian 138

Oken, Lorenz 141

Olshausen, Waldemar 10, 130, 145 (Intro., 17), 151 (II, 15), 154 (II, 34)

Paracelsus 19, 78, 156 (III, 10), 167 (VII, 15)

Pascal, Blaise 38

Passavant, Johann 140

Pfaff, Christian Heinrich 132, 134, 153 (II, 28)

Pixberg, Hermann 151 (II, 15)

Platner, Ernst 150 (II, 3)

Plato 74, 106, 163 (VI, 14)

Plotinus 41, 45, 78, 93, 103, 106, 141, 163 (VI, 14)

Prochaska, Georg 21

Rabelais, François 170 (VII, 44)

Raphael 67 f.

Rehm, Walter 10

Reil, Johann Christian 141

Richter, Jeremias Benjamin 166 (VII, 14)

Rilke, Rainer Maria 62, 69

Rimbaud, Arthur 37, 138

Ringseis, Johann Nepomuk 140, 141, 143, 169 (VII, 38)

Ritter, Heinz 144 (Intro., 3), 145 (Intro., 7), 155 (III, 5), 157 (III, 28)

Ritter, Johann Wilhelm 41, 116, 117, 132-135, 143, 154 (II, 38), 167 f. (VII, 23-24)

Röschlaub, Andreas 11, 28, 29, 49, 72, 104-110, 154 (II, 28), 156 (III, 18), 159 (V, 6), 161 (V, 16, 21), 162 (V, 23, 29), 169 (VII, 38), 170 (VII, 45)

Romanell, Patrick 146 (I, 2)

Rousseau, Jean-Jacques 35, 80

Rush, Benjamin 25

Sade, Marquis de 2

Samuel, Richard 8, 79, 152 (II, 16), 157 (III, 28), 158 (IV, 15)

Schaeffer, Johann Ulrich G. 148 (I, 31), 159 (V, 4)

Schelling, Friedrich Wilhelm Joseph 11, 12, 13, 14, 23, 24, 28, 38, 39-45, 46, 47, 48, 49, 54, 64, 66, 79, 88, 91-93, 97-100, 102, 103, 108, 116, 117, 132, 136-137, 141, 143, 145 (Intro., 10), 148 (I, 23), 151 (II, 12, 15), 152, (II, 16-17, 19), 156 (III, 12), 158 (IV, 16-17, 19), 159 (V, 5-6), 160 (V, 9), 161 (V, 13), 162 (VI, 6), 168 (VII, 27), 169 (VII, 42), 170 (VII, 45)

Schiller, Friedrich 4, 15, 35, 73, 93, 149 (I, 42), 150 (II, 6), 161 (V, 12)

Schipperges, Heinrich 146 (Intro., 20)

Schlegel, August Wilhelm 77, 167 (VII, 15), 169 (VII, 38)

Schlegel, Friedrich 4, 7, 8, 38, 53, 74, 77, 80, 86, 88, 91, 129, 141, 142, 151 (II, 11, 14), 154 (II, 38), 157 (III, 28), 165 (VII, 6), 169 (VII, 38)

Schlegel, Karoline 28, 91, 154 (II, 38), 167 (VII, 15), 168 (VII, 24)

Schleiermacher, Friedrich E. D. 86

Schmid, Heinz Dieter 162 (VI, 3)

Schocken, Salman 8

Schopenhauer, Arthur 6

Schubert, Gotthilf Heinrich von 139, 141, 143, 169 (VII, 38)

Schulz, Gerhard 164 (VII, 2)

Scott, Sir Walter 26

Selle, Christian Georg 166 (VII, 14)

Shakespeare, William

   Hamlet 157 (III, 24)

Shelley, Percy Bysshe 1, 34, 47, 58

Sömmering, Samuel Thomas 46, 98, 166 (VII, 14)

Sprengel, Kurt von 166 (VII, 14)

Spinoza, Benedict 39-42, 44, 151 (II, 15), 152 (II, 16, 17)

Stahl, Georg Ernst 19, 146 (I, 7)

Stark, D. Johann Christian 159 (V, 4), 166 (VII, 14)

Steffens, Heinrich 91, 92, 141, 143, 170 (VII, 49)

Sterne, Laurence, 95

Striedter, Jurij 121, 162 f. (VI, 3, 7)

Strohschneider-Kohrs, Ingrid 62, 66, 155 (III, 6)

Tieck, Ludwig 5, 7, 8, 114, 116, 129, 142, 150 (II, 1), 152 (II, 17), 165 (VII, 5), 168 (VII, 28), 169 (VII, 38)

Tiedemann, Dietrich 41, 78, 85, 150 (II, 3), 156 (III, 10)

Trahard, Pierre 95

Treviranus, Gottfried Reinhold 141

Troxler, Ignaz Paul Vital 141

Unger, Rudolph 10

Van Helmont, Johann Baptist 19, 167 (VII 15)

Volta, Alessandro 132, 133, 134

Vordtriede, Werner 144 (Intro., 4)

Wackenroder, Wilhelm Heinrich 67-68

Wagner, Lydia Elizabeth 145 (Intro., 18)

Wagner, Richard
    Tristan und Isolde 157 (III, 24)

Wasmuth, Ewald 76

Weikard, Melchior Adam 27 f., 49, 139

Werner, Abraham Gottlob 80-83, 87, 116, 131, 135, 167 (VII, 22)

Wetzel, Friedrich Gottlieb 139

Whytt, Robert 20 f.

Wiegleb, J. Christian 47

Windischmann, Karl 140-141, 169 (VII, 42)

Wolff, Christian 85

Wordsworth, William 1, 12, 30, 34, 68-69

Zinzendorf, Nikolaus Ludwig von 130, 152 (II, 17), 165 (VII, 7), 166 (VII, 8)

Zola, Emile 170 (VII, 44)

www.ingramcontent.com/pod-product-compliance
Lightning Source LLC
Chambersburg PA
CBHW020758160426
43192CB00006B/366